I0605480

FUJI FIRE

FUJI FIRE

Sifting Ashes of a Forgotten U.S. Marine Corps Tragedy

CHAS HENRY

POTOMAC BOOKS
An imprint of the University of Nebraska Press

Manufactured in the United States of America.

For customers in the EU with safety/GPSR concerns, contact:
gpsr@mare-nostrum.co.uk
Mare Nostrum Group BV
Mauritskade 21D
1091 GC Amsterdam
The Netherlands

LIBRARY OF CONGRESS CONTROL NUMBER: 2024058204

Designed and set in Minion Pro by Katrina Noble.

In memory of
L. C. Malveaux, Tyrone C. Elem,
Thomas J. Breunig, Colin Miller,
Philip E. du Pont, Robert V. Smith Jr.,
Robert L. Brees, Stephan R. Turner,
Orlando E. Sandoval, Gregory L. Hassel,
Rodger A. Larson, Willie Davis Jr.,
Ernest E. Gutierrez, and Willie J. Hamilton Jr.

For
all whose lives
were altered by the Fuji Fire

Semper fidelis

For every battle of the warrior is with confused noise,
and garments rolled in blood;
but this shall be with burning and fuel of fire.

—Isaiah 9:5, King James Version

The rain has let up.
In the sky vacant without my son,
well, how damnably disgusting,
like a shabby worn-out bathrobe,
Fuji!

—Mitsuharu Kaneko, Mount Fuji

CONTENTS

List of Illustrations ix
Introduction xi

1. Burn Ward 1
2. Seagoing Marines, Choppy Waters 5
3. A Disturbance 16
4. The Camp 21
5. Fuel Farm 31
6. Super Typhoon 45
7. Friday, October 19, Morning 56
8. Friday, October 19, Afternoon 62
9. Friday, October 19, Evening 112
10. Saturday, October 20 126
11. Sunday, October 21 152
12. Brooke 172
13. Back at the Camp 229
14. An Informal Investigation 238
15. Aftermath 253

Addendum 1: Those Who Died 281
Addendum 2: Those Who Were Injured 283
Addendum 3: Those Who Received Awards 289
Acknowledgments 293

ILLUSTRATIONS

MAPS

1. Japan and surrounding Pacific region xii
2. Camp Fuji and Fuji Maneuver Area xiii
3. Typhoon Tip superimposed over continental United States 55
4. Camp Fuji training camp 111

PHOTOGRAPHS

Following page 228

1. Training camp Quonset huts at base of Mount Fuji
2. Marines in their training camp Quonset hut
3. Typhoon Tip at its peak
4. Marines battered by Typhoon Tip
5. Breach in long berm above training camp
6. Marine wielding a portable fire extinguisher as hut burns
7. A Quonset hut exterior after fire
8. Two Marines sift through burned hut interior
9. Medical personnel transfer burned Marines to a U.S. Navy helicopter
10. Interior of U.S. Air Force C-141 evacuating Camp Fuji Marines to Texas
11. Captain Deanna Cox treats Lance Corporal Tom Breunig during MEDEVAC
12. Aerial view of Brooke General Hospital
13. Intensive care "cube" inside burn center
14. Aerial view of training camp after fire
15. M-60 tank being retrieved from trench above the training camp
16. Fire incident memorial stone
17. Colonel Allan W. Lamb

18. Lieutenant Colonel John H. Redgate at Camp Fuji
19. Sergeant Major Robert Hendrix at Camp Fuji
20. General Robert H. Barrow

INTRODUCTION

THE VOLCANO HAD not erupted in 272 years. It was not lava that scarred its lower reaches on Friday, October 19, 1979—rather, a deluge of gasoline. Had the U.S. Marines billeted on the slopes of Mount Fuji been back home, they would have been pumping the same blend into muscle cars and motorcycles.

The remains of an unparalleled super typhoon slammed their camp, prompting a fuel spill. Gasoline flooded Quonset huts. Open-flame kerosene heaters inside sparked flash fires. Throughout the tumbledown encampment at the base of one of the world's most majestic peaks, the *whoomph* of ignition spread.

Amid tumultuous winds and rain, seventy-three were injured in the flames, fifty-four suffering burns. Of that number thirteen lost their lives—one immediately, twelve others within fifty-four days thereafter. Among survivors, dozens faced years of reconstructive surgery and lasting physical and emotional disfigurement.

What really occurred at the dilapidated combat training outpost? Had a "freak accident," as headlines posited, been viciously foisted on the Marine battalion there? Was it the "act of God" official investigators quickly surmised? Where did a second deadly "freak accident" at the camp—less than a month later—fit into the calculation?

The questions have lain out for decades, mulled by the relatively small number who remember the events that autumn at Camp Fuji, Japan. Even at the time, news cycles conspired to quickly push the barest dispatches about what happened to the back pages of most newspapers, if they appeared at all.

This book culminates a four-year, two-continent gathering of documentary evidence and recollections—toward the end of understanding what Marines of the time came to call the Fuji Fire.

CHAS HENRY
Captain, U.S. Marine Corps (Ret.)
Washington DC

MAP. 1. Japan and surrounding Pacific region. Created by Scott Gannon, based on materials included in the 1979 incident investigation.

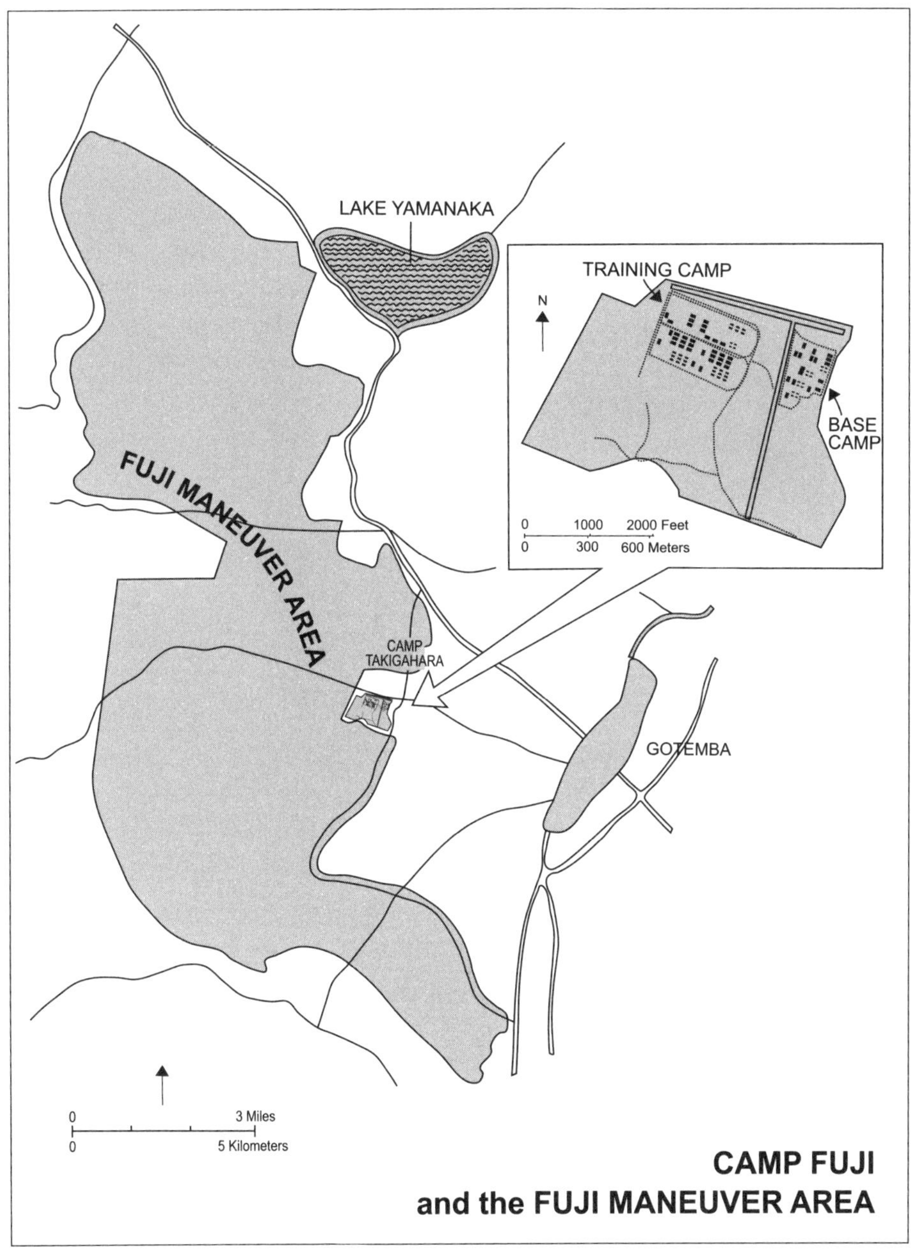

MAP. 2. Camp Fuji and the Fuji Maneuver Area. Created by Scott Gannon, based on materials included in the 1979 incident investigation.

FUJI FIRE

1

BURN WARD

Having witnessed a lot of bad things, ugly things, none can compare to that experience.

—*General Robert H. Barrow, Twenty-Seventh commandant, U.S. Marine Corps, on meeting Marines injured in the Fuji Fire*

THERE WAS NO mistaking it, observed Army lab technician Justin Gragg. When nurses picking up blood and plasma had come from Ward 14A, "you could smell them as soon as the elevator door opened." The acrid odor of charred flesh—"truly disturbing," the Soldier would later recall—infused their uniforms, their hair, their skin.

They were almost always sweaty, too. Temperatures on that burn ward and others were kept above 90 degrees Fahrenheit. When you stepped off an elevator into one, heat wrapped your face, rose through the soles of your shoes, then engulfed you completely. With humidity levels elevated as well—to 80 percent or higher—the wards often manifest their own weather: a moist indoor fog.

As medical team members perspired through protective hats, face masks, and wraparound gowns, patients shivered. Twenty-one-year-old Marine Lance Corporal Mark Bedwell—suffering second- and third-degree burns to his face, arms, and back—was among those pleading for warmth. "It's 110 degrees in there," Bedwell explained, "but we didn't have skin to keep our heat in." An Army corpsman positioned a heat lamp at the bedside of the young man from Burkburnett, Texas, then brought extra blankets.

At 2 p.m. on Monday, November 5, 1979, thirty-three U.S. Marines lay in beds at the hospital. Only a handful had made their way to Ward 13B, where patients ready to undergo long-term skin grafting could focus on recovery and rehabilitation. Most were on Wards 14A and 14B, where treatment space had been expanded to allow all-at-once admission of so many with second- and third-degree burns. Those teetering between life and death filled "the cube," Ward 14A's cramped, sixteen-bed intensive care unit. While the remainder may not have faced imminent fatality, their grasp on life was far from guaranteed. Out of patients' earshot, a doctor cautioned a chaplain from the young mens' unit about the perniciousness of burn injuries. The Marines, the chaplain recalled being told, "could easily die of shock; or, if not shock, it's infection; and if it's not that, it's renal failure; and if it's not that, they just die."

The gravity of their injuries was inescapable. Even some combat-hardened generals—ordered by their commandant to visit the burned men and ask themselves, "How did this happen?"—were taken aback. Nurses had become adept at anticipating shocked reactions to the Marines' flame-disfigured forms. It was not uncommon for visitors, wrapped in protective clothing, amid the stifling heat and smothering humidity, to tip toward unconsciousness. When necessary nurses discreetly guided senior officers or others to a nearby restroom, allowing them to weep, vomit, or otherwise compose themselves out of view.

In the cube ambient light was keeping Issac Williams awake. Sleep, he felt, would help him escape the agony of a body more than 90 percent scorched. "Lying in bed," an observer remarked, "the nineteen-year-old Marine looks like one massive burn." Lance Corporal Williams had convinced surgeons to slice away his fire-fused eyelids. "I said, 'Listen, cut my eyelids,'" he remembered. "I didn't want to be blind." The procedure *had* provided him limited sight. Now, though, the Alexandria, Louisiana, native was literally shut-eye deprived.

A Marine nearby, third-degree burns encircling his torso, lay suspended on a Stryker frame bed, flipped to face the floor. The device allowed nurses and corpsmen to turn him over without distressing skin-burned-away portions of his body. When morphine doses waned, the young man's mind registered blurry linoleum, and the shoes of doctors and nurses shuffling around him.

The Marines had been in San Antonio, Texas, for two weeks—at a military hospital on Fort Sam Houston. The post, first occupied by U.S. Soldiers 102 years beforehand, had over the decades evolved into a hub for military medical training. In 1947 a group of Army researchers began work at the post's Brooke General Hospital. Among their missions: treating and studying burn injuries.

By 1979 the forty-two-year-old hospital building had seen better days. It was not uncommon for staff members there to battle ant infestations. Outside window ledges were frequently caked with pigeon droppings. The burn injury treatment provided on Wards 13 and 14, by contrast, was esteemed in medical circles as the world's best.

The young men now filling those wards had been forced through an explosive gauntlet of flames. It had happened at a ramshackle U.S. training camp in Japan. On the lower slopes of Mount Fuji, seventy-three people had been injured when an immense typhoon triggered a fuel spill that flashed into a fiery maelstrom. Sixty-nine of those hurt at the camp—including the thirteen who would die from their injuries—were American Marines.

One had burned to death at the camp; three others died at a U.S. Air Force hospital in Japan. Thirty-eight of the casualties—badly injured, but thought to have reasonable chances of survival—had been wheeled onto two Air Force C-141 Starlifters and flown to San Antonio. One had not survived the flight. Already four others who *did* make it safely to Texas had succumbed to thermal injury or infection—including, the night prior, twenty-year-old Lance Corporal Orlando Sandoval of Pueblo, Colorado. More death lay ahead.

The incident was already being spoken of as the worst-ever peacetime disaster in the history of the U.S. Marine Corps.

In Japan Lance Corporal David Luttenberger had served in the same company as most of the worst injured. He, too, was shaken by the fire and its aftermath. Good fortune, though, had allowed the nineteen-year-old from Cedarville, Ohio, to escape injury. Transferred shortly after the incident to a Marine Corps base in North Carolina, he flew first to San Antonio. Spending two days with his hospitalized comrades, Luttenberger was disconcerted by an inability to identify even close friends.

"They were unrecognizable—by shape, by size," he said, "no hair, no facial features." Their faces were covered by a patchwork of temporary skin grafts. “Many of them had breathed in the fire and it seared their lungs and seared their throats, so their voices were gravelly, if they could even talk.”

As he prepared to sit at each bedside, a nurse would whisper to him the name of that particular patient. Not being able to distinguish one buddy from another felt disloyal. “A lot of them, I’d lived with for a year—close quarters in barracks, on ship, in tents.” The visit—“a horrific experience”—left Luttenberger hollow: “It was worse than the fire, I think.”

Robert Barrow had not known the Marines personally, but he left meetings with the burn-injured young men feeling similarly gut punched. A veteran of combat in World War II, Korea, and Vietnam, Barrow had been appointed Marine Corps commandant 110 days before the blaze. Twelve years after he spoke with survivors in Texas, memories of the bedside conversations continued to evoke emotion. “To this day when I think about it,” he admitted in 1991, “it is difficult, as I’m right now experiencing, to not have tears come to my eyes.”

Across the globe in the fall of 1979, U.S. Marines were asking the same question Barrow had put to his generals: “How did this happen?”

2

SEAGOING MARINES, CHOPPY WATERS

We need your help to prevent violence and disorder in this town. Please cooperate.

—*Sign posted in Henoko, Okinawa, just outside Camp Schwab, 1979*

AS THE SUN rose on Sunday, September 30, 1979, three U.S. Navy warships drew near the southern- and westernmost island in Japan's Ryukyu chain. Two would navigate into Okinawa's Nakagusuku Bay. Americans called it Buckner Bay, after an Army general killed on the island during the closing days of a World War II battle there. At 8:21 a.m. USS Thomaston (LSD-28) tied up on the port side of Northwest Army Pier, which jutted out from White Beach. Seventeen minutes later—some twenty miles to the north—the flat-bottomed USS Tuscaloosa (LST-1187), built to push onto shorelines with no docks or piers, moored on a ramp in the Kin Red Beach Training Area. As midday approached, the small flotilla's lead ship, USS Juneau (LPD-10), made its way toward White Beach. At 11:38 it berthed opposite Thomaston—on the Army Pier's starboard side.

That day and the next, Marines and Sailors of the 2nd Battalion, Fourth Marine Regiment—"two four" in Marine jargon, written "2/4," part of the "Fourth Marines"—would begin streaming toward the vessels from Camp Schwab, their base on Okinawa's northeast coast.

In many respects the mobilization mirrored 2/4's movement early in the year to train near South Korea's demilitarized zone, or its trek during July to undertake muddy field exercises in the Philippines. This time the destination was Japan's largest, most-populated island: Honshu. There the battalion would disembark for several months at a training outpost on the lower slopes of Mount Fuji. At Camp Schwab handmade signs taped to doors indicated that the Magnificent Bastards had deployed.

Yes, the Magnificent Bastards—a unit nickname Marines and Sailors of 2/4 did not necessarily proclaim loudly in proximity of their mothers, but that they hoped might dispirit potential enemies. The nom de guerre had been permanently embroidered on the battalion's flag since 1964.

The Marines were serving in a Corps rebounding from a quality crisis. Eminent military historian Allan R. Millett assessed the situation harshly. "In 1975," wrote the Marine colonel and distinguished Ohio State University professor, "the Marine Corps had become a dumping ground for the refuse of military recruiting." The degradation had been self inflicted, Millett suggested, when the Corps during the early 1970s set aside a requirement to recruit mostly high school graduates. Many who enlisted without a diploma served admirably; a significant number, though, did not. Radical reform, begun in summer 1975, included rapid discharge of some five thousand Marines deemed chronic troublemakers. While the purge left a force of arguably higher quality, the work expected of the Corps had not diminished. Those remaining would have to pick up the slack.

Assignments to Okinawa—"the Rock," Marines called it—typically lasted one year. With almost no housing available for family members, most Marines and Sailors traveled to the island alone. Twelve months later each would return to the United States. Like other overseas-based Marine Corps units, 2/4 dealt with the challenges posed by the individual rotation system.

"You turned over one-twelfth of your people every month," recalled Jeffrey Bearor, in 1979 a first lieutenant and company commander in 2/4. "It was quite a churn. It was very hard to get to know your kids. . . . They knew they were only going to be there a while." Senior-ranking officers rotated in and out quickly, as well. "Just in the time I was in 2/4," Bearer observed, "I had two battalion commanders."

The perpetual, noncoordinated arrivals and departures impeded units' ability to coalesce. Battalion records from late 1978, for instance, noted that "during October, seventy-five percent of the experienced Supply personnel rotated to [the continental United States]. Although rotating personnel were replaced almost man for man there was little if any overlap to permit proper training of new personnel by the outgoing personnel." A unit deployment program just being initiated would help in some measure mitigate the problem. Soon, longer-intact battalions from the California-based 1st Marine Division would—one at a time—rotate to Okinawa for six-month deployments. They would be assigned as one of the Okinawa-based Fourth Marines' three battalions.

On Monday, June 18, 2/4 had been expanded to Battalion Landing Team (BLT) status. On its own, it was made up of three infantry companies—E (Echo), F (Fox), and G (Golf)—and a headquarters and service company that included Marines trained in administrative work, intelligence, surveillance and sniping, motor transport, and the firing of large mortars. In BLT configuration the unit added an artillery battery; two tracked vehicle platoons—one operating the Marines' iconic amphibious assault vehicles, the other M-60 tanks; a combat engineer platoon, and a platoon of reconnaissance Marines.

Three days later a new commanding officer was assigned to lead the BLT. Forty-three-year-old Lieutenant Colonel John Hollister Redgate had grown up in Connecticut, where he studied at Fairfield College Preparatory School. President of his class at the Catholic academy, he had graduated second in scholarly standing. While studying at the Jesuit-priest-led Fairfield University, he embarked on a Marine Corps officer candidate program that led to his commissioning upon graduation in 1959. His career had included combat in Vietnam and a stint as aide to the general commanding all Marines in the Pacific. Redgate had excelled in military scholastic settings, and his recent graduation from the Marine Corps Command and Staff College had included academic honors. The Fourth Marines commander when Redgate assumed leadership of the battalion had known the officer for some time. "He had a calm, professional demeanor," retired Colonel Warren Wiedhahn remembered years later, "not boisterous, not bombastic. He was the kind of a Marine officer leader you just highly respected."

A challenge for the new commanding officer was following in the footsteps of the battalion's departing leader, Lieutenant Colonel John P. Brickley. "Brickley had everybody's respect," recalled David Corderman, then a second lieutenant in 2/4. Similarly popular had been Major George W. T. O'Dell, the battalion's operations officer during Brickley's term in command. "Digger" O'Dell's exploits on shadowy classified missions had made him something of a Marine Corps legend. In a service that placed great stock in physical strength and athletic appearance, both Brickley and O'Dell exhibited muscular prowess. John Redgate was very fit, but of slighter build. When Captain Leon Craig Jr. reported into the battalion, he remembered wondering, "What's the battalion commander going to look like? Is he going to be some great big strapping person? But he looked like he could be on [the family-oriented TV show] *Father Knows Best*. He was just a nice guy . . . a very sincere, genuine person . . . with this voice like Gregory Peck." David Corderman shared the positive assessment of their new leader. The lieutenant colonel, though, he said, seemed "always in that shadow, being compared to Brickley."

One week after Redgate assumed command—as part of yet another aspect of Corps-wide transformation at the time—dozens of 2/4 Marines who had been trained to employ the more powerful infantry weapons would be consolidated into a separate company within the battalion. "When I got to Okinawa," recalled Mike Cummings, in 1979 a lance corporal and 81 mm mortarman, "I was in the Headquarters and Service Company." The new Weapons Company he and others would join would include fellow 81 mm mortar crew members as well as Marines trained to fire 50-caliber machine guns and M-47 Dragon missiles. Redgate assigned First Lieutenant John Seal to lead the company. It was a place-holding assignment; Seal was set to transfer to another post on October 23.

The battalion's senior enlisted Marine was Sergeant Major Robert Hendrix. The forty-four-year-old was the sort of person whose personality so quickly filled a room that you would later be surprised to realize his diminutive stature. "He was, I'd guess, five-foot-five or five-foot-six," recalled Mark Bedwell, "and he might have been maybe 140 pounds." Hendrix's confidence prompted fellow senior Marines to nickname him Rooster. "Squared away" was how younger Marines described the sergeant major, setting the example of perfect uniform, haircut and physical fitness—seemingly able to do anything that would be asked of any Marine in the battalion, probably better. The African American staff noncommissioned officer had risen to the top enlisted rank during decades in which some Marine Corps leaders would not have welcomed such advancement. Though a sergeant major's principal job was advising the commanding officer on troop-related issues, Hendrix also served as a father figure, mentor, protector, and disciplinarian. Bedwell recalled one exemplary evening just outside Camp Schwab. He had wandered into a noodle restaurant where Hendrix was already dining. The sergeant major invited the young Marine to join him at his table. Before long a commotion outside drew their attention to a 2/4 Marine involved in an altercation with a Japanese police officer. Hendrix unhurriedly rose from his seat, walked outside, and calmly defused the situation. On his return Bedwell remembered the sergeant major "started talking like nothing had happened. He was that smooth and that cool."

Those preparing to deploy who had recently begun their overseas tours packed dress uniforms and other personal belongings into storage on Okinawa. Those near the end of their one-year stints in Japan mailed larger items home. They would carry everything else with them to Honshu. When their transfer dates arrived, they would return to the United States directly from their deployment site, Camp Fuji.

Senior Marines in the unit understood that, not long after the BLT arrived at the camp, its battle skills would be formally judged in a combat readiness evaluation test. Most lower-ranking Marines knew only that recent training schedules had included more "humps" than usual—increasingly lengthy hikes with full packs and weapons. Their CRET would culminate in a timed, twenty-five-mile battalion forced march. Though occasionally grueling, and frequently blister-inducing, the hikes—a shared hardship—built esprit de corps and nurtured friendships.

It was on one such trek that Steve Neal met fellow aviation enthusiast Stephan Turner. "He was in 81 millimeter mortars," Neal recalled. "And we'd be out on these route marches. He'd be playing with his E6B—which is a little circular slide rule that pilots use. And he was just trying to master it, because he wanted to be a pilot when he got out." Neal was similarly motivated, "so we kind of chummed it up."

Pierside on Okinawa temperatures hovered in the 80s Fahrenheit. Marines and ships' crew members sweated as they loaded weapons and other supplies. Vehicles and gear that would be needed first when troops disembarked were packed in last. Inside cargo holds, and on decks topside, everything was tied down. Heavy weather was prowling the Pacific; it could create choppy seas. Issac Williams had joined 2/4 after the battalion's Philippines deployment. This would be his first time at sea. He was awed by the massive warships. Boarding USS Tuscaloosa, though, he wondered to himself if "it was bad for us to go on a ship when we know there's a big old storm sitting out there."

Marines carried their rifles and seabags down into troop berthing—tightly packed sleeping spaces stacked six high. Each "rack"—"a very small bunk," noted then–Private First Class Frank Huerta—was a heavy piece of canvas lashed taut to an aluminum pipe frame. As arguments ensued about the respective merits of racks toward the top, middle, or bottom, sleeping bags and nylon poncho liners were laid out over each piece of canvas. When racks were occupied, the canvas sagged, making it difficult for those sleeping below to turn over. The quarters were cramped, Huerta recalled: "You had so many men in there, breathing and sweating." Officers had it a bit better, though lieutenants and captains were packed six to a small stateroom.

The three ships were all bound for an area on Japan's central east coast, just off the city of Numazu. They would be sailing independently, though; two of the three would pause along the way for a bit of relaxing sightseeing on Kyushu, an island north of Okinawa and south of the BLT's eventual destination on Honshu. USS Thomaston, carrying Marines from Echo Company, was first to pull away. At 10:52 a.m. on Monday, October 1, it left White Beach, underway to Kyushu's northeastern coast. Those onboard would enjoy time ashore at the city of Beppu.

The voyage for Marines embarked onboard USS Tuscaloosa would be more straightforward. They—some from Fox Company, others from Weapons Company—would enjoy no port calls on the way toward the Numazu coastline. Over the course of that Monday, Tuscaloosa Sailors and Marines operating "Landing Vehicles, Tracked" practiced launching and reembarking the amphibious tractors. At 7:30 p.m. the ship got underway. Just over an hour into their voyage, the Marines were shocked by alarm bells signaling that an electrical fire had broken out in the enlisted galley. It took just four minutes to extinguish the blaze, but sobered the Marines about potential seafaring dangers.

At 7:52 the following morning, USS Juneau—carrying the BLT command element, Golf Company, Headquarters and Service Company Marines, and others—pulled away from Northwest Army Pier, setting a course for Kagoshima, on Kyushu's southwestern tip.

With all three ships underway, Mike Tuttle, then a Weapons Company private first class, remembered the Marines' routine devolving to "sleeping, working out, or waiting in the chow line." To the extent possible, they migrated to the ships' weather decks—those exposed to outside elements—to escape cramped berthing, breathe fresh air, and enjoy magnificent vistas. Andrew Bonwit, a twenty-year-old lance corporal from Abington, Pennsylvania, recalled USS Thomaston's voyage as mostly calm. He spent evenings lying on the ship's flight deck, looking up. "There's nothing like the sky at sea," he enthused. "Some of the best star-watching ever."

Just before 8 a.m. on Wednesday, October 3—after having traveled some eight hundred miles north—Thomaston anchored at Beppu. Most on board were granted time off from work—in the nautical lexicon: *liberty*. "From what we heard," Echo Company Marine Thomas Moquino recalled, "we were the first Americans since World War II to be docking there." It was made clear that Beppu was not the sort of city that attracted seafarers with rows of raunchy seaside bars and strip clubs. "People were friendly," Moquino avowed, though language barriers limited communication. He joined friends riding a funicular up Mount Tateishi. The view at its peak, "was awesome," the twenty-year-old from Santo Domingo Pueblo, New Mexico, recalled. "You could see the ocean that was south and then the city itself."

Famous for its geothermal springs, Beppu also offered Japanese bath house experiences new to most of the visiting Marines and Sailors. The tiled center Andy Bonwit and his friends visited resembled a family resort, with indoor play areas and water slides. Men and women bathed in separate sections. "The funny thing was," he remembered, "they had lady locker room attendants. So the men were getting undressed and getting ready to go in, and the ladies were going about their business. I was kind of shocked by it, but the ladies couldn't possibly care less."

Less than an hour after Thomaston arrived at Beppu, USS Juneau anchored off the southern Kyushu port city of Kagoshima. Like Beppu it was not a frequent stop for U.S. warships. Mike Tuttle, eighteen, recalled unit leaders admonishing: "'Hey, let's not screw this up.'"

The area's abundance of deciduous trees reminded one Marine of an island off the coast of Washington State. A significant portion of the city's bay was occupied by the imposing Sakurajima—Cherry Blossom Island, an active stratovolcano. Its proximity required city residents to frequently sweep up dustings of volcanic ash. The battalion's physician noted that children in the city wore safety helmets on their way to and from school. During an eruption a few years prior, he was told, a number of youngsters had died after being stuck by volcano-spewn rocks.

Kagoshima's extensive system of street cars powered by overhead wires brought to Lance Corporal Mike Burbo's mind trolley buses he had seen on the U.S. West Coast. In a letter to his family in Roanoke, Virginia, the then-twenty-year-old called the city "the San Francisco of the East." Two California-born Weapons Company Marines—seventeen-year-old Frank Huerta of City of Commerce, and Lance Corporal Ernie Gutierrez, twenty-one, of Moorpark—joined friends watching a game at a baseball stadium. Greeneville, Tennessee, native Bill Dyer spent time playing the vertical pinball machines at pachinko arcades. He redeemed winnings in the form of individually wrapped caramel candies—"the best ever made," he declared. Tim Howell wrote his mother in Immokalee, Florida that the city's residents

> were as nice as they could be. . . . A few friends and I were invited to a junior high school. . . . The principal took us around to their English classes. It's mandatory to take six years of English. We each got up in front of the class and stated our names, age, hobbies, and what state we were from. Most of them never have seen an American before. They would ask us questions in English about the United States, etc. We went to three different classes and each one enjoyed our presence there. Afterwards they asked for our autographs, which shocked me.

A group of BLT 2/4 officers was hosted ashore by an American who taught at a Japanese university in the city. On a pub crawl of sorts, he took them to a very different sort of bar. "Along one wall," noticed then-Major Lance Woodburn, BLT 2/4's executive officer, "they had all these uniforms, Japanese uniforms from World War II. And the Japanese would come in and put these on, and talk about the war. There were three or four of us that went with him to this bar. And we got some, what I would consider to be, maybe, hostile looks. We didn't stay there long." The professor's point, Woodburn remembered: "The Japanese have very different memories of World War II than we do."

A set of more junior officers was surprised, while wandering the city, to be approached by a dignified elderly Japanese man asking if anyone in the group spoke Spanish. "Hey, Martinez! Turn around!" they called to a friend who had been walking some distance ahead. "This guy wants to talk to you!" Second Lieutenant Adolfo Martinez, a Golf Company platoon commander, was puzzled by the request, but stepped over. In slightly accented Spanish, Tadashi Nogashira introduced himself to the twenty-four-year-old who, at age seven, had emigrated to the United States from Cuba. During World War II, Nogashira had served as a Japanese diplomat in Peru. Over the remainder of the day, the older gentleman showed the group around the city. Their unexpectedly hosted itinerary included lunch at a Japanese restaurant, sightseeing and shopping, then dinner at Nogashira's home.

As Marines lucky enough to have embarked on Juneau and Thomaston walked city streets that day, those onboard Tuscaloosa remained at sea, underway. Their ride was rough. In some measure that was the natural state of things on ships with so shallow a draft. "A flat-bottom that floated like a cork" is how Jeffrey Bearor described the vessel. Add roiling prompted by the nearby-roving Tropical Storm Roger, and things got choppy. Louis Sanford recalled recurring nausea: "After awhile you got tired of standing in line to eat, and watching the food float around in the water on the mess deck. You stopped eating." Further disconcerting, the corporal found, was a frequent lack of fresh water onboard; that precluded opportunities to shower. Allowed to observe on the vessel's bridge, Weapons Company's Steve Neal saw Navy watch standers responding to rough seas, on occasion *over*reacting to test the Marines' sea legs. "They'd go, 'What do you think? How far can I tilt the ship?'" Neal remembered. "The wave would come up and they'd spin the tiller as hard as they could." In sum, Jeffrey Bearor remembered, "it wasn't a pleasant crossing."

Mercifully, it was not extraordinarily long in duration. At 6:53 a.m. on Thursday, October 4—some two and a half days after it had pulled out of port on Okinawa—Tuscaloosa anchored in sixteen fathoms of water off Numazu and began off-loading its embarked Marines and Sailors onto

Imazawa Beach. The process did not take long. By 2:09 p.m. that day, Tuscaloosa was underway on a mission to Busan, South Korea.

As that first contingent made its way to Camp Fuji, those who had embarked on Juneau and Thomaston continued sightseeing, consuming beer and noodles, and engaging in language-impeded flirtations. Their liberty calls came to an end on Saturday, October 6, when Juneau pulled away from Kagoshima and Thomaston did the same at Beppu.

Two mornings later—at 7:24 a.m. on Monday, October 8—Thomaston anchored off Numazu. Just after noon its LCMs began shuttling to Imazawa beach. The "Landing Craft, Mechanized"—"Mike Boats," in slang applying the military's phonetic alphabet—were loaded with Marines, their vehicles, and their gear. The disembarking extended through the following morning (Tuesday, October 9), when USS Juneau pulled into the bay, anchoring at 7:37.

As they had approached the coastline, it had been impossible for the BLT 2/4 Marines and Sailors to miss Shizuoka prefecture's defining geographic feature. Lance Corporal Joe Macdonald of Quincy, Massachusetts, watched Mount Fuji grow "bigger and more incredible-looking." David Luttenberger joined friends admiring "the sun coming up, and the top of Fuji breaking through the clouds." Eighteen-year-old Mike Cummings was among those awestruck. "It seemed to be kind of fairly flat around there, you know," he remembered, "and Fuji just—was out there by itself. Bam! Just stickin' up, you know, snow-covered."

Under bright sunshine the complex off-loading process continued throughout that Tuesday. "We go from the sea and the fresh air, the salt air in our face," Mike Burbo recalled, "[to] the crunch of the sand and the drop of the ramp: 'Charge the beach!'" The Marines and Sailors were urged to hustle as if they were making a landing in combat.

From the shore, some would drive to Camp Fuji in their military trucks and jeeps. Most were guided toward commercially rented buses for the forty-minute-to-one-hour journey. Their tanks and tracked vehicles followed, loaded onto low-bed trucks.

Mike Cummings—who had grown up amid wide open spaces in Emory, Texas—was struck by the tight crowding of buildings in rural towns they passed on their way. "Everything was just stacked on top of each other," he recalled. "The Japanese just lived 'compact.'"

By the morning of Wednesday, October 10, everyone and everything was ashore. The Marines and Sailors of BLT 2/4 were eager to learn what life would be like at the base of the globe's most recognizable volcano.

They focused inland, unaware of the warm water, evaporation and gusting air currents conspiring beyond the ocean horizon.

3

A DISTURBANCE

The wind goeth toward the south, and turneth about unto the north; it whirleth about continually.

—*Ecclesiastes 1:6a, King James Version*

THE FIRST HUMANS to notice it were likely more than 1,000 miles away—U.S. Air Force lieutenants on Guam, working in lower-floor rooms of a building on Nimitz Hill. Huddled over light tables, they squinted through the same sort of magnifiers a jeweler would use to scrutinize a precious gem. At 10 a.m. Chamorro Standard Time on Wednesday, October 3, they compared that day's satellite images with those captured the day before. Loupes held to their eyes like protruding monocles, the imagery analysts peered into an active monsoon trough extending some 2,600 miles from the Marshall Islands through the Caroline Islands to Luzon in the Philippines. Those thunderstorms at that point *right there*: Were they persisting, becoming more organized? It was probably time to alert the TDO—a typhoon duty officer.

Typhoons. It took time for some of the Americans to get used to the term. Back home they had been aware of hurricanes. In different parts of the world, the aberrant weather—inward-spiraling winds rotating around a low-pressure zone—went by different names. In the southwestern Pacific and southern Indian Ocean, people spoke of "tropical cyclones." In the northwestern Pacific, west of the international dateline, they were called typhoons. The latter term likely originated from the Mandarin *tai-feng—feng* meaning "wind." A reference dating to 1124 CE—風癡—described "insane wind." A European traveler in Asia during the 1820s chronicled gales "called in the Chinese seas *Tay-Foung*." Whether described as a hurricane, cyclone, or typhoon, the only significant difference among such storms was that if they occurred in the northern hemisphere, they spun counterclockwise; in the southern, clockwise.

In the western Pacific, typhoon activity had been just slightly above average that year. Beginning with Alice as 1979 dawned, sixteen tropical depressions had so far rotated with sufficient vigor to become tropical storms or typhoons. Two more, Roger and Sarah, were a day away from achieving tropical storm status.

U.S. military meteorologists kept an eye on it all. Images transmitted from polar-orbiting satellites provided them twice-a-day views of large swaths of the Pacific and Indian Oceans. Air Force analysts evaluated the high-resolution photos, then passed them to Navy and Air Force TDOs. Air Force weather technicians and Navy aerographer's mates—typhoon duty assistants—took in real-time storm observations, plotted them on charts, and saw to it that completed forecasts were transmitted. In 1979 scores of American men and women in uniform were based on Guam to track typhoons.

Their presence had been demanded by ghosts of World War II. During that conflict U.S. commanders in the Pacific had discounted the value of tracking bad weather and issuing alerts. The result was devastating. Inadequate warning of two typhoons alone—one in mid-December 1944, the other in June 1945—left nearly 800 Americans dead. By comparison, 317 died while fighting Japanese naval forces in the three-day June 1942 Battle of Midway.

Absent sufficient notification of dangerous weather, three destroyers had been sunk, thirty-six other ships damaged. A light carrier was nearly lost when dozens of fighter planes, storm tossed on its flight deck, burst ablaze. Between the two incidents, more than three hundred aircraft were destroyed or damaged. While task force commander Admiral William Halsey dodged formal blame for the meteorological miscalculations, Admiral Ernest J. King, chief of naval operations during World War II, would later confide, "What I had against him was the two typhoons."

The twin tragedies prompted Navy leaders to develop a more sophisticated infrastructure for observing and reporting weather over the Pacific.

Headquartered in Guam, it was over time merged with Air Force units that had separately been surveilling tropical cyclones.

In 1979 twenty-seven-year-old Navy Lieutenant (junior grade) George Dunnavan was one of several TDOs working twelve-hour shifts at what had become the Joint Typhoon Warning Center. It was not unheard of for staffers there to track seventy typhoons a year. "The season was twelve months long," Dunnavan recalled. "You could get 'em any time of the year."

At this moment JTWC forecasters were focused on what appeared to be three cloud circulation patterns between the islands then named on U.S. maps as "Truk" and "Ponape." They compared the most recent satellite imagery yield with that received the day previous. The cloud masses *did* seem persistent—and that *could* be curvature in the cloud pattern, pulling rain bands from the south. TDOs looked through recent days' readings gathered by U.S. National Weather Service contractors on the two small atolls. Pressure measurements were down from the day before—indication of a tropical depression.

It was time to send someone out to take a look. An "invest," they called it, emphasizing the first syllables of investigation flight.

"They'd tell us, 'Okay, go to this place and do an invest,'" remembered retired Air Force pilot Bob Korose. To get a close-up look at sea surface winds, he recalled, they flew below any covering clouds: "We'd do it at 1,500 feet and below."

"We," in this case, included crews of the Air Force's 54th Weather Reconnaissance Squadron (WRS). Unit patches on their flight suits declared them "Typhoon Chasers." Flying from Andersen Air Force Base on the northeastern tip of Guam, the squadron's crews launched multiple missions daily into each tropical cyclone within flight range. They headed out over the water in WC-130 Hercules aircraft specially equipped to allow observation and recording of weather conditions—even from inside a storm's eye.

"Ninety percent of the time your job is mundanely routine," recalled then–First Lieutenant Carol Belt, one of the squadron's aerial reconnaissance weather officers. The remaining 10 percent, though, the ARWO attested "knocks your socks off."

Though much of the meteorological gear the 54th WRS and JTWC used in their work was state-of-the-art for the time, it left capabilities to be desired. For instance, while the sensors dropped from WC-130s to measure conditions within a typhoon's eye did capture temperature, humidity, and air pressure, they were not capable of gauging the maelstrom's internal wind speed. And wind speed sensors employed elsewhere could withstand only so much physical thrashing; one was never certain, when checking transmitted readings, if a device had been ripped apart before the winds it was measuring reached top speed.

Limited computing power on Guam created additional challenges. Help came from a Navy data processing center in Monterey, California. Every six hours it forwarded forecast aids developed by processing worldwide weather observations through several predictive models. The information, transmitted to the JTWC via undersea cable, was beneficial but far from real time. "You usually would *catch* rapid intensification," George Dunnavan conceded with frustration. "You wouldn't *forecast* it."

Sometimes airborne invests would turn up nothing. Whatever TDOs thought they had seen in the imagery had come and gone. Maybe it had never been there in the first place. That was not the case on Thursday, October 4. It took time to measure, but, at 7 p.m. Chamorro Standard Time, 138 miles southeast of Truk, a 54th WRS crew confirmed the presence of four winds that could compel the disturbance to spin. Combined they created what the crew's ARWO recognized as a "closed surface circulation."

The team radioed back its "obs"—observations—prompting the JTWC to issue a Tropical Cyclone Formation Alert. The Air Force crew had confirmed the birth of what would, in one day's time, develop into the forty-third tropical depression of the 1979 Pacific typhoon season. Two days later—on Saturday, October 6, at 10 a.m. Chamorro Standard Time—American meteorologists in Guam certified it the season's nineteenth tropical storm.

"Tip," they named it.

In May, Japanese meteorologists had granted named-storm status to a depression their American counterparts deemed less than a cyclone. That disturbance remained on Japan's storm count. Weather officials in Tokyo reckoned this early October whirlwind 台風20号—Typhoon 20.

In days to come, 54th WRS crews would fly into Tip thirty-five more times—no longer conducting invests, but rather determining "fixes"—reporting the specific location and intensity of an identified storm on the move.

In Guam the TDO added Tip to a watch board, then begrudgingly called for help. It was a point of pride, George Dunnavan declared, for a duty officer to be able to track and produce multiple daily reports on two simultaneous storms. Now, though, there were three. Tip crammed alongside the already churning Roger and Sarah. The proximity caused uncertainty; the storms pushed and shoved one another, greedy for a finite volume of wind and moisture.

Buffeted by Roger's winds particularly, Tip meandered.

Over the next twenty-four hours, the storm limped slowly and erratically in the Western Pacific. After looping around the island of Truk, it stalled briefly, before moving to the northwest and beginning to intensify.

4

THE CAMP

Lowly hut is mine . . .
Thus I choose to dwell—
And the world in which I live
Men have named a Mount of Gloom.

—Kisen Hōshi, ninth-century Buddhist monk

The camp was primitive, to say the least.

—General Robert H. Barrow, Twenty-Seventh commandant, U.S. Marine Corps

RUGGEDLY PICTURESQUE. THAT was one *Pacific Stars and Stripes* reporter's description of Camp Fuji in the late 1970s. There was certainly no gainsaying the majesty of the volcano that towered above and so nearby. "It looked," Mike Cummings recalled, "like you could walk out the gate just a couple miles and start climbing."

From the camp's lower-slope position 2,250 feet above sea level, another 10,139 feet intervened before one reached Mount Fuji's near-perfect cone. Even when atmospherically obscured—which it often was—Fujisan loomed. Throughout the year its visage varied with changes in atmospheric condition and the issuance and receding of mountainside foliage. On clear days it could be seen from Tokyo, sixty-two miles to the northeast. The volcano's size and solitary presence on a massive plain had for centuries awed most who took in the view. For many admiration led to veneration. Early calligraphic renderings of the mountain's name most closely translated to "peerless" or "immortal."

Fuji's lower slopes, bordering Japan's Kanto Plain, had long been attractive to military leaders seeking space on which to practice large-scale warfighting. Samurai of the Kamakura Shogunate had made such use of the area in the fifteenth century. During the late 1930s, soldiers of Japan's Imperial Army trained on what they termed "the East Fuji Maneuver Area." After the nation's World War II defeat, U.S. Army forces occupied the space, establishing four individual bases. In 1953 one of those parcels—the North Camp, near the Shizuoka Prefecture town of Gotemba—was ceded to the U.S. Marine Corps. In years subsequent half of that real estate had been returned to Japan's reestablished defense forces, the Jieitai. The American Marines retained a 309-acre camp abutting the 36,000-acre Fuji Maneuver Area. They took turns with Jieitai counterparts using the maneuver area's two large training sites and twenty-five field firing ranges.

That wide open space allowed battalion-sized Marine units to rehearse maneuver—supported with live fire from tanks, artillery and mortars. It was training at a scale difficult to replicate on Okinawa. There many training areas bordered local neighborhoods or farms. Incidents of artillery rounds straying onto civilian property had led to training restrictions. Because Camp Fuji's expanse offered deeper range and maneuver space, leaders at the Marine Corps base on Okinawa—which operated Camp Fuji as a satellite training center—routinely rotated units up to the Honshu site for months at a time.

The camp was parceled into two sections. Closer to the mountain, on terrain with a pronounced downward-sloping grade, was the training camp. Its 140-some structures served as temporary quarters for visiting units. The site could accommodate 1,300 individuals. In October 1979 the quarters would be occupied by 1,206 enlisted Marines and 49 Marine Corps officers—augmented by five Naval officers and 44 enlisted Sailors.

Below the training camp, on more level terrain, an expeditionary-type airstrip cut horizontally across the camp. Downhill from that was the base camp, headquarters of Range Company: nearly one hundred Marines and Sailors stationed at the camp on one-year tours, and forty-three civilian employees, most of them Japanese. Led by the camp commander, a Marine colonel, Range Company maintained and scheduled the site's facilities.

Portraying the camp's living conditions as "rugged" was gracious; "ramshackle" would have been more precise. "Even for those days," Mike Tuttle said, "it felt like living in a time gone by."

"You've seen third world countries?" Frank Huerta laughed. "We're almost there." General Robert H. Barrow, appointed the Corps' top officer on July 1, 1979, had visited as recently as November 1978. Reflecting in 1991 he described the site as appearing to have been "put together by infantry carpenters."

Six dirt roads guided movement around the training camp—one crossing its top, another at the bottom, and four running parallel up and down the hill. Sunshine and blue skies could at times offer the landscape a bit of color, as could stands of evergreen trees south and downhill from the training camp. In fall and winter, though, the palette was largely monochromatic—"depressing-looking . . . no color," thought twenty-one-year-old Joe Macdonald. "Everything was that steel gray and the ground had kind of a grayish-blackish look about it."

Accommodations were austere. Almost all buildings on the camp—whether used for lodging or office space, or to shelter showers or toilets—were corrugated steel and plywood Quonset huts. "It was right out of *Gomer Pyle, U.S.M.C.*," Corporal Glenn Roberts thought, evoking a popular CBS television network show of the mid-to late-1960s. In a letter home to Somerset, Pennsylvania, nineteen-year-old Roger Miller described his platoon's World War II–era hut as "a half-a-tin-can-looking thing."

Many were 20 feet wide by 40 feet long, 10 feet tall at the uppermost point of the arc. That yielded about 400 square feet of usable floor space. Slightly larger huts—at 20 feet by 48 feet—offered 480. Corrugated steel sheets surfaced the huts' tops and sides. Sergeant Rob Ahrens recalled them being "covered with tar to try to stop the leaks." The huts' interiors were insulated and lined with pressed wood. Those inside walked on a wooden floor. Each hut was positioned on a rectangular concrete base.

Three windows were built into each side of the rounded huts—each 16 inches tall by 42 inches wide. They were placed high on the wall, recalled Lyal Miller, in 1979 a twenty-year-old infantry corporal assigned to Range Company. A tall person, standing, could look through them and see outside; others might have to step up onto something. One of two panes in each window frame could slide aside. Most often they were kept shut, Miller said, because "in the winter it was too cold, and in the summer, too many bugs." A corrugated steel awning jutted out above each window, shielding the aperture from rain or sun.

Some of the huts—those requiring particular security—were accessed through doors fitted with lockable doorknobs. Most, though, were entered and exited via more flimsy coverings: "nothing but a piece of painted 3/8th-inch plywood on a hinge with a spring to keep it closed," Miller explained. "Some of the springs," remembered Bill Meyers, at the time a twenty-five-year-old first lieutenant in Fox Company, "were actually pieces of bicycle tire inner tube." Handles had been screwed onto each side of the plywood. Hook-and-eye kits had been added to keep some doors secured to their frame when closed; on others a hole had been drilled near an upper edge of the thin wooden sheet—opposite its hinged side. A length of communications wire would be looped through the hole and tied off. The loose end of the wire could then be lashed around a nail pounded into the doorpost.

Eighteen to twenty young men would be squeezed into each of the barracks. They would lock seabags full of clothing to steel-frame bunk beds—again, "racks"—fill wooden footlockers with other personal effects, and pile flak jackets, helmets, and other combat gear wherever they could. "Overall housekeeping is poor," wrote fire inspectors who worried that the cluttered conditions could obstruct occupants' escape should they ever encounter an emergency.

Corporals and sergeants—who were traditionally granted more, and more private, space—found themselves at Camp Fuji cheek by jowl with the lower-ranking men they supervised. "I'm twenty-one," recalled Anthony Senatore, in 1979 a sergeant assigned to the BLT's amphibious assault vehicle platoon. "The kids are seventeen, eighteen. Even though you're still in your early twenties—right?—you're the old guy." As best they could, some noncommissioned officers tried to regain a semblance of cloistered privacy by blocking off a small portion of a hut with metal wall lockers. On nights when younger Marines were "being wild and stuff," Senatore and three fellow sergeants would decamp to hammocks in their respective heated amtracs.

Given the training camp's placement on land inclining down toward the airfield and base camp, it had been necessary to terrace its terrain. Four or five lengthy retaining walls, built of cinderblocks and wooden railway ties, had been required to create generally flat expanses. Walking from bottom to top, or top to bottom, required significant steps up or down when reaching each wall. Mike Cummings noted that many Quonset huts sat very near a tier's end: "We're thinking, 'Damn, if somebody falls out of the back of one of those doors at night, it's about a three feet drop to the next level.'"

The sloping topography invited rainwater to flow downhill through the camp. In 1973 an earthen berm had been bulldozed into place about 350 feet uphill from the uppermost training camp huts. Some 440 yards long, 10 feet high and 15 feet thick, it was designed to divert rainwater toward the camp's northern and southern edges. It had been effective in some measure, though water deflected around each end of the berm still often wended its way back into living and working areas. Sometimes it flooded into huts—particularly those positioned with doors facing uphill. "Water would just flow right through," Lyal Miller recalled, "in one door and out the other."

Erosion was a perpetual threat, given the porous character of the area's soil, which had devolved from the mountain's eruptions of lava, basalt rock, and ash. Centuries of harsh weather had disintegrated the layers of pyroclastic material. Decades of explosive live-fire military training, and near-constant maneuvering of tracked vehicles, had further pulverized it into an abrasive admixture of gravel, sand, silt, and clay. In an effort to reduce the volume of sediment washed away by rain, a system of drainage ditches—inlaid with formed, U-shaped concrete or steel pieces—had been installed throughout the camp.

Because temperatures at the base of Mount Fuji could, in the height of winter, dip below freezing, a rudimentary heating system had been installed in the camp's Quonset huts. Each hut was fitted with two liquid-fuel heaters.

"They looked kind of like old potbelly stoves," David Luttenberger recalled, "kerosene heaters that were fed through a pipe coming from the outside." The heaters reminded Mike Tuttle of stoves at deer hunting camps in his native Maine, "especially the way the smokestack came up from the stove and went through the ceiling of the hut." "Once those things were lit up," Mike Cummings said, the huts—despite limited insulation and drafty cracks—"warmed up pretty quick," if unevenly. As heat rose inside the rounded-arch structures, "the top bunk," Lance Corporal Roger Miller observed, "was about 15 degrees warmer than the bottom bunk." The flat upper surface of each barrel-shaped heater could be used to prepare in-hut meals. Canned foods, or noodles in water in a metal canteen cup, were often warmed up atop the appliances.

In 1979 Corporal Lyal Miller and two Marines he supervised were tasked with ensuring that the heaters worked. Yellow-painted kerosene tanks, he recalled—each holding a hundred gallons or so—stood six feet off the ground at the end of each row of Quonset huts. Galvanized pipes, buried underground, carried the fuel to each hut, where copper tubing fed it into a burner.

"So it's simply gravity that's forcing the kerosene to flow through the galvanized pipe, into the copper tubing into the regulator," Miller recalled. "The regulator has a little float valve like you would find in the back of a toilet. . . . When it's below a certain level, it allows more of the kerosene to flow into the regulator."

A dial on the front of each burner let hut occupants turn the devices on—and raise or lower the generated warmth. Each furnace had a latched door on the front; Miller remembered it being perhaps six inches wide and eight inches tall. "You open the latch," he explained. "Once the fuel is running in there, you throw in a match, or something to ignite the fuel—and it starts burning. And then you close the door and the latch." When new units arrived, Miller and his team would show one person per structure how to operate the heaters; those Marines would teach their hut mates.

Camp Fuji offered few personal comforts. Because it was rare for a woman to visit the camp, conveniences—such as they were—were limited to male necessities. If a Marine or Sailor needed to urinate, for instance, he stepped outside. Between every hut, a concrete tube protruded. Four or five inches in diameter—set in at a 45-degree angle—each extended three or four feet above the soil surface. "I thought they were some kind of vents," Joe Macdonald recalled. "And then I saw some guy relieving himself into one. I was like, 'Okay, we're pretty primitive here.'" *Piss tubes*, the Marines called them. They contributed, eighteen-year-old Lance Corporal Bill Dyer noted, to a wafting aroma of "ammonia and volcanic dust."

Other hygiene facilities were enclosed, but, at best, merely functional. "If you had more serious business to do," Lyle Miller explained, "you had to hike about a hundred meters down to the end of the row [of huts], and either up or down the hill." The trek took one to a Quonset hut full of commodes. "They didn't even have dividers," he said. "It was just a row of toilets and everyone is in there doing their business."

Showering involved similarly long walks across volcanic dirt roads to huts fitted with overhead-mounted water pipes. Joe Macdonald recalled the downward-spraying water as only intermittently warm. If it was raining as one trudged to and from the showers, Mike Cummings remembered, "you were going to get wet—going and coming." Even under dry skies, Anthony Senatore would dress fully for the walk. Those who did not, he avowed, ended up back in their huts "pretty dirty again and needing another shower." Dropping temperatures created additional annoyances. Hospitalman First Class Murray Simpkins, the BLT's senior corpsman, found that shower shoes "would freeze to the ground [and break apart]" as he returned from taking a shower.

Breakfasts, lunches, and dinners were provided in Building T-115. Officially the training camp dining facility, to Marines it was the "mess hall" or "chow hall." Like everything else at the camp, getting to, then into, the structure for a meal involved time outside, even in bad weather. "We had to bundle up," Thomas Moquino recalled, then "wait in line to go into the building." Lines were usually long.

From its very first days under the shadow of Mount Fuji, though, BLT 2/4 did what it had come to do: the unit trained. "We hit the ground running," Jeffrey Bearor affirmed.

"Colonel Redgate was really good in that regard," then-Captain Richard DesLauriers remembered. The commander of the attached artillery battery recalled that Redgate had dispatched a liaison officer to the camp in advance of the BLT's departure from Okinawa. "We planned a lot of our training before we ever left Okinawa."

A key portion, it turned out, would involve heading out on long hikes. Mike Cummings recalled that "the battalion commander, Redgate, loved to hump. And we hadn't been there a few days when he took us on a hump around the base camp."

Companies, platoons, and detachments began heading out to maneuver areas and ranges for days at a time—wargaming, live-firing. Support organizations began their work, as well. Motor transport mechanic Joe Macdonald and his crewmates erected a giant tent over a large floor of steel plating. "There was always a line of vehicles waiting to be fixed."

Many elements of the BLT began the training with fewer people on hand than called for on their organizational charts. Golf Company Second Lieutenant Adolfo Martinez noted that his platoon mustered 37 to 50 percent of its authorized strength.

As was the norm at the time, Marines and Sailors kept joining the unit to replace others who had completed their overseas year. Some who had arrived on Okinawa after the BLT boarded ships for Camp Fuji were flown to Honshu. As buses carrying the first such group neared the camp on Tuesday, October 16, they began to hear what First Lieutenant Duane Schattle recalled as "a faint, barely audible drone in the distance." As they entered the camp, the chant, voiced by hundreds, became clearer: "Newbies! Newbies! Newbies!"

Others in 2/4, short-timers like Steve Neal, bided the last few weeks of their assignment abroad. "I had my head down, and I was running for the finish line," he remembered, ready to "go home and start my new duty station." He faced the essential dilemma of someone nearing the end of an individual rotation system tour. "These were all new people," he recalled. "They *would* have been my friends. . . . Nothing against them, they were all great people, of course. But all my friends were gone."

When Marines and Sailors at the camp were not working or training, they did have opportunities to shop. The Navy Exchange (NEX) operated a number of businesses on Camp Fuji. Products and services were offered in a main store, which included space for a vendor that processed and printed photos the Marines had taken. A souvenir shop and snack bar were close at hand. Rounding out the operation were a laundry, barber shop, and cobbler shop.

The latter vendor provided a service made necessary by the camp's gritty soil. "It would eat the soles off of boots," Mike Cummings recollected, "just wear 'em down to nothing." The cobbler tacked on tread salvaged from old tires. "You could actually grow an inch wearing those things," Bill Dyer remembered. Marines dubbed the resoled footwear "Frankenstein boots."

A logistics support unit that had deployed to the camp from Okinawa provided a field laundry service. "You'd turn your stuff in in a laundry bag and you'd get it back," Mike Tuttle said. "But if you wanted that stuff pressed, there was an outlet there at Fuji." That laundry was run by a contractor named Kiyoshi Hama. The business owner Americans had dubbed "Charlie" also owned an on-camp snack bar. "It was like a deli, almost," Anthony Senatore recalled. The kitchen's *hayaku* [quick] burgers, Leon Craig attested, were "the best in the world. The bread made the difference." Beers could be purchased through a window of the small shed, then enjoyed—if one had dressed warmly—at nearby picnic tables: the "beer garden." Serving a somewhat captive consumer population was profitable. From July through December 1978, NEX sales had totaled $669,340.91.

There were also four hut-housed "clubs" on Camp Fuji, where the young men could enjoy beer or soft drinks, play coin-fed game machines, and listen to recorded music. Two were operated at the training camp—one for Marines ranked sergeant and below, a second for senior enlisted Marines and officers. Two similar clubs were situated downhill at the base camp. A theater of sorts had been set up at the training camp—"an outdoor, big movie screen with all these benches," Joe Maconald described, though he did not recall it being used during the cold months of BLT 2/4's stay.

Almost every weekend groups of Marines and Sailors would visit a nearby Catholic orphanage, the Yamanaka Seibi Home. There they would play with the resident children and undertake site improvement projects directed by an Italian nun, Sister Mafalda Morando, and others of the Salesian Sisters (FMA) who operated the home.

Early in the BLT's tenure at the camp, Marines worked out—or ran through what Lance Woodburn remembered as "ankle-deep volcanic ash." Some read. Many listened to music. "In the evening we had our little boom boxes," Fredric Britton Jr. recalled. "We'd sit there, we'd play cards."

As days went by, the Marines and Sailors took more notice of their surroundings. Corporal Jon Jurgen, who had trained at the camp in 1978, noticed that fuel bladders were positioned differently. In October 1979 three were sited directly uphill from training camp Quonset huts. Previously, he recalled, fuel tanks above the camp had been placed near the camp's northern gate. "If you stood and looked at the Quonset huts, toward Mount Fuji, it was off to the right," he recalled of the previous site, "a good distance from the end of the line of the Quonset huts."

Jogging uphill, Mark Bedwell thought back on the fuel storage site he had observed when 2/4 exercised in South Korea: "It was a good thousand meters from where we were bivouacked." If the battalion was training as it would fight in combat, he thought, storing fuel so nearby didn't make sense. "Hey, you want to wipe out a whole battalion of Marines? Hit the fuel dump."

But, he figured, "what do I know?"

5

FUEL FARM

> You may choose a [fuel supply] site in low hills or rolling country, but never choose one uphill or upstream from other installations which would be in the path of escaping fuel.
>
> —*U.S. Army Field Manual 10–69, October 31, 1977*

IN YEARS BEFORE World War I, cavalry mounts and pack animals had accelerated armies' movement across battlefields. As the U.S. military adopted a new sort of horsepower in advance of the war, petroleum products became an increasingly crucial warfighting resource. During World War II, motor gas—slanged as "MOGAS"—powered most American military vehicles and propeller-driven aircraft. Eighty-six octane was pumped into tanks, trucks, and jeeps—100 octane into airplanes. When jet aircraft screamed into skies during the 1950s, they burned a liquid more kerosene-based, designated JP, for "jet propellent." Its variants were referred to by numbers specifying the fuel's particular formula: JP-5, for instance. By the late 1970s, many trucks and larger vehicles had shifted to diesel. Gasoline, however, was still fueling M151 jeeps, as well as combat-deployable generators and pumps.

The fuels' chemical characteristics afforded effective engine combustion. They also presented risks. "Liquid fuels are dangerous materials to handle as they vaporize easily and burn rapidly," warned a 1977 pocket guide for Marine Corps fuel handlers. "Fuel in the form of vapor must be present when anything burns," a 1973 Navy safety manual explained, "because it is not the actual substance which is consumed by the flame, but the vapor of the substance in combination with the oxygen of the air." An ignition source making contact with a vapor-air compound would result in a fiery explosion more dangerous than would occur if flame was directly applied to the fuel in its liquid form.

Key to determining the danger was "flash point": the lowest temperature at which vapors rising from a fuel's liquid surface combine with nearby air to create a mixture capable of igniting—"flashing"—if exposed to flame. Fuels with higher flash points generally presented less fire risk. Kerosene, for instance, would not flash unless temperatures around it were at least 115 degrees Fahrenheit. For jet propellants such as JP-5 to ignite in this fashion, atmospheric temperatures needed to be around 140. Diesel flashpoints, depending on the fuel blend, ranged from 126 to 205 degrees. MOGAS vapors, on the other hand, could flash into flame at most any temperature above -45. The advantage: MOGAS could get military engines started even in very cold environments. The danger: it could flash in the range of temperatures normal over much of the earth. "Products which give off flammable vapors at or below 80 degrees Fahrenheit, such as gasoline," the Navy manual made clear, "are the most hazardous of all petroleum products to handle."

Fire safety was a concern at Camp Fuji. Early in 1979 maintenance crews had been forced to demolish the training camp Quonset hut designated Building D-218 after extensive fire damage rendered it irreparable. The camp lacked a meaningful firefighting capability—a vulnerability pointed up during a two-day, late August inspection by Okinawa-based Fire Chief J. L. Livermore and Fire Inspector T. Ohashi. Livermore and Ohashi found only two standard fire hydrants at the camp. Dry chemical fire extinguishers were evident in the base camp where permanent staff lived and worked; "however," they reported, the "training camp side lack of extinguishers is wide spread." Water barrels that would ostensibly supply ad hoc bucket brigades in the event of a fire could easily turn into blocks of ice during winter; they recommended adding antifreeze chemicals. Finally, the inspectors faulted the camp for having "no program to inform personnel of fire safety," and insufficient means of alerting residents in the event of a blaze.

Echo Company's Fredric Britton Jr. recalled receiving only scant instruction before standing "fire watch" in the training camp—a sentry duty dating back to the days when troops would bed down around a campfire; someone needed to ensure that the fire remained lit, but did not spread and hurt anyone. Britton was told to sound an alarm if he observed fire danger. "There's a triangle with a little thingee," he explained: a metal beater to create the triangle's high-pitched ringing tone.

While the few available extinguishers and barrels of water might potentially allow fire watches to knock down small fires, the inspectors worried about the camp's ability to respond to a larger blaze. "Mobile fire apparatus response," Chief Livermore confirmed, "is limited to verbal agreement of response from Japanese Self-Defense Force adjacent to the camp and local village approximately five mile distance [*sic*]." Due to "lack of adequate fire protection," he recommended that camp leaders immediately begin teaching staff and visiting units "use of available first aid extinguishers, fire reporting procedures, and strict fire prevention measures." In forwarding the inspection results to the Range Company commander on September 12, the Camp Butler commanding general did not apply pressure for rapid change. He directed that "appropriate action relating to recommendations should be initiated in accordance with normal command, support and funding procedures."

Conversations about where visiting units would store and dispense fuel at Camp Fuji involved the Range Company staff and combat engineer officers attached to the units arriving to train. It was not unusual for such units to want to place their "fuel farm" alongside the dirt road directly above the training camp. Vehicles traversed it frequently while heading to weapons ranges and the Fuji Maneuver Area. Fueling vehicles "on the way," some contended, was more efficient than requiring them to drive elsewhere, fill up, then double back. From 1976 to 1979, however, at the insistence of the Range Company staff, diesel and MOGAS had been stockpiled just inside the camp's far northern gate, which fronted less occupied space. Aviation fuel had been made available on level terrain near the small runway.

On Tuesday, June 19, Colonel B. T. Chen—who had overseen Camp Fuji since August 23, 1978—relinquished command of Range Company. Because Chen's replacement had not yet arrived, Major W. E. Hudson, who had served for eight months as Range Company's executive officer, its second-in-command, assumed interim authority as camp commander.

The following day, a small advance team of officers and senior noncommissioned officers from Battalion Landing Team 3/9 arrived from Okinawa.

The unit was next in queue to train below Mount Fuji. It would be receiving additional assistance on this deployment from a separate command being simultaneously deployed to Camp Fuji.

Logistics Support Unit (LSU) Foxtrot had been assembled on Okinawa on March 5. Under a concept in place at the time, LSUs would provide support services needed when battalion landing teams and associated aviation units were deployed around the world. In weeks to come, LSU Foxtrot would be redesignated LSU 3/9, reflecting its support of the similarly-numbered BLT.

The support unit was commanded by thirty-eight-year-old Major John F. Brosnan Jr., who arrived at the camp sometime around July 2. By then a fifteen-year career artillery officer, Brosnan had served two combat tours in Vietnam. In January 1970 he had trained at Camp Fuji while assigned to 4th Battalion, Twelfth Marines. During half of his year with 4/12, Brosnan had acted as the artillery battalion's logistics officer. Based on that on-the-job experience, the Marine Corps had amended his qualification record to indicate a professional competence in logistics. Assigned again to Okinawa in 1979, Brosnan was selected to lead the LSU. Its Marines and Sailors provided such disparate support services as combat engineering, motor transport, vehicle and equipment maintenance, payroll disbursing, postal services, and dentistry.

The job of the seven bulk fuel specialists incorporated into the LSU's Landing Support Platoon was to ensure BLT 3/9's easy access to all the fuel its vehicles would need to sustain training at Camp Fuji. Brosnan determined that they would do so using a movable fueling station system his Marines had carried to the camp. "It was my decision to set up a fuel farm," Brosnan explained in 1979, "because we only had one tanker refueler [truck] with us and the LSU had bulk fuel people attached to it. I felt I had a duty to train them and make use of our bulk fuel capacity."

The concept of a transportable fuel storage and dispensing system evolved in the wake of World War II. Fighting their way onto enemy-held Pacific islands during that conflict, Marines had found themselves relying primarily on 55-gallon drums and 5-gallon cans to fuel amphibious tractors, tanks, trucks, and jeeps. Warfighting engines moving inland quickly burned away the modest quantities. When supplies depleted forward momentum slowed. Unrelenting demand for petroleum placed massive burden on Sailors and Marines coordinating delivery of supplies from ship to shore. The more time they spent pushing metal barrels across unshielded shorelines, the greater their exposure to enemy fire.

During the late 1950s, new technologies promised more efficient fuel-handling, in the form of rubberized fabric tanks. They had been developed in Akron, Ohio, by a Goodyear Tire and Rubber Company department famous for fabricating blimps and cartoon-character-shaped parade balloons. When filled, a Goodyear news release noted, the sizable liquid containers looked "like giant-sized pillows." The firm marketed them as "pillow tanks." Portability was a key attribute. When the tanks were empty, advertisements touted, each could be "rolled up like a rug." Set up, pillow tanks taking up the space of about one hundred barrels could hold the liquid equivalent of a thousand. At a Goodyear plant in Rockmart, Georgia, the tanks were fabricated through precise assembly of calendered fabric, specialty rubbers, and precision hose attachment fittings. After complex seaming and closure work, each tank was vulcanized in a huge heater.

Army engineers and Air Force logisticians were first to make military use of the rubberized reservoirs. By March 1962 the Marine Corps was purchasing pillow tanks. The Amphibious Assault Fuel System LSU 3/9 Marines unpacked at Camp Fuji in 1979 included 20,000-gallon fabric tanks. Empty, each weighed 275 pounds. When laid flat—like the "rug" sales brochures had described—a single unfilled "pillow" spread to 24 feet, 4 inches wide, and 28 feet long. Set up, and filled to capacity with a liquid fuel, a 20,000-gallon bladder would swell to 5 feet, 9 inches tall. That would pull in the sides and end a bit, shrinking the bladder's ground footprint to 22 feet, 3 inches wide and 25 feet, 8 inches long.

An elegance of the AAFS was that no tools were needed to get the system up and running. Suction-type hoses with quick-disconnect coupler and adapter fittings attached the bladders to powerful, trailer-mounted centrifugal pumps. The pumps' engines, built by GMC Detroit Diesel, could pull and transfer six hundred gallons of fuel per minute.

"That's what was provided for you," Brosnan recalled. "There was nothing else to use," he noted, other than the unit's single M-49 refueling vehicle. It could hold only 1,200 gallons. "If we hadn't have used them, we wouldn't have had any fuel."

Advice on where to set up an AAFS could be found in a pocket guide for bulk fuel Marines, which recommended selecting a location that balanced battlefield requirements with safety considerations. It "should take advantage of natural cover," the handbook continued. "The most level and easily accessible fuel routes should be chosen. Fuel lines should be near and parallel to an existing or planned road or trail, when possible. . . . Location of the system should minimize construction requirements and maintenance difficulties." It also recommended taking prevailing winds into account, "so that if a fire were to start, flames would blow away from most of the fuel containers."

A 1971 Defense Department petroleum operations handbook recommended placement "with the contour of terrain being such that it will confine spillage and [in event of a storage tank leak] permit recovering of fuels and prevent flow into open streams." To ease any potential need for firefighting, it directed that a fuel farm's "main outlets [be] so located that flow is away from a congested area and toward a harmless area where fire extinguishing agents can be applied en route or at destination."

Terrain-related guidance offered in two U.S. Army instructions of the time was even more specific. An Army field manual published in 1977 suggested selecting sites "reasonably level and well-drained to prevent water damage. . . . Look for a tank site without slopes," the manual's authors advised, as a "large slope may cause filled tanks to roll sideways, backwards, or forward." Most strikingly, the Army field manual directed that while sites in low hills or on rolling terrain might be acceptable, "never choose one uphill or upstream from other installations which would be in the path of escaping fuel." Interestingly, the language of that prohibition had—in the five years preceding the field manual's publication—been strengthened to *never*. Wording in a 1972 Army technical manual had instructed that fuel farms "*should not be* uphill or upstream from other installations" (emphasis added).

The principal instruction guiding LSU 3/9 bulk fuel technicians was a set of regulations published in October 1978. Marine Corps Technical Manual 3835–15/1 encouraged that fuel farms be "level with good drainage to prevent damage to containers by water" and "isolated from living quarters and at least 250 feet away from buildings or structures such as a fuel operations hut." Terrain incline was not otherwise included among factors influencing storage site selection.

It is not clear that the seven young bulk fuel specialists assigned to LSU 3/9, nor the combat engineer leaders to whom they reported, would have been aware of prescriptions beyond those detailed in the Marine Corps technical manual. Importantly, while the Marines would have been expected to comply with Department of Defense and Navy Department regulations, their operations were not governed by Army field manuals. It was TM-3835-15/1, therefore—and a bit of corporate memory—that guided the LSU Marines as they set in place their fuel bladders and pumps.

John Brosnan recalled that in 1970, when he had last trained below Mount Fuji, he had been told to dispense fuel from a location directly above the training camp. "The battalion commander, when we took 4/12 up there, said, 'This is where I want it . . .' You know, the training areas are all uphill and everything. So the fuel farm—being there—was a good place to put it."

"Based upon that experience," Brosnan explained, and the existence of the long—seemingly protective—berm he had found in place during this deployment to the camp, "I made the decision to put the fuel farm there when we moved in with 3/9." In 1979 he described the location as "at least 100 meters [~329 feet] from the nearest building and 250 to 300 meters [~820 to 984 feet] from the closest barracks buildings."

The site allowed easy filling of the rubberized fabric tanks by commercial tanker trucks that delivered fuel to the camp. Visits by the ten-thousand-gallon tankers were less disruptive when the vehicles made their way in and out without backing up or turning around—maneuvers that could rip up the camp's graded-dirt roads and potentially endanger Marines walking about.

"They didn't want those refuel trucks driving through the middle of the compound," Jacob Evans Jr. called to mind. In 1979 Evans was a first lieutenant commanding the LSU's landing support platoon. "Basically," he remembered, "they wanted them on the outer perimeter all the time." With the fuel bladders just above the road-hugging long berm, trucks could enter the camp through one gate, fill the bladders, then—making two simple ninety-degree turns—skirt the periphery of the training camp and exit via another.

Major Hudson, the acting Range Company commander who would complete his assignment at the camp on July 19, did not override the placement decision.

From Tuesday, July 3, to Thursday, July 12, LSU 3/9 combat engineers and bulk fuel specialists leveled ground uphill of the main berm and added soil to reinforce the elongated mound. Lieutenant Evans oversaw the work, under the watchful eye of the LSU's executive officer, Captain Joseph Bryant. On the newly flattened space, Evans's Marines laid out two large rubberized fabric ground cloths to protect against rocks and other sharp objects. Then, on top of each, they unrolled a fuel bladder. "The bladders were inclined slightly forward," Evans noted—downhill facing—"to allow for gravity feed."

Soil berms were built up around each bladder to protect against spread of potential spills. The 1978 Marine Corps technical manual codified the precaution, prescribing that "as a general rule" berms built around each individual fuel bladder "must be able to hold one and one-half to two times the contents of a filled tank." Evans explained that "our guidance was that the bladders would never be filled with more than 10,000 gallons of fuel, so we built [each] berm to hold 15,000 gallons."

One now-retired Marine Corps officer—who began his career as an enlisted bulk fuel specialist during the 1970s—remembered a good deal of berm construction at the time being less than substantial, even given commendable training provided by instructors at the Marine Corps' East- and West-Coast fuel-handling schools. "Sadly," he recounted, "once I got to the fleet, I realized that other staff noncommissioned officers were not following the book and had us build berms on top of the surface instead of digging down. . . . They would not hold up against a rupture or deluge. Instead of digging into the ground, per the manual, [they had us] merely pushing dirt to build a berm wall."

The berms surrounding LSU 3/9's fuel bladders, Jacob Evans affirmed, were constructed in proper fashion. "Dig out and create a valley, if you want to call it that," he said. "And that's what we did."

On Wednesday, July 11, the bulk fuel Marines took delivery of 10,000 gallons of diesel fuel. The battalion landing team they had been deployed to support began moving into the training camp the next day. Some 5,200 gallons of MOGAS arrived for transfer to a bladder on Friday, July 27.

The fuel farm sat atop a soil mixture that had long frustrated Marines shoveling foxholes. "I'd dig out a handful of ashes," Thomas Moquino would later sigh, "and more would go back into the hole."

Major Brosnan had considered the camp's sharp and crumbly volcanic soil as the fuel farm took shape. "I knew the type of soil presented an erosion problem," he noted in 1979, claiming, though, that "an alternative [fuel farm] location would have required the clearing of vegetation, making the erosion problem worse." Also bolstering his confidence in the site: Brosnan and his bulk fuel team believed that the long roadside berm, and the raised perimeters they built up around each bladder, were solidly packed.

There was engineering logic behind the view. "When they are properly designed and constructed," geotechnical engineer Rolando Orense contended in 2022, "compacted volcanic soils can serve well as embankments." Strength and erodibility, observed the University of Auckland professor, determined the robustness of such berms, road abutments, and similar support structures. If soil particles can be tightly compacted, maintained Orense—who spent fifteen years consulting on soil-related aspects of engineering projects in Japan—friction between them can establish a solid bond.

Achieving sufficient densification with volcanic soils, though, can be more complex than doing so with other earthen materials. Compaction and densification is often created using vibration energy from heavy equipment rolled over successive layers of an under-construction berm. In a structure constructed of volcanic soil, this process can sometimes, Orense noted, crush and compact "the upper part, but not the lower part of the lifts." Moreover, he added, "the low density of volcanic soils makes them erosion-prone." If particles of pyroclastic materials are not well-interlocked through proper compression, seepage might develop underneath a berm constructed of the material. Another susceptibility: "piping"—duct-like holes developing in the structure, through which liquids might flow. "For the embankment to hold," Orense emphasized, "the foundation of the dike needs to be improved as well." That, he said, would require additional heavy equipment rolling over berm layers—reorienting soil particles into a denser configuration and, to the extent possible, driving air out of the compressed soil.

The degree to which the long berm had been compacted is not clear. Japan's Defense Facilities Administration Office (DFAO) had coordinated its 1973 construction as a flood-control measure.

No efforts, though, were made to densify the berms LSU engineers built to surround each of the bladders they installed. "We had no way of compacting other than a dozer running over it," Evans recalled. "But we didn't do that. We just dug it out, bermed it up, and set the bladders in," The rush resulted from a tight deadline. "When we got there," he recounted, "we were in a crunch—3/9 was right on our tail. I knew they would need fuel for the tanks and the jeeps and all the vehicles. We also provided fuel for the base camp."

The fuel farm, as constructed that early July, placed the bladders and a fueling site for tracked vehicles uphill of the 440-yard berm. Two pumps—each weighing more than one and a half tons—had been placed atop the berm. Just below the man-made ridge was a fueling site for vehicles traveling on rubber tires. Bulk fuel Marines sat in a box-like wooden structure alongside the road there, awaiting customers. "They'd pull up," one recollected. "We'd give them the nozzle, turn the fuel pump on, pump 'til they had the gas they needed, write down the amount of gallons, have them sign it, send them on their way."

Roadside fueling of the wheeled vehicles required suctioning fuels up and over the elongated man-made mound—arduous work for the pumping system. The 1977 pocket guide recommended avoiding suction lifts in excess of ten feet. "I did not like having the pumps on top of the berm," wrote Corporal David W. Marlow, noncommissioned officer in charge (NCOIC) of the fuel farm during its early months of operation. "It was too hard on the equipment to pump the fuel uphill from the bladders to the top of the berm, and it meant having an extra man on top of the berm to operate the pump."

Still, John Brosnan's experience in 1970 convinced him that the above-camp configuration would best support Battalion Landing Team 3/9. The unit's commander, Lieutenant Colonel Dale Dorman, came to believe so, as well. Soon after the BLT's arrival at Camp Fuji—Dorman's first-ever visit there—he was briefed on the site. Any initial reservations were "alleviated," he noted decades later, "because the berm that was being built was unlike any berm I had ever seen as far as the overall safety of it." The LSU's addition of soil to the Japanese-constructed long berm set Dorman's mind at ease, as did his impression of Major Brosnan as "a super-competent individual."

Dorman's chaplain—thirty-two-year-old Navy Lieutenant Steve Jensen—was less sanguine. He was not an engineer, but the fuel farm placement struck him as ill advised. "I brought it up," one day, he recalled, as he joined BLT officers in a meeting with Range Company leaders. "I said, 'I'm clearly new to all this,'" Jensen remembered, "'but maybe new eyes can see something that people who've been around awhile can't see. It just defies common sense that you would put fuel bladders with the flex-pipe linkages up above Quonset huts where people are living. . . . You've got stoves in there.'" The chaplain remembered a lieutenant colonel at the base camp telling him curtly that "'that's the way it had been done for a long time and it had proven to be safe. So, keep my thoughts to myself.'"

By the time Colonel Allan W. Lamb assumed command of Range Company on Wednesday, July 18, the fuel farm above the training camp had been in place for a week. The forty-nine-year-old determined the site suitable. "I had seen many fuel farms before," he recalled, "and they had all been constructed like this one, even in sand or in areas subject to flash flooding." Lamb was inclined to allow visiting commanders significant latitude in how they configured their unit's equipment on the camp. "Insofar as is practicable," he wrote in 1979, "it is my policy not to interfere with the training of the BLT."

Lamb's confidence in the new fuel farm location was seemingly affirmed when, on August 27, the camp passed an inspection conducted by Colonel James A. Poland, the assistant chief of staff for logistics and facilities at Camp Butler, the Marines' senior command on Okinawa. Camp Fuji fell under Poland's operational purview.

It would be surprising if Colonel Lamb was not at some point informed of objections to the site selection raised from within the camp's supply department. They came from Masao Satoh, an eleven-year camp employee whose day-to-day duties included ordering and overseeing delivery of petroleum products. "I objected to the fuel farm being moved because of drainage problems," Satoh explained in 1979.

> I told Lieutenant [Steven C.] Miller, the Range Company Supply Officer, that this was a bad location because the rain that drained out of the impact area above Camp Fuji washed toward that site and then through the Training Camp further downhill. I also mentioned that the soft volcanic soil in the area contributed to the water run-off. Lieutenant Miller agreed with me and about a week later talked to someone in the BLT about putting the fuel bags on concrete blocks. This was not carried out, however.

The supply specialist may have found a degree of solace in an engineering project begun in early September. At Colonel Lamb's order, LSU combat engineers filled a sizable opening in the long berm. It had been plowed to allow passage of tracked vehicles. "Water runoff through the break," noted the camp commander, had been "flooding a stand of trees and uprooting them."

In mid-September—again, on Lamb's instruction—LSU 3/9 Marines began extending the long berm's northern end. Having watched more than a decade's worth of storms pass over the camp, Masao Satoh believed the latter effort "would have very little effect on water drainage." Eroding floodwaters, he explained, would typically "flow around the south end of the berm." In Satoh's view the most useful potential engineering project would be creation of a new "wall" or "drainage control ditch" three hundred yards uphill from the existing man-made ridge. Such a structure, the supply specialist contended, "would cause more water to flow around the camp to the north and south"—reducing flooding in the camp proper. He discussed the idea with a DFAO representative, who told him that work on a project of that sort was scheduled to commence in 1980.

The Marines continued their berm extension project, which, it turned out, had not been motivated by drainage-related apprehensions. "I had the north end of the berm extended to conceal a burn pit in that vicinity," Lamb wrote. "I had received complaints from the DFAO that the dump was unsightly as it was visible from Gotemba Trail [Route 23, the road that bordered Camp Fuji's northern edge, separating it from Camp Takigahara, a Japanese military post]. I had the burn pit covered and the berm extended to prevent access to it."

Though unclear if it was prompted by Masao Satoh's expressed concerns, records imply that an inspection of the fuel farm was conducted on September 18–19 by combat engineer Lieutenant Colonel John G. Fitzgerald. As facilities maintenance officer of the Marines' principal base on Okinawa, Fitzgerald was also responsible for ensuring upkeep of Camp Fuji's buildings and grounds. His visit—during which he apparently assessed the site as stable—would have been made amid adverse weather. Strong showers had hit the camp on Saturday, August 18. By day's end the rainfall had totaled 7.72 inches. The greatest measure had come between 8 a.m and 2 p.m., accompanied for a time by winds averaging twenty-two miles per hour.

More bad weather was to come. During the overnight hours of Sunday, September 30, and Monday, October 1, the camp felt the last effects of

Typhoon Owen, which had blasted over Japan's main island with winds of up to sixty-three miles per hour. Across Honshu Owen would be blamed for twelve deaths and eighty-three injuries. By the time the storm reached Camp Fuji, its impacts were more related to wind than rain. Breezes began to accelerate at 11 p.m. on Sunday. Between 1 and 2 a.m. Monday, wind speeds at the camp were averaging more than twenty-nine miles per hour. At 3 a.m. they were still blowing beyond twenty miles per hour.

The two incidents of heavy weather had required repairs at the fuel site. "The small berms around the bladders had washed away," Jacob Evens noted, "so they were level with the tops of the bladders." David Marlow recalled that each "had filled with water." The long berm, Evans said, "had washed out slightly."

John Brosnan's stint at Camp Fuji nearly a decade before had not been stormy. "It was just cold and dry when we were up there with 4/12," he recalled. Weather conditions nine years later, though, did not lead Brosnan to reconsider his site selection. "Yes, we may have had some hellacious rainstorms," he recalled decades later, "but I don't remember it causing any significant damage, or any significant change in the way we were thinking about things."

About a month after Lance Corporal Rickey Lamon had been assigned to Okinawa in mid-1979, he volunteered to deploy with LSU 3/9. "They said there was a float gonna go all over the South Pacific," he remembered. "There was going to be a two-week stop at Mount Fuji. That would be one of the stops." The travel sounded fun; he jumped at the opportunity. After arriving at the camp, though, he learned that not everyone was heading on to a succession of exotic ports. "They said, 'Well, we're only going to take two people from each unit.'"

On Monday, September 10, when BLT 3/9 returned to Okinawa, most of its accompanying LSU remained at Camp Fuji. "The reason we stayed longer was because of a shortage of personnel within FSSG," Jacob Evans recalled. The Okinawa-based 3rd Force Service Support Group—from which the LSU members had been drawn—could not pull together another complete unit to assist the next BLT headed to the training camp. "We were already intact," Evans recalled, so FSSG leaders decided: "Just leave them there."

While most of the LSU remained, some of its members would be called back to Okinawa for other assignments. Corporal David Marlow was one. When he departed the camp, Rickey Lamon was left as the senior bulk fuel Marine.

It was work for which he had not been formally trained. After having gotten "a little sideways with a couple of instructors" while studying to be an aviation electronics specialist, Lamon had been reassigned to a Marine Corps air station in southern California. Working alongside bulk fuel specialists there, he trained on the job for several months before being ordered to Okinawa.

In early October BLT 2/4 began moving into the training camp. As the new group of Marines and Sailors crowded into Quonset huts, Lamon and his team unfurled a third fuel bladder uphill of the large berm. Into the nylon fabric tank they pumped JP-5 that had previously—and poorly, they believed—been stored in an airstrip-adjacent bladder below the training camp. At that site it had been set atop airfield matting, with no surrounding berm. "My concern," Jacob Evans remembered, "was that if this thing ruptured, all that fuel could flow into the base camp or the Japanese camp across the street." Because bulk fuel team members would not be dispensing aviation fuel while supporting BLT 2/4, they did not connect the resituated bladder to a pump.

Now settled in, the LSU Marines felt themselves in a useful routine. The newly arrived battalion would need the same sorts of support they had successfully provided the last. More of the same, they surmised.

Wild winds over the water would ensure otherwise.

6

SUPER TYPHOON

> Once the other ones got out of the way—Sarah and Roger—Tip took over. Ultimately, it dominated everything from the Japanese islands practically to the equator. And then from the Philippine islands eastward, well beyond Guam.
>
> —*George Dunnavan, U.S. Navy meteorologist*

AS BLT 2/4 settled in at Camp Fuji, Tropical Storm Tip ranged the Pacific, pushing toward Guam. With Tip headed their way, U.S. military commanders on Guam began to worry about damage the storm might cause to aircraft and ships there. Paying close attention to JTWC forecasts, they directed the submarine tender USS Hunley (AS-31) to leave port for open seas and ordered aviation units to fly most military aircraft to safer terrain. Seventeen of twenty-four planes at Naval Air Station Agana departed the island, as did all aircraft based at Andersen Air Force Base—B-52 bombers and KC-135 refuelers among them. Many of the Guam-base aircraft made their way to Kadena Air Base on Okinawa.

No longer moshing with adjacent storms, Tip intensified quickly. The storm's sustained surface winds accelerated. It drew more moisture from the sea. The girth of the maelstrom grew. At about 8:15 on the evening of Tuesday, October 9, Tropical Storm Tip passed some thirty miles south of Merizo—Guam's southernmost village. Sustained winds of sixty-three miles per hour brushed over the island territory, gusting as high as seventy-three. Its roaring winds and rain left behind flooding, power outages, downed foliage, and washed-out roads.

In 1979 meteorologists had yet to adopt the now-familiar numerical categories used to describe cyclone intensity. They instead classified windstorms under four headings: tropical disturbance, tropical storm, typhoon, and super typhoon. After Tip's outer reaches washed over southern Guam, its winds pushed beyond seventy-four miles per hour; it was designated a typhoon—Category 1, by modern reckoning.

Over the next two days, its gales surged to greater than 130 miles per hour, then beyond 157, pushing the storm into current-standard Category 4, then 5—the realms in which tropical cyclones are deemed "super typhoons." By Thursday, October 11, it was tracking toward Okinawa. Guam-based aircrews that had taken refuge there returned to home base flight lines and hangars.

On Thursday, October 11, a 54th WRS aircraft jarred and jolted its way into the eye of the havoc-wreaking storm. Onboard to take measurements and get a firsthand look at the storm's center was Carol Belt, an Air Force first lieutenant and ARWO well experienced in measuring typhoons from within.

Crews from the 54th were beginning to realize that this storm was unique. The tack they took to study it, though, was routine and continuous. "Each crew that flew into [a typhoon] would be there for three to six hours or so," Belt remembered. "And then they would go back to Guam, the Philippines, or wherever." As soon as one crew departed the storm, another would make its way in. "Meteorologically, we tried to take what's called an official 'fix' of the typhoon eye every three hours." The process kept multiple crews aloft for long periods.

Flights *to* storm sites were typically routine, once aviators overcame muscle-memory compulsion to steer clear of bad weather. On approach crews increased safety precautions. "In those days they still allowed you to smoke," Bob Korose remembered. Cigarettes had to be extinguished. Anything that might fly about inside the aircraft had to be tied down. "Then you had to be strapped in."

Turbulence became likely when aircraft began pushing into a typhoon's eye—flying through "feeder bands" of wind and water being drawn to its center. The most violent of such instability was experienced when penetrating storms still forming—or those collapsing. Think of an old-fashioned toy top, 54th WRS crew member Roger Ritchie analogized. "When you spin the top, you know, it starts out wobbly, and then it's going, and then it starts wobbling again as it falls over." Storms were the same, he explained. Counterintuitive though it might seem, it was easier to fly through one that was fully spun up.

Tip, by this time, was powerfully developed and holding shape. As she and colleagues pierced its eyewall, Carol Belt recalled instability no worse than one might experience on a typical commercial flight. During a penetration several hours later, ARWO Patrick Giese would describe similar stability. "From about 150 miles out," he recalled, "it was like somebody turned a fire hose on your windshield." He discerned no feeder bands; the storm was steady, "light turbulence the whole way through."

Making their way in, crews assessed the perpendicular access point that would get them most directly into the storm's center. Because north-of-the-equator cyclones spin counterclockwise, aircraft flying into storm eyes in the earth's top half are constantly buffeted by strong winds from the left. Patrick Giese watched pilots fight against the inevitable rightward drift by "kind of crabbing into the wind. Keep turning left, keep turning left, keep turning left."

Pilots would set turbulence penetration speed: just over two hundred miles per hour. "If you fly in too fast," Bob Korose explained, "then you get more structural forces on the plane and that can cause damage. And if you're flying too slow, you can lose airspeed and possibly stall." Maintaining desired speed was not easy, he said: "When you get an updraft, you're going to lose speed. When you get a downdraft, you're going to gain speed." The fluctuations could be significant, quickly altering a plane's airspeed by twenty-three to thirty-five miles per hour. Keeping the WC-130s level, their speed steady, often required two pilots on the controls simultaneously. Navigators on the aircraft carefully eyed radar screens, directing pilots around potential rough spots. In the end such journeys did not usually take long. At penetration speed aircraft were flying close to three miles a minute.

Having broken through to the comparative calm of the storm's eye, air crews had to pay immediate attention to the typhoon's internal "atmospheric"—also known as "barometric"—pressure. Pressure in the eye is always lower than outside, explained Roger Ritchie, because cyclonic eyewalls "have upward motion and it's sort of like throwing mass out, so air pressure at the center drops."

The 54th WRS crews began their flights into the eyewall at 10,000 feet. The altitude offered a safety benefit to crews piercing the rain bands. If strong downdrafts hammered their aircraft lower, pilots had reasonable time to recover control. At 10,000 feet (outside of the eye) the atmospheric pressure around the WC-130s measured some 700 millibars. Because evaluating storms at a single pressure level allowed easier analysis of findings, pilots would work hard throughout their missions (outside and inside a typhoon's eye) to maintain 700 millibar pressure around the aircraft. Doing so, after breaking through to the lower-pressure environment of an eye, often required an abrupt descent to 9,000 or 8,800 feet above sea level. As 54th WRS missions within Tip continued, the storm's internal air pressure continued to drop. During one twenty-seven-hour period alone, it fell fifty-nine millibars. As October 11 bridged into October 12, typhoon-hunting Hercules aircraft at the storm's center kept lowering altitude.

Meteorologist Carol Belt and her crewmates made their way into Tip during those dark overnight hours. "Couldn't see a thing" at first, she remembered. Navigating by radar they made their way to the calmest point in the eye's center, where they would release a sensor called a "dropsonde." It was the same sort of device weather forecasters had for many years floated *up* in balloons—cylindrical, smaller than a loaf of bread. This one had a small parachute attached, allowing it a smooth descent. "They had a little tube in the aircraft," Navy TDO George Dunnavan recalled, "and they'd just put the device in it and hit the button, and it dropped out." As it floated to the sea surface below, the sonde measured temperature, humidity, and air pressure at every point on the way down, its radio transmitter relaying the data back to the WC-130. Because each device could be set to transmit on a unique frequency, it was possible to release two or three at a time, collecting the measurements captured by each. "The shell of it is a hard cardboard, basically," Bob Korose explained, "so when it hits the water, it will stop transmitting. And that last pressure that it gets is the sea level pressure."

Inside the eye one of Carol Belt's crewmates dropped sondes and took measurements. The WC-130 then broke out on the side opposite of where it had entered. Flying some distance away, pilots made two turns, then thirty minutes later penetrated the storm's center from another point. "Still dark," Belt recounted, "still couldn't see a thing. Took the observation, flew back out." The motif repeated. Had the aircraft's path been mapped over the course of the mission, it would have mirrored the shape of a bowtie or an hourglass. Flying such a pattern allowed measurement of each of a typhoon's quadrants.

While measurements were indicating a very strong storm, Belt remembered, inky night skies had obscured most visual proof. That changed soon after the team broke into the eye for a third time. "I'm busy, taking my observation and coding it, getting ready to send it," she recalled. One of the pilots called, "'Weather, you'd better come up here, look at this.' I said, 'Hang on!' We were a little pressed for time." Their summons became increasingly urgent. "'Weather, *seriously!*' And so I get up and look out."

Skies above the eye had suddenly cleared. Reflected moonlight—indirect, they couldn't see the moon itself—poured through. "There was about a nine mile-wide clear spot at the top of the twenty-five-to-thirty-mile-wide eye," Belt estimated. "The moon was shining in, making the whole eye glow . . . it was an immense, immense fishbowl."

"Fishbowl" was one of three typical eyewall shapes. "If it's not all that strong," the ARWO described, "it'll have what we call a 'barrel eye'—you fly in, the walls are basically straight up and straight down. The better it forms, the tighter it wraps." In eyewalls exhibiting a "stadium effect," the top portion of the wall flares outward, mimicking the shape of an outdoor stadium's upper tiers. In well-tightened cyclones, the top can pull inward, causing the opening to become narrower than the eye's main body—not unlike a rounded fishbowl with a narrow circular opening at its top.

Through the acutely constricted opening atop the "fishbowl" in which they flew, moonglow illuminated Tip's myriad cells—individual thunderstorms that had been seized into the storm's interior orbit. From within, brief-but-intense lightening bolts added radiance. The flashes allowed Belt quick glimpses of how the power-merged storms had been stacked and intertwined. "In each cell," she noted, "there was a double helix of circulation. All these little double helixes going around. Oh, my gosh, probably a dozen or more." Adding to the crew's sensory overload: electrically-ionized air molecules—St. Elmo's fire—began washing over the WC-130's windscreen and wings. "It looked like a thin skim of colorful water," Belt reminisced, "pinks and yellows and oranges. *Everything* was glowing! It was stunning."

Then there was the view downward. "Below the eyewall, where the strongest winds are," Belt observed, "there was phosphorescent algae on the sea surface. *It* was glowing." The ocean surface below, she remembered, was "absolutely calm right at the very center . . . and in that little millpond, there are styrofoam coolers that have blown off of fishing ships, there are seagulls who are just sitting there because they can't get out. There's a lot of junk that pools in that calm center, and it just swooshes around." That calm disappeared as one looked toward the edges of the within-the-eye sea surface. Nearer the wildly twisting cyclonic winds, Belt emphasized, "the swells and so forth are quite dramatic. . . . The sea surface turns a blue-green with the air that's been churned into the water itself and then the wind sheeting over it."

Finally impressive, she marveled, was what she saw to be the storm's triple eyewall, its interior wall, then two additional—the second, five or six miles out from the inner wall; the third, about ten or twelve miles distant. "It was so tightly wrapped," she remembered, "that it had the eyewall, and then there was—outside of that—a concentric, complete eyewall, and outside of that about a three-quarter eyewall, which constitutes basically a third eyewall." Observing an eyewall developing beyond a second was highly unusual.

The storm had astounded the crew nearly to the point of distraction. "We almost missed the fix," Belt confessed. "We were just flying around and around on the inside going, 'Oh, my God, look at this!'" As Belt radioed her observations to the JTWC, she offered the best description possible under deadline: "To say it was spectacular is totally inadequate . . . . 'Awesome' is a little closer."

In the morning hours of October 12, Belt and her crew mates exited Tip, passing the monitoring mission to the next-in-line 54th WRS crew. By midday, as aircraft commander Lieutenant Colonel Edward Darcy piloted a fresh team of typhoon chasers into Tip's eye, the storm had intensified even further. The resulting interior pressure drop required Darcy to quickly push his WC-130 into a descent more drastic than typically required. "In this case," recalled then-Captain Patrick Giese, the new team's ARWO, "we were only flying, say, 6,000 to 6,500 feet—somewhere at that range, above the surface of the earth" in order to maintain 700 millibar pressure altitude.

On this mission Darcy's crew manifest included more names than usual. His primary mission team consisted of Captain John. R. Harris II, the navigator; Giese; Master Sergeant John Hancock, the flight engineer; and dropsonde operator Senior Airman Roger Ritchie. (While the mission almost certainly included a copilot, the individual's name was not obvious within available records.) Beyond this core crew, ARWO First Lieutenant David Rosenblit was onboard to audit the mission as a flight examiner. Major Bob Korose had also climbed into the WC-130. He had joined the 54th in August. This would be his first observation flight with the squadron.

Flying into the storm during daylight, Darcy's crew would experience Tip's drama differently than had teams earlier in the day. Surrounded by storm chaos, they looked upward into a sunny blue sky. The wall had evolved in shape since Carol Belt's overnight observations. It was still tightly compact—"a solid wall, all the way around, no breaks in it," Roger Ritchie recalled—but its top edges had flared outward in stadium fashion.

Sunshine flooding in from above gave Patrick Giese a clearer view of the double-helix phenomenon Belt had reported. He observed extra bands of clouds sticking out from the inside of the wall—"like a cloud band or cloud streak that was along the wall cloud. Both of them were spiraling upward, around, and it went around three or four times before it would exit out of the top. Like a road going up a mountain with a fifteen-degree incline or something."

Looking downward to the eye's sea surface center, the crew observed typically placid waters. Surrounding that circle of tranquility, though—rising all along the eye's interior perimeter—were massive swells. "I was looking," Roger Ritchie gauged, astonished, "at a hundred-to-two-hundred foot wave."

Because dropsondes could not measure wind speed, ARWOs of the time employed a best-guess system. Whenever a flight mission flew through a break in clouds, or the sea surface became visible, weather officers would jump from their seat on the flight deck and peer at the sea through a sizable plexiglass window. Observing sea surface conditions, they would consult a collection of photographs depicting all manner of waves, whitecaps, and green-water streaks. Each photo was marked with the wind speed measured when it was taken. Current wind speed would be recorded based on which photo most closely resembled the sea state below.

"Waves are developed by the wind and the stronger the wind, the bigger the waves," Patrick Giese indicated, "up to a point. They think that point is somewhere between 120 and 150 miles an hour." That meant the photo album approach was less reliable assessing winds of a typhoon well into Category 5. "Once it gets to that speed," he said, "the wind shears off the tops of the waves. You no longer *have* waves. Anything sticking up, of course, gets blown over. So it looks like white and green streaks, foam and froth. . . . When you get to a hundred knots [115 miles per hour] it's all just spray." While satellites and other technology now offer more precise wind speed determination, Giese noted, in such agitated seas states *then*, "you didn't know if it's 100 knots, or 150, or 160."

Giese had never seen whitecaps as enormous as those within Tip's eye: "Once in a while, you would get two or three of 'em come together at the middle, with a clash. And the thing would splash up at two hundred, three hundred feet. At least that's what it looked like from where we were flying up there."

The physics of a rapidly intensifying typhoon escalated temperatures inside Tip's eyewall to 86 degrees Fahrenheit. "You could feel the heat in the cockpit," Giese affirmed. "I mean, we were sweating, and unzipping flight suits. It was extremely hot."

Key to recording the mission's first fix would be pinpointing—as exactly as possible—the very center of Tip's eye. Once the WC-130 was positioned at that point, it was time to release a dropsonde. Roger Ritchie unstrapped from his seat and moved to the launch tube. Uncapping the four-inches-in-diameter opening at the bottom of the plane, he slid the device through the tube. Once outside its small antenna extended, its parachute opened, and the sonde began transmitting data while descending to the ocean surface. "It fell a lot quicker because we were [flying] so low," Ritchie remembered. "It didn't take too long to get down there."

Forecasters on Guam—and crews flying missions into Tip—had been paying attention to the storm's progressively lower sea level pressure readings. Excitement was building about the possibility of documenting a pressure lower than ever before recorded.

Dropsonde data began arriving almost immediately. "We had a tape—an old system—prints out a four digit number just about every second," Ritchie explained. "So it's tickin' off." He entered the numbers into a computer about the size of a large, modern iPad. Programmed algorithms, he noted, "would calculate pressure, temperature and humidity for every level that you put in." Ritchie calculated carefully and, he thought, rapidly.

It was not quick enough for his crew mates. “They all kept yelling back: ‘Drop! Drop! Have you got it yet? Have you got it yet?’” They all knew that whatever figure emerged would contrast significantly with the 1013 millibar average sea-level pressure across most of the earth.

Ritchie concluded his review. “Okay, drum roll,” he teased. “870 millibars.”

The measurement—made at 1:53 p.m. Chamorro Standard Time; 12:53 p.m. Japan Standard Time—*was* record setting. 870 millibars was the lowest sea-level pressure ever officially observed—not just inside a tropical cyclone, but anywhere on earth. Four and a half decades later it remained a record. “You have to drop 90 millibars from ‘normal’ to get down to a Category 5 level,” Patrick Giese explained, awe still evident. “And from there, it’s a drop of another 50 to get down to 870.”

Because of a basic truism—the lower the pressure at its center, the stronger a typhoon—the measurement implied even more about Tip. Giese contended that it allowed extrapolation of the storm’s wind speeds at the time. “If you’ve got the lowest sea level pressure, you happen to have the strongest winds ever recorded,” he claimed. “Therefore, it is the strongest *storm* ever recorded.” His estimation of Tip’s winds at that moment: “two-hundred-plus” miles per hour.

The unsurpassed low pressure was recorded early in the crew’s mission inside Tip. On subsequent penetrations readings would start to tick upward. The storm was beginning to weaken, though almost imperceptibly. The crew’s final eyewall passage was smooth, though pilots did have to apply near-maximum power as they, outside the eye, brought the WC-130 back to a ten-thousand-foot cruising altitude.

Based on the radius of gale-force wind from its center, there had never before been a cyclone as widespread in aerial extent. At its height, winds spinning from Tip’s eye stretched 690 miles in every direction—1,380 miles edge to edge. If a storm of similar size was set atop the western continental United States, it would cover most of Washington, Oregon, and California; all of Idaho, Nevada, Utah, Arizona, Montana, Wyoming, Colorado, New Mexico, North Dakota, South Dakota, Nebraska, and Kansas; most of Oklahoma; half of Minnesota, half of Iowa; one-third of Texas; and one-third of Missouri.

As it was, in the Pacific, Tip stretched halfway between Guam and the Philippines. With its scale came system-controlling power. “They sometimes talk about tropical cyclones being 'steered' by the upper level wind flows," George Dunnavan noted. "But Tip was so massive that it was dominating the entire weather situation out there for two or three days at least." Patrick Giese believed that, beyond grabbing moisture from nearby typhoons, the storm's pull had reached into the southern hemisphere. "Fifteen hundred to two thousand miles away," the ARWO asserted, "it was stealing moisture from across the equator, which kind of blew our minds."

In the end, for all the scientific amazement, each of the typhoon chasers knew the dark clouds they had encountered were ominous. "On one hand," Roger Ritchie reflected, "you want to jump up—'Yay, we did it! We broke the record!'—you know. And on the other hand you're thinking: Now how much damage is this storm gonna do?"

On Thursday, October 18, people on Okinawa were warned that Tip was set to impact the island with sustained winds of at least 115 miles per hour, gusting to 143 and beyond. Most sought cover inside and braced. Four young U.S. Marines, though, found themselves unable to resist the temptation to witness storm-powered monster waves. Twenty-one-year-old Lance Corporal Norman Schultz of Milwaukee and Corporal Lawrence Soares, twenty, of Fairhaven, Massachusetts headed to Bolo Point, about three miles north of Kadena Air Base. Corporal Jeffrey LeBlanc, twenty-one, and twenty-year-old Private First Class Diane Wilcox joined them atop steep, rocky cliffs near the Zanpamisaki lighthouse. As the four marveled at the progressively surging surf, it reached out. Schultz and Soares were swept into the sea. After a hectic search, LeBlanc and Wilcox discovered Schultz in the water—dead. Soares was lying amid rocks, his right leg badly mangled. The two uninjured Marines grabbed the corporal, applied a tourniquet, and rushed him to Naval Regional Medical Center, Kuwae. A search and rescue team was dispatched to recover Schultz's body from the beach. As Navy surgeons determined it necessary to amputate Soares's rock-shattered limb, Super Typhoon Tip twisted north toward Honshu.

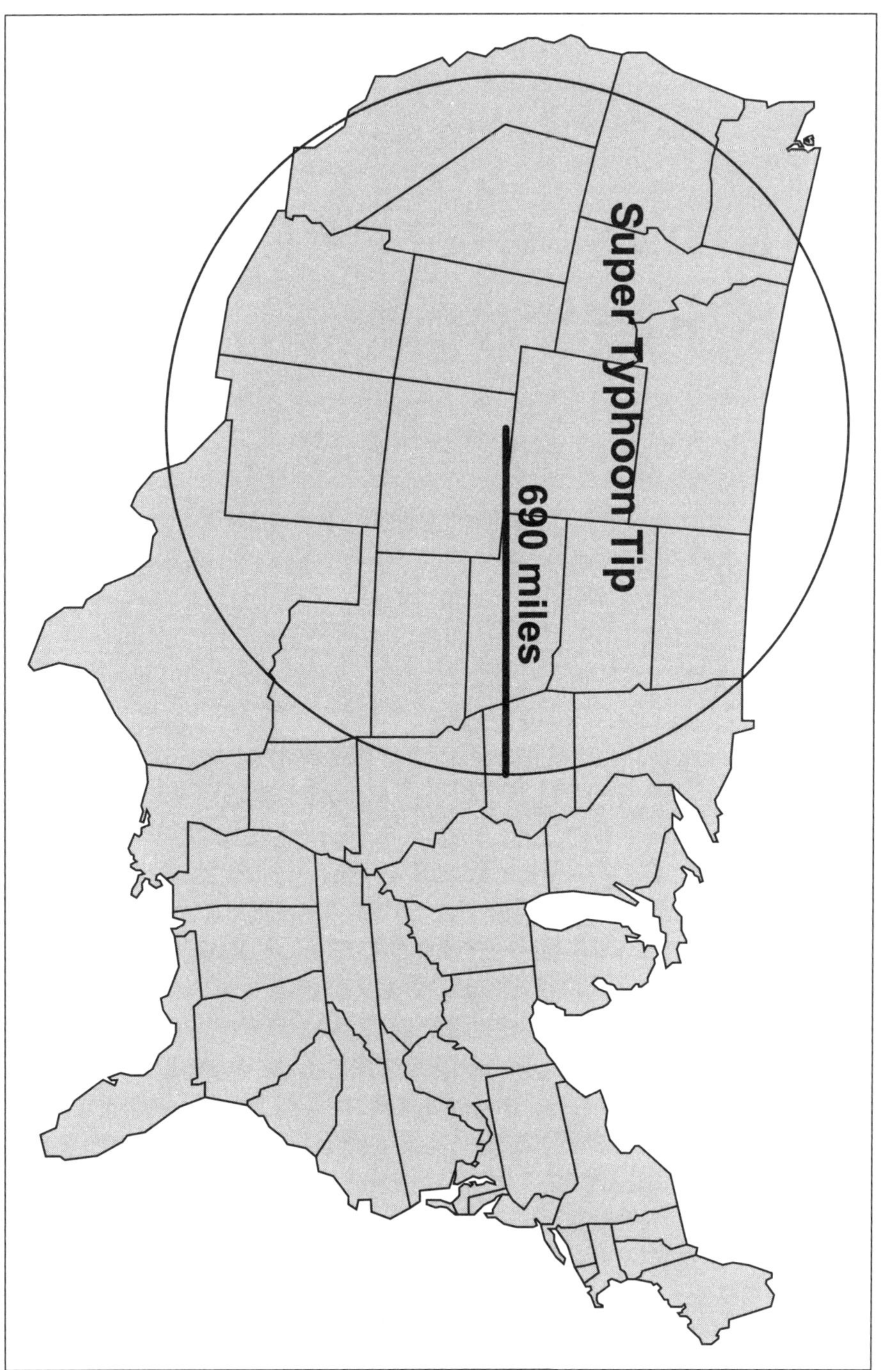

MAP. 3. Typhoon Tip superimposed over the continental United States, illustrating the massive space it occupied in the Pacific. Created by Scott Gannon, based on a U.S. National Weather Service image.

7

FRIDAY, OCTOBER 19, MORNING

Storm should pass us by at 2100 tonight.

—*Note taken during BLT 2/4 morning staff meeting by Captain Leon Craig Jr., commanding officer, Echo Company*

"REVEILLE, REVEILLE. C'MON! Get up!"

It was 4 a.m. on the 292nd day of 1979—the year's 42nd Friday. Cloudbursts over Camp Fuji had briefly ceased, replaced by a persistent drizzle. Nearly two and a half inches of rain had fallen the day before—another inch since midnight. Lieutenant Bill Meyers stepped outside into what struck him as a "spooky fog."

Inside Quonset huts squad leaders shook their men awake. After several days of field exercises, rumor had it that everyone would have the weekend off. First, though, there would be a long-anticipated pay call, then a ten-mile conditioning hike with weapons and gear-heavy packs. Marines and Sailors stumbled into consciousness. It was 62 degrees outside as they headed out for morning ablutions—in Marine Corps alliteration, to "shit, shower, and shave." As the sun inched above the horizon at 5:53, many, cleaned up and uniformed, were polishing off breakfast at the mess hall.

In the nearby town of Gotemba, firefighter Haruhiko Katsumata watched TV as he prepared for the day. "It was around 6 a.m.," he recalled. On-screen weather maps showed Typhoon Tip at sea, powering its way north toward Honshu. "According to the news," Katsumata remembered, "the typhoon was about to land in the proximity of Osaka . . . I was thinking, even if the typhoon doesn't hit Shizuoka prefecture directly, because of its size, it would likely create some damage in our area, so I headed to work at the Gotemba Fire Station."

At Camp Fuji's base camp, downhill from where BLT 2/4 was billeted, camp commander Colonel Allan Lamb began his workday reading teletype-delivered messages that included weather updates. One, transmitted at 6:29, ordered him and other commanders at U.S. naval facilities in the area to set Tropical Storm Condition Two; they would pay closer attention to the storm's developing track.

Another, issued at 7:45, provided a Camp Fuji–specific weather forecast. In it Navy meteorologists at Yokosuka, 45 miles to the east and south, noted that Tip, was "expected to pass 30 miles northwest of Yokosuka about 2100 [Japan Standard Time] Friday night." It called for a day of "overcast cloudiness with moderate to heavy rain" at the camp. After midnight, they predicted, the rain would gradually clear. The forecasters anticipated that the day's storm-driven winds would begin at 21–28 miles per hour, with gusts up to 46. Gradually, wind speeds would increase to 35–40 miles per hour, with gales gusting to 69. Like the rain, their predictions concluded, winds would calm after midnight, dropping to 14–21 miles per hour with gusts accelerating 6–12 miles per hour beyond.

In the training camp, at the daily 8 a.m. meeting of BLT 2/4's senior officers, word was passed about the possibility of an evening storm. A disaster control center was being set up in the BLT's communications hut, they were told—manned by an officer, a corporal or sergeant, a corpsman and five lower-ranking Marines. Should the storm cause damage, the DCC team would coordinate response and cleanup. It was still hoped that everyone would be given the weekend off. A tour bus to Tokyo was set to depart the camp the following morning at 7, and an orphanage visit arranged for early Saturday afternoon.

At 8:30 a.m.—as rains resumed, and sustained winds at the camp boosted beyond twenty-five miles per hour—the naval forces commander at Yokosuka declared the alert status Tropical Storm Condition One. Range Company staffers would continue to keep an eye on the weather; training, though, would likely continue. In weeks prior there had been other storm warnings; none had proved particularly disruptive. The BLT 2/4 officer of the day oversaw a communications check. "Radio and land lines operational," he logged.

After 9 a.m. winds receded to a more breezy average of eleven miles per hour. The temperature approached 68. Rains began to grow heavier. Most Marines uphill at the training camp had no clue of evolving forecasts. Few had radios, Mark Bedwell explained. "We didn't have TV." The previous day's edition of *Pacific Stars and Stripes* had reported that Typhoon Tip was bearing down on Okinawa, but made no mention of mainland Japan.

Even with the prospect of a ten-mile hump in the rain, a sense of optimism prevailed. There was the promise of weekend liberty—*and* it was finally payday.

Camp Fuji paydays differed from those on most bases. First, with no banks nearby, the Marines and Sailors would not receive paychecks; they would be paid in cash. Second, they would not receive their pay, as was usual, on the 15th and 30th day of each month. Commanders bringing units to the camp would schedule field training Monday through Thursday; Marines and Sailors would return to camp Friday mornings. After cleaning up they would be afforded time off to leave camp and explore Japan—beginning Friday afternoons. Every-other-Friday paydays put money in their pockets just prior.

Making forward-deployed paydays possible was another of LSU 3/9's disparate support services. The unit deployed with lots of cash. As October 19 approached, its disbursing officer, Captain Sam Sanders, had stockpiled a million dollars or so in U.S. currency and about half that value in Japanese yen. It was enough to cover one pay period, with a bit left over, in case he could not immediately draw more from a bank at Yokosuka. The money was kept inside two safes in the Quonset hut that served not just as the disbursing office, but also as living quarters for the sergeant and four other pay clerks on Sanders's team. "Of course, when you've got money like that," Sanders noted, "you've always got a guard." He carried a holstered .45 caliber pistol, as did the sergeant on his team. Clerks would take possession of the sergeant's pistol when their turn came up in the guard duty rotation.

In days beforehand junior officers from each of the units that made up the BLT had provided lists to the clerks, indicating every Marine and Sailor on hand to be paid, and what percentage of their pay each wanted in dollars and in yen. The work of gauging exchange rates and reconciling due pay was complex—computed with calculators, then noted in pencil or pen onto paper pay records.

Even before most Marines were wiping sleep from their eyes, a gaggle of lieutenants and a sprinkling of captains had lined up in the Officers Club hut. Sidearms on their hips, they carried empty ammunition cans. At a table in the club, Sanders and his sergeant counted out each unit's total; the lieutenants and captains signed for the money, stashed the cash in the ammo cans, then dashed back through the elements to their units' huts. There they set up their own pay tables.

This payday—the first of a new federal fiscal year—brought with it, for most U.S. service members around the world, a 7 percent military pay hike. For the transitioning-to-cash BLT 2/4 and LSU 3/9, several weeks would go by before manual readjustments put the boost into their pockets. The basic pay for a private with less than two years' service had been raised to $448.80 a month; privates first class would make $500.10 monthly, and the monthly gross for lance corporals with two to three years in the Corps had been upped to $548.10.

Each payday meted out just half those amounts, of course—and total cash-in-hand was further reduced by withholding for social security and taxes; savings bond purchases, which military leaders encouraged; and allotments some Marines and Sailors had arranged to support family members, make car payments, and the like. Also deducted from most handouts each payday was $1.50 for a Servicemen's Group Life Insurance policy. If a Marine paying that $3-a-month premium died, his or her beneficiary would receive $20,000.

Despite deductions, and still being paid on the old scale, it was nice to slide the dollars and yen into wallets—or squirrel them into padlock-secured footlockers. No one walked away feeling rich, but with no training scheduled for Saturday or Sunday—pay call had seemed to confer useful weekend spending power. "Everybody had big plans," Mike Cummings recalled. "Everybody that was not on duty was going to Tokyo for the weekend."

Around 10 a.m. Typhoon Tip made landfall sixty-eight miles south of Osaka—some three hundred miles from Camp Fuji. In Japanese coastal waters, eight grounded or sunk commercial ships lay in the typhoon's wake, forty-four of those vessels' crew members dead or missing. Moving inland, deprived of the moisture that powers cyclones when they are over water, Tip's wind speeds diminished from their phenomenal peak. Given the storm's massive girth, though, it remained destructive—and on a path that would place it over Shizuoka Prefecture.

For the next forty-five minutes, slowly accelerating rain and winds at Camp Fuji presented only minor nuisance. "Until [the storm] got close," Rickey Lamon remembered, "it was just a normal workday."

At 10:45, in a message titled "Typhoon Tip Warning Number Five," the commander of U.S. Naval Forces, Japan ordered a heightened alert status: Tropical Storm Condition One Caution. The message would have been received at the Camp Fuji communications center. Considerable time apparently passed before word of the change reached uphill to the BLT 2/4 duty officer.

Worsening conditions, though, led to cancellation of the day's scheduled training, and the off-base sightseeing that so many had looked forward to thereafter. "They said, 'All liberty has been canceled,'" Mike Cummings recalled. "And, I mean, that just took the wind out of everybody's sails."

Marines and Sailors were told to wrap up work outside. They were to begin moving to berthing areas or indoor work spaces for protection from the storm. In some cases time would be spent cleaning weapons or reviewing training manuals.

In one of the Weapons Company huts, Marines recently returned from practice-firing shotguns and machine guns sat on racks, talking as they cleaned the M-16A1 rifles each carried. Lance Corporal Ernie Gutierrez was composing a letter to a girlfriend named Frances, back home in Southern California. He wanted to write her in Spanish, but found it a challenge. His friend and bunkmate Frank Huerta helped.

Most of the Marines had experienced a typhoon or two while based on Okinawa. Reactions to the prospect of another were based on those experiences.

Issac Williams was wary, thinking back on a lunchtime storm that had come up as he and a fellow Marine left the Camp Schwab mess hall: "I had a friend named [Jesse] Lugo, he was a little bitty dude—and the storm was so strong that it took him. And when it took him, he grabbed on to a pole. And I got him off that pole and brought him in. That was the first time I'd ever really been in a real storm." The typhoon image that stuck in the mind of Weapons Company Private First Class Terrence Stokes was of a bulky soft drink machine flying through the air.

Steve Neal, on the other hand, recalled previous cyclonic events as having created opportunity for outdoor play. "We would lean into the wind," he said. "You would fall on your face sometimes, but you would more or less be 'flying' into the wind." Inside reinforced concrete buildings, Neal recalled, storm days on the Rock had involved "just sitting around, drinking coffee, and throwing darts." Fredric Britton Jr. looked back on a relaxing three or four days riding out a typhoon, his unit's squad bay well stocked with toilet paper, food, and beer. Marines in another Okinawa barracks had famously laid a wall-locker on its side during a storm, repurposing it as a massive, drink-filled ice bucket. Those experiences led some Marines to equate "typhoon" with "day off."

When the mess hall opened at 11:30 a.m., Issac Williams and others donned rain gear and headed there to grab lunch. Orders had gone out that they should wear helmets and flak jackets under their ponchos and walk with a buddy, each looking out for the other. They slogged through steadily intensifying showers and winds averaging eighteen miles per hour. Others headed to the NEX or its affiliated snack bar. Fresh pay was spent on luxury items that had earlier caught the eye—and on provisions useful for riding out the storm.

Earlier in the morning, Colonel Lamb had sent home all Japanese civilian employees under his command. Those working at the exchange found themselves bureaucratically isolated. They reported to Navy managers at Yokosuka, who at the time anticipated little potential storm impact. Keep working, they had been told. Marines and Sailors preparing to ride out the storm were glad they did.

"I bought a *Playboy*," Mark Bedwell remembered. "I bought a new watch—it was over a hundred dollars, a Seiko divers watch—a bag of Doritos, and a large Coke." Glenn Roberts's shopping list was similar: "What's the old term? 'Gedunk'? I mean, candy bars, potato chips, soda—things that will sustain you for the long haul."

They were ready, it seemed.

8

FRIDAY, OCTOBER 19, AFTERNOON

Being burned to death, being killed that day, was the furthest thing from anybody's mind. I think in some ways that can be more of a traumatic or shocking event than it can be for a Marine that's out on a combat patrol.

—Sergeant Major Mike Tuttle, U.S. Marine Corps (Ret.)

The water was up to your knees, and the fire was on top of it. When we opened the front door to try to go out, we were already burning up.

—Lance Corporal Issac Williams, U.S. Marine Corps

BY NOON NAVY Exchange managers at Yokosuka had recognized the potential threat posed by Typhoon Tip. They telephoned Camp Fuji NEX supervisor Akira Yamada, telling him that he and the store's three clerks should close early. First, though, they would have to serve the many Marines and Sailors by then queued up to purchase ride-out-the-storm provisions. As they sold snacks, boom boxes, music cassettes, and the like, wind gusts well beyond the by-then-twenty-two-mile-per-hour average noisily slammed the store building. "Suddenly the roof starts roaring like it's going to fly off," Mark Bedwell remembered. "I noticed the Japanese women working there were getting scared."

Some in the camp turned for information to the U.S. military's Far East Network radio station. Via a 50,000-watt transmitter in suburban Tokyo, it usually offered English-language music and news. At some point, though, the station's frequency, 810 AM, began yielding only static. Tip's winds had toppled FEN Tokyo's 300-foot antenna.

Fox Company commander Jeffrey Bearor double-checked his unit's preparation. His Marines had "pulled everything possible into the huts," he said. "Any supplies we had outside had been covered with tarps."

It was at this same time that Private First Class Ki Lewis Smith, a communications specialist with LSU 3/9, was assigned sentry duty at the fuel storage area. He was placed on his post by Corporal Andrew L. Stowell, the LSU's corporal of the guard that day. As Smith recalled, Stowell instructed him to "walk along the large berm in front of the fuel farm and occasionally to walk along the small berms around the fuel bags."

At 12:15 p.m. camp commander Allan Lamb declared a Tropical Storm Condition One Emergency. This indicated that the camp was being hit with wind gusts of between fifty-eight and sixty-nine miles per hour. The declaration restricted all but essential operations and directed that everyone not involved in such operations move indoors.

Combat engineer officer Jacob Evans peered out the window of his hut. Driving rain poured all around. Looking upward he glimpsed the passing of the storm's eye. "That was calm as it comes," he remembered. "The sun was shining right though." He ran to get a camera. By the time he returned to the window, the serene center had accelerated beyond view.

Within fifteen minutes rain and winds were pounding fuel farm sentry Smith so ferociously that he radioed for permission to retreat inside a steel cargo container just downhill of the large berm. On his last walk around the area, he would recall, the small berms around the three pillow tanks "were getting soft." There was, he reported, "about two or three feet of water around each bladder and the water almost covered the MOGAS bladder." The doors of the metal storage structure in which Smith hunkered faced northeast; from just inside, as visibility permitted, he could observe a portion of the large berm's downward-facing edge

By 12:45 p.m. conditions were such that the LSU guard officer determined it unsafe to leave the sentry in place. He told Stowell to retrieve Smith.

Stowell did so. The two returned to the LSU's duty office in Hut D-407. There Smith was able to change from rain-drenched clothing into a dry uniform.

At the BLT 2/4 headquarters, the officer of the day logged: "Storm condition 1 caution set." Ten minutes later: "All companies notified of storm condition." The level 1 "caution" had been received at the base camp two hours beforehand; thirty minutes previous, the base camp had set the further escalated "emergency" status. For whatever reason storm condition information was not moving quickly uphill.

Between 11 a.m. and 1 p.m., more than three inches of rain had fallen. With the ground saturated, the liquid film on its surface became slippery. "So when you walked on the water," Bill Dyer recalled, "the volcanic dirt underneath it would roll—kind of like BBs. It was like you were walking on ice."

Some Marines had been ordered to do what they could to keep their huts from flooding. "We were supposed to be filling sandbags and setting them around our Quonsets," said Charles Dickerson, then a private first class with Weapons Company. "And we did pretty good on ours. We had 'em about four high—pretty much all the way around except the doors." Hut to hut such preventive measures were inconsistent. "I remember looking to the one to the left of us," the Harrodsburg, Kentucky native reflected, "and they hadn't done nothin.'"

In Barracks D-214 rain began trickling in the back door. "That was the uphill side of our Quonset hut," Mike Tuttle recalled. To keep it dry, Marines lifted gear up onto their racks. Pushing the bunks together, they sat on their mattresses and continued games of spades and the like. Over time the entire floor was covered by an inch or two of flowing liquid. "You could see water moving through the barracks," Tuttle remembered, "from the back door, going out the front door."

In the Echo Company area, Andy Bonwit was eyeing a retaining wall behind his platoon's hut. Water had accumulated behind it. "It smacked down," he remembered, "made a big noise, and suddenly the barracks was flooded." Someone in his platoon scavenged several wooden pallets from outside. "And we started stacking footlockers on those, and seabags on top of those."

In a Fox Company hut, nineteen-year-old Michael Bendt of Charleston, South Carolina, was on fire watch. From noon until 4 p.m. that day, the private was tasked with ensuring the safety of the Marines and Sailors inside. Per the eighth of the Corps' eleven general orders for sentries, he was "to give the alarm in case of fire or disorder." At the moment his attention was focused on stopping the flow of water under their hut's rear door. He grabbed a blanket laying atop a nearby rack. A Marine objected. "He's like, 'Hey, that's my blanket,'" Bendt recalled. "I went and got mine, stuffed it underneath the back door to slow the water down. And it seemed to do a good job."

Sometime around 1 p.m.—as average wind speeds swiftly accelerated toward forty-seven miles per hour—Rickey Lamon's noncommissioned officer-in-charge, Staff Sergeant Henry R. Simmons, braved the elements to make one last check on conditions at the fuel storage site. It appeared intact, he affirmed. The three bladders were in place, as were the two pumping systems atop the long berm.

Wind-hurled raindrops were by this time, as Lamon described, "as big as nickels. You felt like they were stripping the skin off of you." Private First Class Mark Ferrara likened the feeling to being blasted with shards of glass. If one wasn't wrapped in three or four layers of protective clothing, swore another Marine, "you'd have literally gotten bruises from it—it was that bad."

Inside some barracks hard-driven rain sounded like BB shot slamming against the metal roofs. Some of it flowed through crevices in the corrugated sheets. "We had leaks everywhere," Headquarters and Service Company's Rob Ahrens recalled. To catch the dripping liquid, he said, "we were running around putting coffee cans on the floor." As winds rattled huts' loose sheeting, a "kind of metallic roar" filled the spaces, Richard DesLauriers remembered. "You could hardly hear yourself talk."

A few days previous, Lance Corporal Steve Haishuk and a couple other Weapons Company Marines had purchased a thirty-cup coffee pot to use in their Quonset hut. A hunkered-down afternoon seemed the perfect occasion for percolation. Running through rain and wind, the West Allis, Wisconsin native found a faucet from which he could fill the large metal canister with water. "On my way back," the twenty-one-year-old recalled, "the wind got so strong—I don't know if it blew me over, but I do remember dropping the coffee pot and then losing the insert for the coffee grounds."

Nineteen-year-old Private First Class Allen Wheland of Centre Hall, Pennsylvania, was performing what remained an essential duty: standing watch just south of the training camp huts at the "ammo dump"—a fenced-in compound storing explosives ranging from pistol bullets to artillery rounds. "One of us was posted in the tower, and we'd rotate out between the tower and walking posts," he explained. Wheland was taking his turn in the tower as conditions deteriorated. Rain blasted horizontally. Whipping winds howled. "I decided at that point it was time to get out of the tower. As I'm starting to climb down, one of the heavy gusts hit and just threw me off the ladder. I sailed about twenty feet through the air and hit the ground." He landed on saturated sandy soil—overlaid by fast-flowing, if barely inch-deep, floodwaters. "I slid another twenty feet," he recalled, "being pushed along."

At a guard post some distance from the camp's living area, Joe Macdonald and another Marine were told by an NCO passing in a jeep to return to their units' huts. As the two neared their respective barracks, they reached a retaining wall. "And the guy that was in front of me jumped off it like we always did. When he did, he went right through the ground up to like his chest." Standing in shock, Macdonald watched the fellow Marine struggle for some time to free himself from the water-saturated, lower-level soil.

Gusts barreling into some huts would push open the flimsy door on one end while slamming shut the thin plywood hatch at the other. A moment later gales from another direction would do the same in reverse. With the wind came rain and grit. To prevent the problem, unit leaders tried to reinforce some of the doors—in several cases, nailing plywood over the outside of door frames. Mike Cummings recalled that someone came into his hut, explained the problem, "and they nailed the back door closed." In Joe Macdonald's hut, a similar announcement was followed by "the sound of the nails being hammered into the door. . . . It seemed like someone's on the ball. Like someone's out in this crappy weather right now, thinking of the things that need to be done, and doing 'em. I was actually a little bit impressed." Others at the camp barricaded hut doors from the inside, pushing wall lockers against the portals. Padlocks were clamped into hasps securing the east exit of hut D-220 and the west exit of D-316. Other doors were lashed as securely as possible with twisted coat hangers, communications wire, or parachute cord. "If you had to take a piss really bad," Mike Tuttle recalled—an issue since so many had bought large bottles of soda at the exchange—"you're doing a little bit of a dance trying to figure out how to pick apart that knot to get the hell out of the door to run down to the head real quick."

At 1:15 the BLT officer of the day telephoned his base camp counterpart—passing along radio frequencies on which Range Company could reach training camp units in an emergency. Meantime, an updated typhoon advisory radically recalculated the time of the storm's arrival. Tip was moving more swiftly than had been forecast that morning, and along a substantially altered path. Now, U.S. military meteorologists predicted, it "should pass CPA [Closest Point of Approach] 109 miles northwest of Yokosuka" at about 2:30 p.m. local time. That would place its CPA to Camp Fuji even sooner—some seven hours prior to the morning estimate.

In the late 1970s, forecasting errors of this magnitude were not unusual. It was easier to predict a cyclone's movement when it ranged over tropical waters; in those conditions, a storm moved at fairly consistent speeds. Forecasting became notoriously difficult, however, if typhoons neared the jet stream—a river of high-speed air at around thirty thousand feet. The stream's winds could grab and guide a storm, accelerating it to exceptional speeds. During October it was not uncommon to find the jet stream directly over the Japanese mainland. A forecaster could never be certain if or specifically when it might begin steering a storm—and data were not always available to determine the exact speed of its acceleration-inducing winds. When the jet stream grabbed Tip, it was as if the storm was a block of wood floating from a meandering creek into a river's raging rapids.

Between 1 and 2 p.m., 3.03 inches of rain fell on Camp Fuji and the nearby town of Gotemba. In addition to causing flooding, the severe downpour instigated a less intuitive meteorological effect: it pulled even stronger winds down to the earth's surface. The phenomenon was beyond metaphorically breathtaking. Roger Miller gasped after experiencing "wind so strong that you couldn't breathe outside."

Twenty-year-old Private George S. Dye—who went by "Steve"—rushed from the chow hall to Hut D-220; he was on mess duty, so had been cleaning up after breakfast. The Columbus, Ohio, native changed from a wet uniform into a pair of cut-off jeans.

Intensely-pounding rains pared visibility outside to near zero. Water cascaded downhill. Even in structures that had been sandbagged, doorways remained vulnerable to the push of floodwaters.

Mark Bedwell noticed the sloshy deck when he made it back to Hut D-214. His shopping bag was wet, but purchases remained intact. "I still had my Doritos and Coke," he said. He slipped the new watch onto his wrist and tossed the *Playboy* onto his rack.

Warmed by their huts' kerosene heaters, many Marines and Sailors pulled off rain-soaked uniforms, hanging them on makeshift clotheslines. "So they're drying out," Steve Neal remembered. "We're wearing our boxer shorts, with—I think I had a T-shirt—and I was wearing some socks. And we were drinking coffee and playing darts." As others relaxed in the Corps' distinctive scarlet running shorts—"red silkies"—decks of cards, chess sets, and backgammon boards were broken out. Given freshly filled wallets, a certain urge to wager could be felt in the air. Conversations hummed; in barracks vernacular, people were "shootin' the shit." Some lit cigarettes. A handful employed hut furnaces as stovetops. "I remember people heating up corned beef hash," Louis Sanford said.

At 1:20 the BLT 2/4 officer of the day logged: "All electric power is out at this time." In Hut D-215 what struck Lance Corporal Jesse Lugo about the outage was the sudden absence of music. It no longer blasted from barracks boom boxes. "Everyone climbed in their rack," the Weapons Company Marine said, "and talked or read by flashlight."

Five minutes later the battalion OOD noted: "Companies [have been] notified to keep people inside unless an emergency, then helmets will be worn." A five-ton truck had been placed at the ready, he noted, "pioneer tools"—axes, sledgehammers, shovels, and such—piled inside should they be useful for clearing storm debris.

Gale-force winds began to topple small structures at the camp and rip roofs off others. "The storm was just beatin' it up," Issac Williams remembered. Torrential rains pushed eroding soil up against a number of huts—in some cases blocking barracks doors.

In the camp chapel, which—unlike most huts—was set on above-ground cinderblocks, a deafening wind whistled over the roof and under the floors. Inside Chaplain Mel Ferguson felt the sharp cold.

In nearby Gotemba City, "heavy rains and wind were causing serious damage," firefighter Haruhiko Katsumata recalled. Some first responders helped clear away wind-wrought destruction; others filled and stacked sandbags in areas prone to flooding.

Having finally been able to close the Navy Exchange store, Akira Yamada, Taeko Matsuzaki, and two other NEX workers jumped into a small car. Yamada would drive them to their respective homes. First, though, he had to ensure that exchange vendors offering shoe repair, snack bar, and laundry services on the camp had closed their shops, as well.

At 1:40 p.m. Typhoon Tip was as close to Camp Fuji as it would get. Its circulating center was some sixty-two miles to the camp's north-northwest. Though it had been reduced to tropical storm status, the tempest was still—across Camp Fuji, and nearby portions of Shizuoka prefecture—generating winds averaging forty-seven miles per hour. That figure factored sustained winds of at least thirty-two miles per hour, with structure-jolting gusts of eighty-two miles per hour and well beyond. Wind damage in that moment included an overhead electrical line blown to the ground near the training camp laundry.

Massive volumes of rainwater had accumulated in the LSU 3/9 fuel farm area—uphill of the long, road-bordering berm and within the berms surrounding each of the three fuel bladders. Its liquid weight pressed against the earthen barriers. Inundating rains dive-bombed the soil structures from above.

Eventually the pressure proved too much. A portion of the long berm began to erode. Floodwaters carried away dissipating chunks of volcanic soil. The rapid disintegration left a gaping breach fifteen to twenty feet wide. The two trailer-mounted pumps atop the berm—each weighing 1.6 tons—tumbled into the opening, hoses to bladders still connected.

Of the three fuels stored in bladders at the uphill fuel farm, the 86 octane MOGAS contained the fewest carbon molecules. Though all were lighter than water, the gasoline was least heavy of the three. At that moment containing 5,933 gallons of gasoline, the rubberized fabric tank weighed 32,000 pounds.

The bladder—Serial Number P-4449, manufactured by the Goodyear Tire and Rubber Company in July 1969—floated up and over what remained of its encircling earthen embankment. Pulled by the downhill flowing rainwater, the bladder rode the rapid into the razed portion of the 440-yard berm. There it became ensnared, wrapped around one of the fallen pumps.

"The frame of the trailer that the pumping system sat on was just kind of like angle iron," John Brosnan recalled. "And the corner of the angle iron would pierce pretty much anything."

The sharp metal edge ripped a five-foot-long tear about six inches above and parallel to the bladder's horizontal seam. MOGAS gushed from the sliced fuel container. An estimated 5,500 gallons of the fuel—enough to fill 100 55-gallon drums—flowed downhill atop already flooding rainwater.

No one at the camp saw it happen. The fuel farm sentry, for safety purposes, had been pulled from his post. Too, LSU commander Brosnan would explain shortly thereafter, "there appeared no valid reason to suspect unusual drainage problems in the site."

Some of the buoyant gasoline streamed into drainage ditches constructed throughout the camp to channelize rainwater and prevent erosion. Silt had accumulated in the normally two- or three-foot-deep concrete or corrugated steel trenches. Much of the fuel overflowed the now-shallower gullies. It poured over the ground between huts, then under doors, and across the floors of structures in which Marines and Sailors were sheltering.

On the training camp's topmost tier, deep water had accumulated in D-211 and adjacent huts. Trying to keep personal possessions from waterlogging or washing away, LSU maintenance platoon members living in the structures lifted foot lockers, boots, and such onto their racks. Most moved outside. Some broke out their small folding shovels—"entrenching tools" in arcane supply terminology Marines shortened to "e-tools"—and began digging a trench they hoped would divert the deluge. Amid the downpour the effort struck Sergeant Anton Koncaba as of marginal benefit. He told the Marines to simply tie open each hut's uphill- and downhill-facing hatches. Let gravity, he instructed, stream the insistent torrents in one door then out the other. Koncaba watched as the flow issuing from D-211's downhill doorway cascaded over the edge of the hut's concrete base. At first a foot-long waterfall, it grew in length as the soil it impacted washed away.

One level below nineteen-year-old Lance Corporal Jerry Holt, a Weapons Company Marine from Boyle, Mississippi, was among the last to be darting back from shopping at the exchange. He smelled gasoline fumes as he rushed toward Hut D-220, his platoon's quarters. Once inside he shouted, "If any of you guys are smoking, put it out." Glenn Roberts, twenty-three, of Fletcher, Vermont, recognized the petroleum odor, yet it seemed out of context to the corporal: "You don't really think about that in the middle of a typhoon."

Corporal Paul Verdier of Weapons Company had been riding out the storm not with platoon mates, but in the hut of his friend Corporal David

Skaggs. Stepping outside Skaggs's building to check conditions, the twenty-three-year-old from Burien, Washington, looked toward the area where he was routinely quartered. "I could see our staff sergeant," he recalled, "and two, maybe three other guys sandbagging a corner of the hooch, the hooch I lived in. Well, crap, that's my house. I'd better go over and help them." Horizontally blowing rain and groundwater rushed nearly shin-deep over the tops of his combat boots. About halfway to the hut, he remembered, "I looked down and I could see the shininess of fuel on the water. And suddenly I could smell it, and taste it on my lips, because the wind was blowing so freakin' hard.

"And so I picked up my pace, and I ran over—and the first person I grabbed, I grabbed the staff sergeant, and I said, 'Hey! This area is covered in fuel.' And he said something like, 'What?' And then he goes, 'You're right!'"

Anton Koncaba again glanced at the waterfall emanating from D-211's downhill-facing door. It had taken on a prismatic sheen. Koncaba yelled, "Fuel!" in the direction of his platoon commander, Warrant Officer Joe Piper, then turned to warn Marines billeted one tier below. A former machine-gunner himself, Koncaba empathized with the Weapons Company Marines. He had seen them return—muddy and tired—from field exercises the day before. Unlike along the first tier, he did not see many Marines below outside their huts. As the twenty-four-year-old from Scottsbluff, Nebraska, prepared to jump down from the upper retaining wall, a hut on that next lower level whoomphed and flared. Building D-215, he believed.

MOGAS had pooled on the hut's floor. Vapors from the fuel had risen, mixed with oxygen, then flashed. It is not inconceivable that a lit cigarette sparked the first ignition. More likely, though, the vapor-air mixture had ascended to a height at which it interacted with flaming kerosene inside one of the hut's heaters.

Across the upper training camp, an instant of brilliant light burst through windows. In the artillery headquarters hut, "somebody says, 'Geez, is that lightning?'" Richard DesLauriers recalled. "I said, 'I don't know. That would be pretty weird.'" In one of the amtrac platoon barracks, Anthony Senatore remembered, "we heard—thunder. And somebody says, 'It don't thunder during typhoons.'"

Outside Paul Verdier felt a rush of heat as he watched a fireball develop at the back of a hut some fifty feet away. It looked, he recalled, "like somebody dropped a napalm canister on that hooch." The consuming blaze moved forward and upward, fed by millions of MOGAS droplets that had been blown into the air. "The wind was full of fuel," Verdier said. "As the fireball grew, it was easily twice the height of the Quonset hut."

Inside Hut D-215 Marines had been preparing to move outside to join the sandbagging effort. When gas fumes became evident, Jesse Lugo wrote soon after, Corporal Colin Miller stood and turned off the nearby stove. Issac Williams watched as Miller then moved toward the western-facing portion of the building. "He opened the back door," Williams recalled. "Water flushed in so fast that it knocked him off his feet. . . . The water was up to your knees, and the fire was on top of it."

When Donald Fox heard a loud, rushing whoomph, he would later recall, "I turned around to see what I heard. What I saw," the lance corporal from San Jose, California remembered, "was a wall of fire. I also saw Corporal Miller standing beside the rear exit. He turned to face me, and as he did, he put his arms up from his side like a cross, and went up in flames. When our eyes locked, I saw death in his eyes."

L. C. Malveaux of Beaumont, Texas—consumed by the fire—fell to the floor. The twenty-one-year-old lance corporal died, in the words of BLT 2/4's medical officer, "almost immediately." In Beaumont, not quite a year before, the Weapons Company Marine had married Lois Marie Johnson. While he was overseas, Lois had given birth to Adrian Nicole Malveaux. Father and daughter would never meet. Nineteen-year-old Tyrone Elem tried to pull Malveaux to safety. The attempt to save his friend left the lance corporal from Alexandria, Virginia, with life-threatening burns of his own.

As flames swept through the hut, Donald Fox and platoon mate Lance Corporal Philip du Pont ran to the hut's eastern-facing door. "I felt something like a hand of heat pick me up and push me out the door," Fox recounted. "I turned around to see where du Pont was, and all I saw inside was fire and darkness." Fox realized that his own shirt was on fire.

"When we opened the front door to try to go out," Issac Williams recalled, "we were already burning up."

The fireball over Hut D-215 remained airborne for some time, fed by beads of gasoline the cyclonic winds continued to hurl into the air. Eventually, portions of the sky fire settled to earth. They ignited vapors rising from floating MOGAS. Resulting flames surfed the flooded ground. They forced Anton Koncaba into a quick retreat. "The fire burned the fuel on top of the water and chased me up the hill," he wrote soon after.

Koncaba was able to scramble to safety. Two of his fellow LSU Marines—Lance Corporals Michael Freeman and Thomas Glasper Jr.—were not as fortunate. On the training camp's uppermost tier, Freeman had fallen into ground-hugging flames beside D-207. Second-degree burns covered more than half his body before a Marine surnamed Patterson was able to pull him from the fire. Glasper—"Glass" to his friends—suffered worse injury. Sixty percent of his body bore third-degree burns acquired just outside Hut D-208.

"I looked down the row of buildings to my right," Sergeant Koncaba recounted, "and saw that Building 207 was already burning. Then Building 205 caught on fire." The waterborne fire would also enter and consume Buildings 210 and 211. Even as those four top-tier huts were destroyed, Glasper and Freeman would remain the only burn casualties on that level. Gushing water had forced most Marines out of the LSU-occupied upper huts before the fire broke out.

No such luck accrued to Marines billeted on the training camp's second descending tier—site of the first ignition. Fifteen-foot curtains of flame moved to surround huts there, prompting more whoomphs.

"A river of fire spread through the structures," Gunnery Sergeant R. R. Keene would write in the *Okinawa Marine* newspaper, "forcing Marines, many clad only in skivvies or athletic clothing, to flee into the typhoon."

Lance Corporal Robert Turner raced from D-215. For several brief moments, he successfully sidestepped the blaze. Then a fellow Marine—on fire, frantically flailing—slammed into the twenty-year-old from Cassopolis, Michigan. The collision knocked Turner headfirst into flames that scorched 45 percent of his skin.

Inside Hut D-214 Corporal Louis Sanford and other Weapons Company mortarmen had seen and heard a nearby structure explode. "In my mind," Sanford recalled, "I went, you know, 'Did the Russians—? Did we just get attacked?'" Then a rumble drew his attention to the rear entrance of his own hut. "The back door—you know, it's just made of plywood, goes up in flames. Everybody froze," he remembered, watching the door burn.

"Corporal Sanford told us to cut the stove off," Charlie Dickerson wrote shortly after the fire. Twenty-two-year-old Corporal Jon Jurgen responded. "I started to go over to shut the heater off," he recalled, "and then I heard a giant whoosh, sort of like a blast furnace starting up." Looking up, Mark Bedford saw "everybody's faces, illuminated red in the flames."

A Marine sitting on the lower bunk opposite Mike Tuttle jumped up, grabbed an upright bedpost, and swung himself toward one of the hut's hatches. "The momentum of his body weight," Tuttle remembered, "propel[led] him literally through that door." Cords that had been tied to secure the entryway hung loose, but still attached. Fleeing quickly behind the young man who had knocked the door from its hinges, Tuttle escaped safely.

Elsewhere in the hut, Charlie Dickerson's mind generated a high-speed movie. "Everything in my whole life that I'd done, good and bad, people I know, went through my head," he recalled decades later. "It was real fast, and yet everything was so clear. Things I'd even forgot about." For a moment the nineteen-year-old found it calming. Then he couldn't breathe. The flash had consumed oxygen inside the hut. "I remember taking a breath," he said, "and it felt like my lungs collapsed." Glancing toward the hut's front door, he watched as twenty-two-year-old Lance Corporal Stephan Turner of Tipp City, Ohio, threw on a steel combat helmet with a plastic liner. With three or four others whose racks were also near the front door, Turner dashed outside. All of them caught fire. "I just seen 'em go down," Dickerson remembered. "I knew that wasn't good." Lance Corporal Terrence Stokes would later see Turner's helmet liner melted into the injured Marine's burned scalp. Dickerson heard Mark Bedwell's voice: "We gotta get the fuck out of here!" Bedwell bolted out. Dickerson stood with his good friend, Charles Degnim, nineteen, of Franklin, Massachusetts. The two gasped for air. "And Degnim said, 'I'm goin' through the wall.' And I grabbed him by the shirt, and I punched my fist through the window. And that's how I got burnt. Flames rushed in. But then we could breathe, so I guess oxygen come in with it." His face and ears scorched, his hand lacerated by the window glass, Dickerson eventually followed Degnim out the door. Someone would later swear that he saw Dickerson helping others escape the hut, as well. Just beyond the doorway, he fell. "Actually," he reflected, "I tripped over, I think it was somebody."

Corporal Bradley Cope, twenty-one, of Crawfordsville, Indiana, and nineteen-year-old Private First Class George Spotts of Norristown, Pennsylvania, had almost made it out of the hut when they encountered a loud boom and wall of heat. "We both got our faces burned," Cope said—hands, too—"but Spotts jerked me back inside." The two dashed to a window someone had broken out. They pushed and pulled each other through the narrow opening. It was not easy; the broad-shouldered Spotts weighed 206 pounds. Their escape, he recalled, took "a couple of minutes at most, but felt like fifty years."

At least two Marines took a counterintuitive tack. Louis Sanford was briefly stunned after the dazzling ignition flash—"sittin' there," Charlie Dickerson recalled, "with a straight stare." Sanford had watched Dickerson break the window, seen how the fire had "reached in and burned his face." It was in that split second that his mind replayed a public service announcement featuring the comedic actor Dick Van Dyke. He had seen it on Armed Forces Television in Okinawa. "Can you guess why I'm crawling?" Van Dyke had asked, as he made his way through a living room on hands and knees. "I'm showing you what you should do if your house is on fire, and there's smoke all over. Down here you'd be able to breathe." Sanford threw himself to the deck. Because of the sandbags well positioned around the outside edges of his platoon's hut, he landed on dry flooring. "And I just stayed there," Sanford recalled, "wondering if I was going to burn down here, or stand up and suffocate."

Terrence Stokes had also acted based on Dick Van Dyke's televised advice. He, too, dropped to the floor, pressing his nose into the "like two inches of air where there wasn't no smoke." Closer to a door, the floor to which he dropped was muckier. "And so I was down there, sucking up dirt, water, and whatever else." At some point he glanced over and saw that the door nearest him had blown open. Fire rose just outside. "And then a gust of wind came and blew the flames down, and I got up and ran out. And when I got past the flames, I turned back around and looked and the flames went back up."

Smoke obscured Louis Sanford's view of the door. He remained inside.

Flames continued to rise from fuel burning in drainage ditches. Wooden beams built into retaining walls began to smolder. Whoomph after whoomph could be heard in the training camp, reverberations of gas vapor ignition.

As Hut D-220 caught fire, the whoomph was instantly followed by a momentarily blinding flash—"like somebody just turned on a bunch of floodlights," Mike Cummings remembered. "Everybody was freaking out," Lance Corporal Gust Miller recounted. "People started running, people were screaming." As had been the case in D-215 and D-214, the Marines' "bias to act"—obeying the "do *something*, quickly" ethos inculcated in recruit training—spurred them to move. As Miller observed fire inside and outside, his personal risk assessment was grim. "Either I die here," thought the twenty-year-old from the Chicago suburb of Darien, Illinois, "or I run through the fire."

Wearing only his cutoff jeans, Steve Dye took a breath, closed his eyes for a moment, and also bolted outside. "I just kicked open the front door," he said. Because the storm had pushed mounds of sandy mud up against the entryway, doing so had required serious pressure. Dye ran into the wind and rain. After some distance he fell. "Only my hand got in the [burning fuel atop the] water," he later recalled. Before joining the Marines, Dye had studied to be a firefighter. Remembering that training, he kept his eyes closed and tried not to breathe.

When Steve Haishuk saw flames at one end of D-220, he ran toward the other. A padlock had been slid into the staple of a hasp securing the door from the outside. Corporal Patrick Schaefer, twenty-two, of Flint, Michigan, and nineteen-year-old Lance Corporal Steve Neal of Indianapolis were right behind. "Haishuk was a big guy," Neal remembered. "And I think he just busted the damned thing off its hinges. He went through. Schaefer went through. I went through." They yelled to others in the hut. "We're going, 'Come on, this way, this way!' Well, some guys weren't listening. There was just so much noise, they just didn't hear us, I guess." All three escaped the hut, but caught fire as they rolled through flames.

Frank Huerta glanced at the rack above his own. "I started looking for Ernie [Gutierrez]," he recalled, "because he was my bunkie, and we had been talking." Gutierrez appeared still to be cleaning his rifle. "I guess he was like dazed," Huerta said, "and so I put him on a fireman's carry, and ran out." Still inside the hut, though, he tripped and fell. "And so I burned my right arm and my left arm pretty bad." Rising from the concrete floor, he again hefted Gutierrez over his shoulder and raced out the hut door. "By the time I took about fifteen steps with him, he was awake already." Gutierrez began moving on his own. Jerry Holt recalled an officer grabbing him after his dash through the inferno, using a jacket to slap down and smother the flaring blaze that had engulfed him as he ran from the hut.

The Marines had been trained to respond to attacks from nation-state armies and bands of guerrillas. Against *this* enemy weapons were useless. No tactical maneuver could shift the tide. "You just have to try to get the hell out," Alan Crook, then a Weapons Company second lieutenant, explained. "And it doesn't work because you're consumed, you're surrounded."

For a moment shock had left Issac Williams standing bewildered in a D-215 doorway. Then "instincts got ahold of me," he recalled. There was only one way out: "We gotta go through the fire." He maneuvered by memory. "I was burning so much, I couldn't see anything—nothing but fire. I just started praying. And I prayed to Jesus, and I asked Jesus to help me get through this. I was just plum out of it, and I was confused, and I didn't know which way to go. And I saw Jesus Christ. And I reached for him, and he reached out to me and he grabbed me. I know it was him. But what it turned out to be—God works in mysterious ways—it was a corporal, and me and him didn't get along well. When Jesus disappeared, *his* hands ended up being the ones that were pulling on me." Drawn free of the flames, Williams took quick stock of his condition. "My skin," he observed, "was rolling off my body."

Jon Jurgen wrapped himself in a blanket and charged outside. The woolen fabric provided little protection. More than 40 percent of his body was burned. As Gust Miller fled, second-degree burns scorched 60 percent of his body. Steve Dye, who had fallen, got up and kept running—toward a voice calling "Over here, over here!" A friend led him to safety. Though he was terribly burned, his pain was dulled by the short-term mercy of destroyed nerve endings. As driving rain pelted his near-naked body, though, it felt to Dye as if he was being stung by bees. Steve Haishuk, in his underwear, was eventually able to extinguish himself by jumping into a drainage ditch. Patrick Schaefer rolled and crawled until his clothes were no longer burning. Steve Neal fell into a gully created when soil was washed away from a retaining wall. "Everything slowed down," Neal remembered. "'Huh, this is what it's like to die in a fire.' Next thing I know I'm over the wall. Guardian angel did something, God knows. And now my skin's all flayed and it feels like you're being hit with BBs."

Some who fled through the walls of towering flame instinctively covered themselves with military-issued poncho liners made of nylon and polyester. In the intense heat, the synthetic materials melted and dripped. As the Marines suffered burns, liquified goo fused with their charring flesh.

More huts exploded into flame—their draftiness contributing oxygen to the volatile chemical reaction. "You can imagine in a Quonset hut that's got a round top," former Fox Company commander Jeffrey Bearor mused decades later, "when a flash fire like that goes off, the heat that was created in those huts must have been incredible."

"It wasn't like a house fire where the curtains catch on fire, and then the ceiling catches on fire, and then the furniture catches on fire," recalled Weapons Company's David Luttenberger, who had been able to safely escape his hut. "It was fully engulfed, one-hundred-percent filled with flame, in an instant."

A Marine burst into the BLT 2/4 duty office, yelling warning of a fire in the Weapons Company area. The blaze, he told the duty officer, was "spreading down the camp as a result of water runoff." The duty team tried to notify their counterparts at the base camp. "Radio comm down," the duty officer logged. "Runner dispatched."

Inside D-215 Lance Corporal Jesse Lugo tried to get his bearings. He watched some fellow Marines try to escape the hut through side windows. Most hurried out the downhill-facing front door. The Illinois native headed to the door, as well, pulling with him a disoriented fellow Marine. As soon as the two were outside, the Marine broke from Lugo's grasp, ran wildly, then fell into a fortunately not-yet-burning drainage ditch. "Marines from another unit," Lugo said, "pulled him out before the fire reached him again." In his shock—which would linger—Lugo had not yet realized the extent of his own fire injury. "I could only feel pain in my feet," he would recall a year later. "I didn't know I was burned anywhere else." As Lugo dashed downhill, he attempted a jump into the open outdoor theater space on the camp's next lower tier. "I fell on my face in a puddle of fire," he remembered.

The blaze spread west, east, and north—ravaging huts D-212, D-214 and D-219. Older Marines at the camp that day—veterans of combat in Vietnam—felt ripped back to a war zone. "Initially, it was like a rocket attack, a mortar attack," reflected Sergeant Major Robert Hendrix. "It was as ferocious or fierce as any battle."

The BLT's artillery unit—Hotel Battery, 3rd Battalion, Twelfth Marines—was billeted in structures on the same graded tier as the huts housing Weapons Company. The Hotel Battery barracks sat just across a dirt road to the southwest—the left-most grouping of huts as one looked toward the mountain. While the entire tier was likely level when originally graded, stormwater, over time and that morning, had more severely eroded soil around the centered row of living quarters. Gasoline-carrying water gravitated toward structures occupied by Weapons Company and away from the artillery unit. An elevation difference of one foot or less had made the difference.

Having escaped resulting fires, Hotel Battery Marines moved quickly to aid those who had been hurt. They guided a 2.5-ton truck—a "deuce-and-a-half"—in from a perimeter road. Ordering the unit's drivers to start up their vehicles, Fred Christy recalled decades later, was "one of the stupidest things or one of the best things I've ever done in my life." Then twenty-two and the unit's motor transport NCO, the corporal from Carmel, Indiana had worried that firing up engines might spark wafting gasoline fumes. They did not.

The artillery Marines "got mattresses [and ponchos]," Richard DesLauriers said, "threw 'em in the truck and loaded [the injured] on there." The vehicle pulled back to the southeastern perimeter road, then headed downhill. Others arrived to evacuate more. Canvas tenting that usually shielded the truck beds had been removed as the storm approached, to prevent winds from jostling or tipping the vehicles. As the trucks traveled downhill, one Marine recollected, "all you could hear was these guys screaming in the back with the wind blowing over their burns." When one arose from the mattress on which he had lain, Fred Christy remembered, "[the skin from] his back stayed on there."

Floating islands of fire moved across the camp, igniting more huts. Some Marines who had escaped immediate danger began dodging flames, heading toward what seemed safer spaces downhill. Others turned back, wanting to help. "Marines from other companies, other platoons started showing up," Mike Tuttle recalled. Their intentions were good, he noted, but "it got hectic there for a while."

"It was really, really difficult to not let it become chaos," Richard DesLauriers remembered. "So many Marines were out there who weren't hurt—trying to help—that you had to make people just stop what they were doing and get organized." Running back toward the Hotel Battery area to direct another truck toward Weapons Company, DesLauriers suddenly sank into a drainage culvert. Deep, overflowing water had obscured the depression. "I stepped into it and just cracked the hell out of my shin and my knee," he recalled. "I remember a couple of the BLT officers standing up there with their arms folded, being calm and saying, 'You need to calm down.' And I said, 'You need to get out of the way.'"

As the number of injured became more apparent, shouts rang out: "Corpsman up!" The Navy medical technician attached to DesLauriers's battery responded. Grabbing his Unit One bag, the emergency kit each kept close at hand, Timothy Terrell rushed toward the calls for help. Outside the twenty-three-year-old watched flames shoot from hut windows and doors, "like torches." Screams echoed. Young men shrouded in green military blankets rolled in the mud. Straight ahead a lance corporal lumbered toward the Raleigh, North Carolina, native, "walking zombie-like, with his whole body smokin." Skin sloughed from the young man. Most of his right ear was gone.

"Please, Doc, take care of me," he pleaded. "Don't let me die."

As Terrell stepped toward the injured man, he yelled to his battery's executive officer, First Lieutenant Bruce Buckiewicz: "Get my equipment—*now!* Please!" Terrell's larger kit of medical supplies, which included morphine and other controlled drugs, was stored in the hut occupied by the battery's senior officers. For a second the corpsman's stomach dropped. Would he, a low-ranking Sailor, be in trouble for presuming to order around an officer?

Guiding his patient toward an evacuated hut, Terrell noticed a friend running his way. Fred Odom had been a classmate when the two had studied to become combat corpsmen. Just minutes before, Odom had been lying on his rack, writing a letter. Jolted by the whoompf of an ignition that spread across his hut's floor, he had scrambled from top rack to top rack down a series of bunks, escaping through a door just ahead of the fire. For more than half an hour, Terrell and Odom cleared airways, attached intravenous drips to patients they worried were going into shock, and treated Marines' intense pain. They smeared burns with silver sulfadiazine (brand-named Silvadene), an antiseptic that looked something like thick shaving cream. When spread well, it was said to kill most all bacteria for twelve hours. Atop the Silvadene, Terrell recalled, they wrapped "a little gauze, not too tight."

Before long, DesLauriers remembered, Terrell "ran out of that white cream. And he says, 'Sir, what can I do?' And I said, 'Doc, I don't know. You just got to do your very best.'" Eventually, Terrell and Odom loaded their patients onto one of the artillery battery trucks for transport toward the base camp flight line.

Throughout the day Major Lance Woodburn, the second-senior officer in the BLT, had been making forays from the hut where he and Lieutenant Colonel Redgate shared office and living space. On perhaps his third walk out to see how the camp was bearing up under the storm, he had heard Marines yelling, "Fire!" Noting that "staff NCOs were already working on getting guys out of the Quonset huts," he ran back to the command hut, "to alert John that we had a fire. We didn't know what the source of it was. At the initial point of it, there was just a lot of confusion."

In the upper left corner of the training camp, "thunderclaps" had caught the attention of the amphibious tractor platoon. But it was an unusual odor that rallied its members to quickly exit their huts. "You always smelled kerosene," Anthony Senatore recalled, because it fueled hut heaters. "The minute we smelled gas, it was like, 'Get out.'" It was only as the Marines were headed uphill toward their landing craft that they realized the camp was burning. Running to the amtracs staged near the long berm, they donned coveralls kept inside. The platoon's four sergeants initially sequestered most of the team inside the vehicles while one of the NCOs took a couple Marines over toward the fuel farm.

"They had shovels," Senatore remembered, "and they were going to the bladders, to see what was going on." A sergeant he recalled as Donald Baird told him, "'The bladder split open; the moat must be full of water. We're gonna go and make sure the other one don't bust open.' And off they went."

Realizing the potential for casualties from the blaze, the amtrac platoon's corpsman urged the Marines to retrieve supplies kept in the unit's "war block"—containerized materials piled up lower in the training camp. Senatore grabbed two young Marines, had them start up one of the tracked troop carriers, then directed them into the fire and smoke.

"The kid driving," Senatore recalled decades later, "turned to me and says, 'You want me to go through *that?*' I said, 'We'll shut the plenum so we don't suck in anything. The way the amtrac works, when you go off ship, you can close off the air outside. There's an aspirator valve that lets some of the air in to burn the engine. But there's only three of us inside the amtrac. We have enough air to breathe.'" With the vehicle "buttoned up," the sergeant tapped the driver's helmet. "He drove through it like a champ," Senatore praised. "Never hesitated." As the landing craft passed through walls of flame, rubber pads around pieces of its outside armor ignited briefly; rain, though, rapidly extinguished the burning. "We got to the other side of it," Senatore recalled. "We found the war block, we broke it open, and we loaded it up."

Outside his hut now, Charlie Dickerson could not see well. Everything looked blurry. "And I remember these two guys grabbing me. And they kept saying, 'We got you. We got you.'" Platoon mate Terrence Stokes recalled Dickerson having told him that "he had never seen any Black folks before he came in the service." Both Marines who helped get Dickerson to the bottom of the hill were Black. "They stumbled and fell" along the way, he recalled, "but they never let me go down." It was a lesson, he said. "No matter what color you was, the Marines helped the Marines. And they put their own lives at stake, too."

After corpsmen grabbed Ernest Gutierrez, Frank Huerta sheltered for a moment in one of the huts filled with toilets, sinks, and mirrors. It was there, he said, "that I saw myself—all these blisters all over my body, my face. I didn't even feel them when I was carrying Ernie."

In a space between the battalion aid station and the chapel, Chaplain Ferguson and Hospitalman First Class Murray Simpkins stood outside in a harsh, visibility-clouding rain. Ferguson had been drawn out by a seemingly explosive whoomph. In the battalion aid station, Simpkins had heard a radio squawk: voices screaming about a fire, then dead air.

Through the storm curtain, figures begin to appear.

"Before I could grasp what was occurring," Ferguson recalled, "there is a Marine running, screaming, and he is half dressed. And I grab him, because I knew that, exposed like that, he really had to be feeling the pain of the driving rain. I reached out to grab him, to pull him back into the chapel, into our Quonset hut. His skin came right off his shoulders and his arms."

Within minutes more burned Marines had been pulled out of the elements and into the chapel. A couple corpsmen ran in and began assessing injuries. "We were trying to triage," the chaplain said, "as best we knew."

Others of the fire-injured made their way, or were helped, to the training camp mess hall. It seemed sufficiently set aside from where the blaze was at first burning. Inside they were laid out atop long dining facility tables. Corpsmen began tending to the Marines so recently scorched that visible heat waves radiated from their bodies.

Outside Lieutenant Michael Weltsch, the battalion's incoming adjutant, encountered a Marine naked except for boxer shorts. The young man was lifting the shorts above a massive blister that covered most of his thigh. "The skin from it had flopped down," Weltsch recalled, "and there was red tissue underneath." Seeming to disregard the injured leg, the Marine implored Weltsch: "My face, man. Did it burn my face?" The lieutenant was able to assure the Marine that his countenance seemed unmarred.

Leaning in to support the Marine hobbling toward the Battalion Aid Station, Weltsch recalled looking uphill and seeing a rain-jacketed Colonel Allan Lamb examining the breached portion of the long berm.

Twenty-five of the emergency-medicine-trained Sailors at the training camp had been living with the various BLT and LSU companies to which they were assigned. Like Tim Terrell and Fred Odom, many were called upon to help patients nearby. Each had been provided introductory instruction in burn care, but little more. They provided what aid they could, then quickly moved patients toward the camp's principal center of medical care.

Building D-420, a slightly extended Quonset hut, housed the battalion aid station. There care could be provided by the only physician on Camp Fuji and ten additional corpsmen. With six in-patient beds, a single surgical table, one oxygen regulator, and six bottles of oxygen, the BAS was not equipped for mass casualty response. Even while almost immediately inundated, though—and inside a hut itself susceptible to fires sweeping the camp—Dr. Wilbur E. McDonald Jr. and his corpsmen set to work.

Their first patient—a walk-in—was charred over 75 percent of his body. McDonald recalled him "screaming with pain and crying for someone to help him." Others similarly made their own way. "I wonder now how they managed to walk," he reflected decades later. "Their uniforms and their skin were one membrane." Others quickly followed, some carried on makeshift litters. The resulting acrid aroma, McDonald affirmed, "is one of those odors that never leaves you. You will smell it for the rest of your life."

In the few seconds it took Michael Weltsch to guide the Marine with a badly burned leg into the BAS, he caught a glimpse of the battalion surgeon. The doctor—"Mac"—was moving purposefully from patient to patient, assessing injuries and directing corpsmen. "He had a look on his face like, 'Oh, my God. What the hell?' He wasn't overwhelmed, but he was concentrated."

In 1979 emergency medicine was just beginning to be viewed as a discrete discipline. The thought of specializing in such care intrigued McDonald, at twenty-seven not long out of medical school at the University of Virginia. His internship in family practice had not been compelling. "Seeing Mrs. Jones for her chronic low back pain for the next fifteen years," he mulled, "did not excite me." A Navy assignment with a Marine battalion did. As an undergraduate in UVA's school of engineering, McDonald had majored in applied mathematics. As a physician he imagined emergency practice as presenting a steady stream of new problems to be solved.

Into the late 1970s, the first physicians to see and treat patients presenting with emergency health issues were thought of as triage specialists—diagnosing problems, then quickly sending patients on to appropriate specialists. When George R. Schwartz and four other doctors published the two-volume *Principles and Practices of Emergency Medicine* in 1978, the work was a first step in establishing emergency medicine as a practice unto itself. Chapter 39 of the groundbreaking handbooks—"Special Problems in Trauma"—detailed a dozen complex medical dilemmas emergency physicians might encounter. First on the list: burns.

McDonald had ordered the books immediately after arriving on Okinawa and being posted to 2/4. They caught up with him by mail soon after the unit arrived at Camp Fuji. For whatever reason—on October 16 or 17—he had flipped to chapter 39 and absorbed the eight pages of burn treatment instruction. The injuries, he learned, could be complex and treacherous. Counterintuitively the text coached, "The burn wound itself should take last priority in the treatment of an acutely burned patient." While infections penetrating destroyed skin would eventually pose grave danger, that risk would not reach peak for three or four days. Immediately after someone had been burned, McDonald had read, "resuscitation efforts must take priority over local care of the burn."

It had not taken long for injured Marines to fill the BAS. Smoke rose from their clothes, skin, smoldering clumps of hair; the haze hampered visibility. One young man, his vision obscured by bandages, sat atop a stool, swiveling to detect recognizable voices. Thick, tarry carbon deposits clogged some patients' airways. One or two required tracheotomies; grabbing a scalpel, the young physician reestablished their airways. The torso of another Marine gasping for air was grotesquely puffed. Fluids leaking from his blood vessels had collected in the soft tissue of his thermal wounds. The swelling pressed hard against the burn-tightened skin corseting the young man's midsection. McDonald sliced an H-shaped incision though the charred outer tissue. The tourniquet-like tension released; the Marine's breathing improved. The doctor started intravenous drips through leathery burns. Tim Terrell, by then assisting in the BAS, was awed by the precise incisions required to do so, and by the tender dexterity McDonald exhibited as he found and accessed minuscule blood vessels. Applying algorithms memorized from his just-purchased textbooks, the doctor replenished fluids that had escaped the Marines' circulatory systems.

Corpsmen listened for McDonald's direction. More often they watched him, then attempted to replicate basic treatment. They scraped away burned skin, trying to clear wounds of soil and melted plastics. They tapped morphine stocks to mitigate patients' pain. They exhausted jar after jar of Silvadene, smearing the antiseptic over burns they then bandaged.

Strewn-about medical supply wrapping covered the BAS floor. Provisions of sterilized water, sodium chloride, and prepackaged bandages dwindled, corpsman Jack Crystle recalled: "At some point, we were just using the water out of the spigot [to clean wounds] and any bandages we could get our hands on."

Inside the hut Fox Company commander Jeffrey Bearor glimpsed the emergency care effort. Beforehand he had not known what to make of the unit's doctor and corpsmen. "From that moment on," he said, "I never questioned another Navy medical person. They know how to do their business, particularly when it's really hard."

It *was* hard.

"Every corpsman had like a Number 10 can from the chow hall that they were throwing up in," Lieutenant Bill Meyers observed.

"Most of the corpsmen are fairly young, and haven't experienced anything quite this bad before," McDonald noted in days thereafter. "Although some of the corpsmen cried and got sick, they continued to work—tirelessly."

Near the bottom of the training camp, Golf Company corpsman Dennis Zickefoose had been lounging in Hut D-427. The nineteen-year-old was playing an early-generation handheld electronic football game his wife, LaRee, had gifted him.

"Somebody came barging in, saying, 'Doc! Doc! There's somebody burned up at headquarters!'" The corpsman pulled a rubberized rain suit over the T-shirt and boxers he was wearing, grabbed his Unit One bag, and ran.

After fleeing the mayhem of Hut D-220, Gust Miller had made his way down the northeastern side of the training camp, below the mess hall. Someone had ushered him into D-423. Zickefoose entered the company headquarters' back door.

"Miller was at the far end when I came in," he remembered decades later. "I could tell that he was hurting," though he had no idea why. Word of the fire had not yet made it to the Golf Company area. Rushing up, the young corpsman asked the Marine for his name. He would never forget the surname. "I thought of the Steve Miller Band."

Zickefoose felt immediately inadequate. "I mean, I'd only been out of [medical] corps school three months. The first thing I thought of was: we need to get him cooled down. And so, [to] the Marines who had run up with me, I said, 'Get these [dressings] soaked, we need to get him wrapped.'" As Zickefoose bandaged, Gust Miller bemoaned being injured during the last few days of his overseas duty year. "Why did this happen to me, Doc?" the Marine asked the corpsman. "I'm going home soon." Zickefoose tried to reassure the young man as he and several others helped him onto a litter. Four of them, each gripping a handle, ran Miller to the BAS. "And that's," the corpsman remembered, "when I realized, 'Holy Cow. We've got all kinds of burned people here.'"

Throughout the early afternoon, heroism abounded. Lance Corporal Roger Rearick and Private James Barnett extinguished flames consuming the skin of fellow Marines, then carried the injured to the battalion aid station. Barnett did so twice. Corporal David Skaggs slapped down fire burning another Marine and hefted him to safety. Sergeant Richard Hill, a military photographer attached to the BLT, pried apart the lips of a burned Marine, clearing his airway. In a desperate attempt to locate Marines who may have been left inside still-burning huts, Second Lieutenant Frederick Winters, Corporal Mark Tipton, and others ripped open the doors of several. "Somebody said, 'I think somebody's trapped in there,'" Winters later recalled, "so we kept trying to go in. And I remember the time that we got in far enough, whoever was in front of me when we opened it took a step in front of me and went down from the heat." Winters pulled him out.

Mike Tuttle, shocked but otherwise unhurt, stood nearby, wearing shorts and a Converse T-shirt he had owned since his senior year of high school. Mark Tipton gathered him and several others. Moving through D-215 as soon as the fire inside had subsided, they encountered the remains of L. C. Malveaux. "He was on the ground," Tuttle remembered, "and his face was literally melted." In an unburned hut, they found a corpsman treating a badly burned Mark Bedwell. Tipton commandeered a jeep and lashed the Marine to the vehicle's hood. Tuttle then walked alongside as Tipton drove the jeep through wind and rain—and around walls of flame. "I knew who [Bedwell] was," Tuttle recalled. "I recognized some of his facial features. It was kind of odd or surreal for me. I thought that he would be in excruciating pain as badly as he was burned, but I just remember him being somewhat calm." They dropped Bedwell at the mess hall. Similar lifesaving efforts went unobserved except by the Marines and Sailors involved.

The fire's fierce, pitiless consequences for a time stunned the BLT 2/4 commander. One officer recalled observing Lieutenant Colonel Redgate "emotionally distraught" by the harm befalling his Marines. Soon, though, he was working with Colonel Lamb on a disaster response plan.

Surveying the ongoing mayhem from a jeep, the battalion's executive officer, Major Lance Woodburn, passed the chapel, and a Marine standing outside, shirtless, skin hanging from his arms. "And I thought, 'Oh, my God.' I couldn't hear whether he was screaming or not because of the noise of the storm."

After finding the energy to flee the outdoor theater area, Jesse Lugo had resumed his downhill run. Along the way he spotted a platoon mate, Private First Class Craig X. Jackson. Third-degree burns covered more than 40 percent of Jackson's body. Together Lugo and the Marine from Richmond Hill, Georgia, tried to flag down a jeep they saw coming toward them. When it appeared its Japanese driver was not going to halt, Lugo recalled, "Jackson and I got in front of him and made him stop." They jumped in the vehicle, which began carrying them toward safety. "All of a sudden," though, Lugo recalled, "the roadway in front of us caved in like an earthquake." A washout. The jeep could not cross. The two were again on foot.

In the camp's center, Anthony Senatore and two other Marines had completed loading medical supplies into their amtrac. Corpsmen pointed them to the chow hall. As the fire spread, the dining facility and the chapel no longer seemed safe refuge.

Battalion leaders ordered all hands to abandon the training camp. Working his way down from the top tier, Captain Roger Mauer, the BLT logistics officer, directed unit commanders to move their men downhill, across the airstrip, into a large base camp hangar. "I'm not sure how far away the hangar was," Thomas Moquino recalled, "but, man, it took us a while to get there."

A dozen or so Marines wielding e-tools had gathered around the BAS, gouging trenches to divert fuel-laden rainwater away from the building. L. C. Malveaux's body had been carried into the aid station. The corpse was rigid. It reminded Mac McDonald of human remains he had seen at a museum in Pompeii, Italy: bodies petrified in volcanic magma after an eruption of Mount Vesuvius. "Someone came in," Jack Crystle remembered, "and said we had to evacuate. Dr. McDonald said, 'We are not evacuating. We are still treating Marines.' And they said, 'You don't understand, the fire is close to the aid station. You have to get out.'"

The doctor dispatched Murray Simpkins, the battalion's senior corpsman, to set up a triage site downhill at the base camp, inside a small hangar alongside the large one, where the uninjured were being told to assemble. The battalion physician and BAS corpsmen then began loading patients into amtracs for evacuation downhill.

At the dining facility, corpsmen did the same. Crews used blankets to lower them onto the vehicles' floors. "I remember them loading a lot of ice onto the amtrac," Anthony Senatore said, "I guess to keep these guys cool." Corpsmen jumped in to attend to the Marines. The amtracs again sealed up and headed downhill through the smoke, heat and fire. Though well intentioned, icing the burn injuries was not helpful; indeed, it could do damage by slowing the flow of tissue-vitalizing blood to the injured portion of a patient's body. Fortunately, the ride to the hastily organized downhill triage site was brief.

Meantime, fiery fuel continued to surge and meander into lower parts of the training camp. Its seemingly random twists and turns were guided by nuances of grading and erosion. When Lance Corporal Joe Macdonald and fellow Marines noticed a reddish-yellow light flash through their barracks windows, they crowded to look out. "Through the rain and wind," Macdonald recalled, "I could see flames rising from a Quonset hut a few down from ours." Then, a hut even closer began burning. "I got scared, I got really scared," Macdonald recalled. His first thought was to get out; the second, that his hut had been nailed shut. At just that moment, he heard a tremendous crash. Wind rushed inside. The hut's front door, broken off its hinges, lay on the floor inside. "And there was a captain on top of the door, on the ground, and he was still like kind of rolling a little bit. And he just jumped up and yelled at the top of his lungs, 'Run for your life, men. Do it now!'" Outside another strong voice grabbed his attention. "Don't stop! This way! Keep running!" Holding fast against the wind, the Headquarters and Service Company first sergeant directed them away from the nightmarish scene.

Bill Dyer saw one Marine fleeing completely naked, a guitar slung over his back. "Some guy threw him a raincoat," he recalled. Another Marine was directed toward safety by a completely unclothed Marine holding a towel: "He was waving it above his head. He had been ready to take a shower." Lieutenant Bill Meyers, clad in a sweatshirt, utility trousers, and flip-flops, pushed his Fox Company platoon downhill. Noticing Marine Mike Larson escaping in just trousers, Meyers tossed him the sweatshirt.

Pausing only to grab his wallet, boots, and rain jacket, Roger Miller joined friends emerging easily from their quarters. The other half of his platoon, though, "had padlocked themselves in" an adjacent hut. "They can't find the keys," he remembered. "They don't know who locked it—you know, just chaos at this point. The Quonset hut above them is burning. We're ripping these guys out the windows." Most made their way to the base camp hangar. A gaggle of Marines sought shelter in a stand of trees to the south.

Elsewhere in the Fox Company area, firewatch Michael Bendt had heard the ignitions uphill. Earlier, smelling gas, he had turned off the two heaters in his hut. The move had not been popularly received. Now, as he ordered everyone in the hut to evacuate, they pushed back again. "They're like, 'Aw, I'm not going out in this.'" Bendt's position was difficult. He was a private with just six months in the Marine Corps, most of that time having been spent in boot camp and at infantry training school. He had been flown up from Okinawa to join the battalion just days beforehand. His only authority came from his assignment as fire watch. "Get on out of here," he told his barracks mates after hearing the whoomphs. "We didn't realize what was going on," he recalled, "but it sounded like artillery walking in on us." Bendt remained in the hut—conscious of the Marines' General Order Number 5: *To quit my post only when properly relieved*. "I was on fire watch," he explained. "Nobody relieved me, so I stayed."

Flames engulfed disparate swaths of the training camp. Smoke billowed upward, merging into the dark storm clouds overhead. Figures moved about, backlit by the glow of fire. Terrence Stokes ran past two bodies on the ground. "They were burnt from head to toe," he recalled. "One was Black and one was white. The rainwater was washing over them." Stokes ran and found one of his company's lieutenants. "I showed him the two bodies, and he just dropped down on his knees and started cryin.'"

The fire decimated Weapons Company. Forty-three of the individuals most seriously injured in the incident, all Weapons Company Marines, had been in just three Quonset huts: thirteen in D-214, thirteen in D-215, and seventeen in D-220.

At the base camp, Captain John Paparone, who commanded a detachment of tank and amtrac crews kept at Camp Fuji, offered to add his tracked personnel carriers to the rescue effort, including one configured as a command vehicle. Its communications equipment, he said, "would have talked around the world." The Range Company logistics officer, Paparone said, told him, "I'll get back to you." He never did.

Amtracs assigned to the BLT continued to ferry the injured. After the day's first dashes, though, crews navigated into and out of the camp via outside roads, rather than moving up and down its central spaces. Amid the smoke and confusion, Anthony Senatore worried, "I didn't want [the drivers] to hit anybody."

Injured Marines wandered the ground-level hellscape. "It was pretty horrible," Rob Ahrens remembered, "because all their hair was gone, some of them their ears were gone. And you couldn't tell whether they were a Black guy or a white guy." Paul Verdier recalled wind-whipped volcanic ash "sandblasting those guys. They were walking out of the dark with their skin hanging off in, like rags, and just being bead-blasted by this fucking ash. And we had no way to protect them, so guys would huddle around them."

Joe Macdonald was directed into such a scrum. "Somebody brought in a Marine who at the time I didn't recognize, but later I believed to be Philip du Pont." A poncho was spread over the volcanic soil. Those who had carried the injured Marine sat him atop the rubbery rain gear, then instructed those gathered around: "Just try to keep the rain off him." "Everything was burnt off of him," Macdonald remembered. "His ears, his nose seemed to be gone, there was no eyebrows. I couldn't grasp what was going on, but I was wondering why this guy had these trash bags in his hands." It was, he eventually realized, skin that had "melted off his arms and was just kind of hanging there." Macdonald ached. "There was nothing we could do and we were just inches from him. And he was looking up at us, like, 'Somebody save me.'"

Mike Cummings meandered, 75 percent of his body covered with second- and third-degree burns. He watched flames ignite in the middle of gasoline-soaked roads, then recede back into the earth. Seconds later fire would rise from the soil surface six feet further on. Though stunned, he felt oddly normal. "When I first got burned, I mean, it hurt like hell," he remembered. "The pain was something I'd never experienced before. And then, next thing I know, I don't feel any pain anymore. It's like, 'What in the hell just happened?'" He encountered uninjured friends. "The look on their face when they would look at me, I knew it wasn't good. The first guy that I asked for help, he just, 'I'm sorry, I can't.' I remember him saying that: 'I'm sorry, I can't.' And he wasn't burned. So I must have looked that bad, with that skin hanging off my face and hands. Everybody was in shock, whether they were burned or not. You couldn't believe what was happening."

Closer to the center of the camp, "one of my colleagues came up to me," Steve Neal remembered. "He was on mess duty, and he was coming back from the mess hall. And he goes, 'Damn, Steve, you're burned to shit!' And I said, 'Thanks a lot, dude!' He helped me get over to the nearest barracks, which happened to be the Marine recon guys. They had a corpsman there, and he gave me a shot of morphine. . . . I just waved and nodded and went to sleep."

In Hut D-214, where Louis Sanford had hunkered for some time on the floor, "the fire had kind of settled down. You know, it was still burning, but it's like when you put too much lighter fluid on a barbecue, it flames up big, then kind of settles." The experience had blurred the twenty-one-year-old's sense of time. "I don't know how long I stayed on the ground," he said. “Eventually, I reached out and grabbed what may have been a broom handle, something like that. I used it to break open one of the windows—from a distance. I didn’t want to happen to my face what had happened to that other guy’s. I pulled myself up and through.” His ears and nose were blistered over—the latter from having inhaled intensely hot air; his hair had been crisply seared. Amid smoke, noise and confusion, he followed others he could see escaping downhill. “Kids eighteen, twenty-one, twenty-two, never been in that type situation,” Robert Hendrix empathized. “It was as traumatic as hell the first couple hours.”

MOGAS vapors and oxygen flashed in downhill huts D-308, D-316, and D-326. In the Fox Company area, as Michael Bendt worked to dig a trench directing water away from his platoon’s hut, the structure just alongside went up in flames. He went back inside, positioning himself in the middle of his unit’s quarters. Through its windows he could see flames rising all around. Inside the temperature rose. Sweating, he drank the contents of every canteen his platoon-mates had left behind. “On firewatch, you’re supposed to watch for fires and be able to put ’em out,” he remembered. “This was one that I wasn’t going outside to try and put out. I’d say some of the flames were ten, twelve, fifteen feet tall. It came in waves. It would stop one second, and reignite again.”

Rob Ahrens and others in his platoon tried to help injured Marines they encountered, but “every time you touched them,” he said, “they screamed.” Thinking it would help relieve their pain, Ahrens recalled, they lowered some of the injured into drainage ditches, holding their heads above the water. “They were kind of incoherent, and yelling.” Second Lieutenant Ronny Yowell, commander of the amtrac platoon, heard the commotion. “You guys hold on,” Ahrens recalled the twenty-four-year-old officer saying. “I’ll go get a ‘trac.’” Soon an amtrac barreled downhill, forcing its way through sporadically rising flames. It backed into a parking area in front of the BAS, too close to the structure. When its ramp was lowered, it slammed into a plywood-constructed waiting room addition that jutted out from one end of the hut. “We had this amtrac parked there,” Ahrens remembered, “with the ramp going right into sick bay.” He and his men carried the injured they had been tending into the amtrac. It headed toward the base camp hangars, easily fording roadways now flooded or washed out.

Marines in the bottom-most tier of training camp huts were among the last to hear what was happening. Inside Hut D-337, peering toward the uphill-facing back door, Mike Burbo realized that "the cracks around the door are yellow. I'm looking through the back of the building—at fire." He rousted all but one fellow Marine out the front door. To that last young man, slowly lacing his boots, Burbo yelled, "Look, if I don't see you in the next twenty-four hours, I'm going to assume you're dead," then ran out. Finally realizing the urgency of the situation, the Marine quickly bolted past Burbo. They joined the flow of young men running toward the large hanger.

There evacuated Marines were gathering, trying to quickly determine who was accounted for, who was not. "Where's Echo? Where's Fox Company?" Andy Bonwit recalled hearing shouted. "Hey, Golf Company over here! Here's Weapons!"

In the Headquarters and Service Company formation, Bill Dyer could not find his bunkmate, Roosevelt Ross, a private first class from Chicago Heights, Illinois. He dashed back to their hut, D-338. There Ross lay "asleep in his rack, which I thought was odd," he recalled, "because there was a whole lot of noise going on." Dyer woke Ross and helped him put on a few clothes. "And I said, 'Okay, you're dressed enough, let's go.' And I ran out that back door." Double-timing back toward the airstrip, Dyer passed Building D-337, which had housed radio and telephone operators of the BLT's Headquarters and Service Company. As he reached a dirt road just beyond it, a wave of heat burst from the communicators' hut. "I ended up in the street," he recalled, buffeted by the blast, but not burned. Ross had chosen a different path back to the rally point. Flames from the hut's ignition scorched one-quarter of his body.

Akira Yamada had ensured the closing of the NEX snack bar, souvenir store, and shoe repair workshop before the first uphill hut flared. When flames rose his car was near the center of the training camp.

"The first feeling that I had was fear," Yamada recalled. "We were four people in the vehicle, trying to run away from the fire." Feeling obligated to keep his fellow employees safe, he shouted that he would drive them to safety. "But the two ladies in the back seat," he said—photo shop employee

Sumiko Yuasa and a barber shop worker surnamed Sato—"got so scared that they just ran away from the vehicle."

Clerk Taeko Matsuzaki remained with Yamada. She stepped outside to guide the vehicle. Though he could barely see his colleague through rain slamming the car's windshield, Yamada held the steering wheel tight and drove in the direction she indicated. "There was so much water and smoke," Matsuzaki later remembered, "that I couldn't see the road." Wailing winds added to a sense of chaos. Finally, the two made their way uphill to a road that should have allowed them to escape toward the camp's ammunition storage area. It was closed.

An alternate path eventually allowed them to drive in another direction that seemed safe. Ironically, it was at the far southern end of the long berm—"a large place just opposite the gas tank," Matsuzaki recalled, where "some other NEX workers had gathered. We waited there for about two hours."

Yamada never had a chance to instruct workers at the camp laundry to close for the day. Among those inside the wood-frame-and-tin structure—Building T-109—was laundry worker Yasuko Nakayama. The fifty-year-old owned a bar just off-base targeting a clientele of Marine Corps and Navy officers. Yogiri, it was called; in English, "Night Fog." A young woman whose father operated a tavern nearby recalled Nakayama as quite attractive. Because nightclub profits could be inconsistent—lucrative when a thousand Marines were encamped, light during periods when few were in residence—Nakayama augmented her income by working days in Kiyoshi Hama's on-camp laundry. "I was inside the NEX [laundry]," a Japanese newspaper quoted Nakayama as saying, "and suddenly found myself surrounded by fire. When I was totally at a loss about what to do in the flames, I was rescued by an American soldier returning [to where I was]."

That Marine was twenty-one-year-old Private First Class Keith Burleigh. According to an award citation, the young man from the Bronx, New York, had been helping to clean the facility when T-109 became the final structure on Camp Fuji to go up in flames. The conflagration began to consume uniforms and other clothing inside. Burleigh dashed from the building. Hearing screams behind him, he ran back inside. "Groping his way through the smoke and fire," the citation stated, the Marine "located the dazed woman lying on the floor unable to move. Although nearly overcome by the intense heat," it declared, and suffering serious burns to his forehead, Burleigh struggled to Nakayama's side. As he beat out flames on her polyester dress, a fiery piece of the polka dot fabric flew into his face, melting into his burn. Lifting the woman and dodging flames that were consuming the building around them, he carried her to safety.

Sumiko Yuasa also found herself in peril—jeopardy she would have avoided had she not fled Akira Yamada's sedan. Echo Company Lance Corporal Steve Holmes had noticed the fifty-two-year-old woman making her way down the lower center of the training camp. "She had white boots on," he recalled, "almost like those little snow boots that everyone would wear to school. That got my attention when I was crossing the roadway trying to get to the hangar."

As Yuasa, Holmes and several other Marines paused briefly to determine the best way to cross a flooding drainage ditch, the woman fell into the deep, fast-flowing gutter. Distracted by flames shooting skyward uphill, Holmes had not seen it happen. "Two Marines came up behind me," the Topeka, Kansas, native recalled. "They had realized what was going on."

One or both—Holmes could not recall precisely—jumped into the ditch. The water seemed two-to-three feet deep. "And they said, 'You stay there. We're going to hand her up.' She was completely submerged. I can't believe she didn't drown, actually."

Yuasa was lifted to Holmes. "I had two hands on her—was eye-to-eye with her—trying to just get her elevated up to the level of the road," he remembered. Yuasa struggled to gain the toehold. "I was trying to pull her, then back away so she didn't fall back in.

"At that point—I assume, static electricity, maybe?—something immediately sparked her. We had her out, and we had her up on the road, and then it was just like someone had taken a match and lit her from her feet. She was immediately engulfed in flames."

Holmes and four or five other Marines who had run up to help pushed Yuasa to the ground. As they rolled her along, some used pieces of their own clothing to smother the fire. Andy Bonwit recalled seeing a Marine pour water from his canteen over the woman's arms. The effort "took some time," Holmes remembered. "That fire did not want to go out."

When a small sedan driven by Japanese workers pulled up, Marines maneuvered Yuasa into the vehicle's backseat. Holmes, just days away from his twentieth birthday, watched the car drive off. "My mind said she wasn't going to live. I really didn't expect her to live." Taking stock of himself, he felt no injury: "You know, my hands weren't burnt." There were, though, images seared into his mind. "She never closed her eyes once," he recalled decades later. "She never made a sound, never spoke, never cried out in pain, or anything. But she appeared to be burnt extremely badly."

Indeed, Yuasa's clothing had been scorched. And she had suffered burns below her knees, on her back and one arm, and behind her left ear. Most of the thermal injuries, though, were first-degree. They would be treatable without hospitalization. The photo shop employee knew that the rapid response of those around her had been the saving difference. "I would have been killed," a United Press International dispatch quoted Yuasa as saying, "if a U.S. Marine did not rescue me."

Forty-four-year-old Kimio Hata also incurred minor burns to both of his arms—the right worse than the left—as he escaped downhill. The Kyoto native had moved to Gotemba some years earlier to buy and operate the gift shop on Camp Fuji. His family had remained on the more southern island, supported by the shop earnings Hata would deliver while visiting them every three months.

Extreme weather conditions and a lack of heavy firefighting equipment prevented Marines and Sailors at Camp Fuji from quickly countering a large-scale fire. The chaos at the camp would test the "handshake agreement" with nearby Japanese firefighters.

Even amid the dangerous weather conditions, responders arrived quickly. "The first really effective fire fighting efforts began within a half hour of the first explosion," Captain Roger Mauer noted at the time, "as the heavy equipment arrived."

Earliest on the scene, arriving ten minutes after the fire had first flashed, were five Japanese airfield firefighters. Their pump truck had been staged within the Camp Fuji enclave, alongside the camp runway. Ten or fifteen minutes later, they were joined by five responders in a pump truck from across the road at Camp Takigahara. Early in the 2 p.m. hour, six more firefighters arrived in a pump truck and a tanker from the Gotemba-Oyama station four miles away. "I mean, they were there amazingly fast," John Brosnan remembered.

Over time teams of volunteer firefighters from two nearby villages responded, as well—two platoons, ten or twelve individuals from Inno; and a single platoon of five or six from Tomaho. Confusion at access gates kept some of the volunteers from getting in to help.

The response was ad hoc and unrehearsed. City fire crews had not previously been allowed onto Camp Fuji to exercise how best to respond to a fire crisis there. "We didn't have any information as far as structure of the camp, or where the buildings were located," Haruhiko Katsumata recalled, "or where any hazardous materials were stored or where water sources were available." Such information was important to strategizing a response and keeping firefighters safe. Most significantly, they had not been told they were being called to fight a fire fueled by gasoline. They arrived with water tankers.

"Water alone is a last-resort method of controlling fuel fires," instructed the Marines' 1977 fuel handlers' pocket guide. "The stream of water hitting the fuel tends to spread the burning fuel over a larger area. Fuel floats on water and the floating burning fuel spreads rapidly through any gaps, holes or cracks." A 1973 naval safety manual explained that a petroleum product fire is best smothered with "foam extinguishers and carbon dioxide."

"If we had known it was a fuel fire," Katsumata reflected, "we would have taken our chemical vehicle rather than a water truck."

Decades later Katsumata's mind still held vivid images of the "horrible spectacle" he and fellow first responders encountered at the camp. At first he believed he was witnessing the result of an arson incident or terrorist attack. "I saw injured Marines with their skin charred," he recalled. "The sight was so shocking I forced my eyes to turn away. I had to keep my composure."

Inside the tanker Katsumata drove and operated, the seven-year veteran firefighter monitored firehose pressure, keeping in radio contact with colleagues handling the attached lines. After about half an hour of putting water on the fire, the supply began to deplete. Compelled by the tragedy around him, and still not aware that the fire they were fighting was gasoline fueled, Katsumata sought another source of water to pump. He found it in the camp's open drainage gutters.

It was a move not taken lightly. "Pumping dirty water or rainwater is the last thing you want to do as a firefighter," he affirmed. The sand and dirt it contained could damage a tanker's pumps and hoses. Looking around, however, he saw no choice. "I could see all the Marines and Sailors who had been basically charred, and some of them were naked. . . . We had to do whatever was necessary to put the fire out."

It is not clear if MOGAS was still flowing atop the rain run-off as Katsumata—working feverishly outside in the storm—pushed a hose into one of the ditches and began pulling water to a pump that then sent it on to lines wielded by fellow firefighters. "I couldn't smell anything," he recalled.

Inside the base camp hangar, more than a thousand displaced Marines and Sailors stood, sat, milled about—"just numb, in shock, disoriented," Echo Company's Fredric Britton Jr. recalled. "It was almost like being homeless in seconds—not even a minute, seconds." "Nomads" was the word that came to the mind of Captain Leon Craig, Britton's company commander. "We're nomads."

Micheal Bendt had rejoined fellow Fox Company Marines, finally relieved from his fire watch post. "It was about 1430 [2:30 p.m.], maybe a little after that, that Lieutenant [Mark] Fornaciari returned back to the barracks to get me out of there. They couldn't come back into that area until the fire was down." Searchers had also retrieved Roger Miller and others who had sheltered in nearby woods.

Each Marine and Sailor was handed a piece of paper. "Whether we wanted to or not, we were all required to send a message back to our families," Mike Tuttle recalled: "I'm fine, I'm okay. More later." The brief notes, along with loved ones' contact information, were collected for transmission home via a network of military communicators and amateur radio volunteers.

The atmosphere in the hangar altered from anxious to somber when Weapons Company Marines arrived hefting the remains of L. C. Malveaux. The body was wrapped in a green wool blanket, the letters "U S" stamped on the fabric. Lance Corporal Rob Krumwiede remembered one of Malveaux's legs hanging slightly off the stretcher; burned portions of his black skin, the tanker said, "looked pink like the inside of your lip."

"It got hushed," Echo Company platoon commander Jim Stallings remembered. "These were eighteen-year-old kids. I was a twenty-three-year-old lieutenant. It was our first time seeing a dead Marine."

As Murray Simpkins oversaw setup of the downhill triage space, corpsmen opened "war stock" supplies battalion logistics officer Roger Mauer had helped them retrieve from cargo containers. What they found in the cases was neither plentiful nor fresh. "IV solutions were out of date," Dr. McDonald would later write, "the water purification kit was a disintegrated mass, and drugs and equipment for modern resuscitation techniques were lacking." Absent any alternative, much of it was put to use.

Truck drivers and amtrac crews began delivering a steady stream of patients to the base camp's small hangar. Some were injured Marines who had been waiting outside the BAS, unable to fit inside. Weapons Company's Paul Verdier walked behind a truck that carried that group to the lower triage site.

"For lack of anything else to do, I just started wetting bandages for the docs," Verdier recalled, emotion welling. "They were wrapping these guys in wet gauze as fast as they could. So I would just wet a roll of gauze, and hand it to someone else and they'd be wrapping somebody."

"I remember lightning," said Steve Neal, who had been carried to the hangar. "Or it was a flashlight, I'm not exactly sure. I remember seeing faces, *concerned* faces. They were probably just checking our vitals."

Lieutenant Miles Wilhelm and Petty Officer Third Class Keith Norred joined caregivers there. The LSU 3/9 dentist and dental technician had been sheltering in their small dental clinic at the base camp, Norred recalled, when "three Marines showed up at the clinic door. They were burned . . . bluish-gray-looking." Guiding the Marines to the small hangar, Wilhelm and Norred began helping to administer painkilling medications. The dentist secured a sleeping bag for use as a more dignified container of Lance Corporal Malveaux's remains.

Miles Wilhelm's path to dentistry had been unconventional. After college he had followed in the footsteps of an admired older brother, earning a commission in the Marine Corps. His service as an infantry platoon commander had included wartime duty off the coast of Vietnam. After mustering out he had completed dental school and returned to uniformed service in the Navy.

With only rudimentary medical supplies on hand at Camp Fuji, it was clear the injured Marines needed care in a better-equipped setting—quickly.

In most circumstances military helicopters would have been available to evacuate those who had been hurt. While none were permanently based at the camp, they could have been hailed from American bases to the camp's northeast. Amid Tip's continuing barrage, though, most aircraft on Honshu had been grounded.

At 2:45 p.m. a telephone rang in the office of Lieutenant Commander George Gregory. Nearing the end of a career in Navy medicine that had begun when he trained as an enlisted corpsman in 1956, the hospital administrator friends called "Greg" was now officer in charge of the clinic at Naval Air Facility Atsugi.

Gregory answered. On the other end of a garbled line—from Camp Fuji, thirty-some miles to the southwest—was the corpsman assigned to Range Company. Excitedly, the petty officer described a horrific ongoing mass casualty incident. One Marine was dead, he said, and more than a dozen severely injured. Atsugi should stand by to receive casualties.

As part of the clinic's typhoon preparations, an extra crew was already on hand. While the air facility had experienced heavy rains and high winds, damage had been lighter than in other parts of Honshu. Gregory ordered the recall of remaining clinic staff, then began making calls of his own. The naval hospital at Yokosuka, he learned, was still being battered by Tip. "There was nothing they could do. They couldn't drive, they couldn't do anything."

The medical service corps officer explored convoying members of his team to the camp. Road wash-outs and other storm dangers, he was told, would make that difficult. Next he looked to the skies, dark though they still were. NAF Atsugi served as an operations and maintenance hub for U.S. military aircraft operating on Honshu. Perhaps aircraft currently on the flight line could help with a rescue.

Gregory called the base operations office, only to learn that, given storm-imposed flight restrictions, many air crew members had retreated to the base clubs. "I was told," he said, "'The pilots are having a typhoon party.'" With flight rules requiring preflight sobriety—eight hours "from bottle to throttle"—it appeared unlikely that a complete flight crew could be raised.

Gregory queried the aviation detachment at a nearby U.S. Army base. It yielded a similarly disheartening response. Army aviators at Camp Zama, he attested, "said, 'We can't fly.'" The Atsugi clinic OIC then rang medical counterparts on Camp Zama.

Major Lewis Gold had finished his regular workday at U.S. Army Health Clinic, Honshu and headed to the on-base duplex he shared with his wife. Tired after a busy shift, the Army pediatrician had laid down to get some rest. As the hospital's duty physician, he could still be called back. He had barely fallen asleep when Gregory's call was patched through to his quarters. The description of an unfolding disaster grabbed Gold's attention. He wanted to help, but faced a dilemma.

"I was on call," he recounted. He was supposed to remain at or near the hospital. Senior leaders he would typically consult were not immediately available. "I had to make a decision," he said. It did not take him long. He was not a surgeon—surgeons treated serious burn injuries—but he and others could help with triage. Gold activated an emergency plan that would ensure care at a Japanese hospital for anyone arriving at Camp Zama seriously ill. He then gathered a physician assistant, nurse, and group of Army corpsmen. Packing what limited clinic supplies might help with burn treatment into two ambulances, he and the others embarked on the five- or six-mile drive to Atsugi.

At the Naval Air Facility's operations office—"base ops"—the crew on duty could not shake off the alert Greg Gregory had shared. A Marine at Camp Fuji had died; others were at grave risk. There had to be *some* way—using aircraft hangared at the NAF, or tied down on its flight line—to get help to those Marines. They began making calls; runners were dispatched.

Two of the aircraft at Atsugi that day were CH-46 Sea Knights assigned to the Navy supply ship USS White Plains (AFS-4). At sea the helicopters would fly vertical replenishment missions, lifting pallets containing anything from toilet paper to frozen meat to jet engines. During transfer from White Plains to the forward-deployed warships they pulled alongside, the loads of up to ten thousand pounds dangled from lines hanging beneath each CH-46.

The two aircraft (tail numbered 153389 and 154832) were flown and maintained by Detachment 106 of Navy Helicopter Combat Support Squadron-3. Each time White Plains emptied its cargo holds, the ship would return to port to replenish. Most often that was to Yokosuka, where flight operations were not allowed while the ship was pier-side. In order to continue flight training and take advantage of heavy maintenance facilities during those periods, Detachment 106 would fly off of White Plains as it neared the port, temporarily relocating to NAF Atsugi.

Given the airfield's closure as the storm blew through, Lieutenant Commander Greg Rhodes, who led Detachment 106, had declared Friday a day off. "We just secured everything," recalled D. C. Ray, at the time a lieutenant and one of the HC-3 pilots. "We tied [the helicopters] down and sent everybody on liberty."

Having been designated detachment duty officer, Ray avoided stopping by the club in the bachelor officers quarters building and was riding out the storm in his room. High winds had knocked out power at the BOQ, but the room's landline could still ring. A caller, from base ops, was blunt and beseeching. He and colleagues were trying to find a crew that could fly. Marines were dying, the Sailor told the Ray. He pleaded for a MEDEVAC.

"When he said that," Ray recounted, "it just clicked. I said, 'I'll attempt to round up a crew and see what we can do.'" His problem was finding squadron mates. No one remained at the airfield Quonset hut where they worked while at the NAF. Rhodes had gone to dinner, but Ray was not sure where. Sprinting through the wind and rain, the lieutenant crossed the base, exiting at the nearest gate. In the adjacent Japanese town, he peered into three restaurants before locating Rhodes and a few other crew members. If the situation was as desperate as described, the lieutenant commander affirmed, "we'll launch."

Ray dashed back onto the naval air facility, confirmed the gravity of the situation at Camp Fuji, then began gathering detachment Sailors from their barracks. Both of the team's aircraft had in some measure been pulled apart for maintenance. Getting them flight-ready would involve serious mechanical work. "It wasn't a fifteen-minute evolution," Rhodes recalled. "It was probably a couple hours."

Base ops runners had continued in their effort to chase down air crews. At the club in the BOQ, some aviators had been drinking and could not fly safely. Two Marine pilots in the group were willing to go, but their CH-53 Sea Stallion was short an engine.

From early September to early October, Captains Bob Shillito and Dan Scandalito had been part of a four-helicopter detachment supporting BLT 3/9 artillery exercises at Camp Fuji. On Friday, October 12, they and others from Marine Heavy Helicopter Squadron-361 had begun flying back to Okinawa. When one of the detachment's helicopters developed engine trouble, the two were left behind to oversee its repair, then return it to the southern island.

If a Navy crew could be assembled to fly to the camp, the Atsugi base operations officer asked the Marines, could they help the other pilots navigate? "Sure," Scandalito said. "We know our way out there."

"I've got all the call signs on my knee board," Shillito added. "I'll bring that along."

Back on Camp Fuji, 3:45 p.m. found John Redgate shifting his battalion command post to the base camp, where he could access a better communications capability and coordinate with Colonel Lamb on a postfire action plan. The BLT CO left his executive officer, Lance Woodburn, to organize security watches throughout the mostly evacuated training camp.

Lamb and Redgate—as best they could, given storm-related communications problems and the necessity of language translation—conferred with commanders at nearby Japanese military bases. From the moment they had been called on to fight the fire, Jieitai leaders had begun to ready other assistance potentially useful to the devastated Marines. The nearby headquarters of Fuji Gakku—in English, "Fuji Schools," the Japanese ground force's training command—immediately agreed to admit injured Marines to its Fuji Sector Hospital. Doctor McDonald would follow those patients and assist Colonel (Dr.) Ryogo Sato, the hospital director, in their care

On receiving word of the patient evacuation plan, Murray Simpkins began directing trucks and jeeps into a convoy column on the airstrip. Japanese trucks and drivers dispatched from nearby Camp Takigahara joined the queue.

Amid winds still sustained at twenty-five miles per hour, with drizzle being hurled about, corpsmen moved patients from the small hangar toward the trucks. Hoisting them onto the vehicles' beds—five feet above the ground—was not easy. Marines lifted Issac Williams into the grip of young men standing on the back of the truck. The move, Williams remembered decades later, "pulled all the skin off my legs, and my skin was just rolling everywhere."

Soon, the vehicles were packed with the injured, accompanying corpsmen, and friends hoping to reassure their buddies. Miles Wilhelm jumped into the cab of the first vehicle. The Navy dentist would lead the convoy.

The column consisted of four or five trucks, Wilhelm recalled. "We just got the fellows and put them in rows on either side, sitting there, and we took off."

On arriving at Fuji Gakku, Wilhelm and the others learned that the Fuji Sector hospital could provide care—superior care, it would turn out—but to only ten patients. Technical and linguistic glitches, it seemed, had inhibited communicating the full extent of what had happened at Camp Fuji. The ten worst-injured were off-loaded, as was the body of L. C. Malveaux.

It was decided that remaining patients would be delivered to civilian hospitals and clinics in Gotemba and other nearby communities. Injured Marines on the trucks shook and shivered as drivers made their way through local communities. Though rainfall was drizzling to a stop, it was 66 degrees out and sustained winds of twenty miles per hour buffeted the vehicles. They moved along roadways impacted by Typhoon Tip, some of which had been closed to traffic by Japanese public safety authorities.

At 4 p.m., near the entrance to a main highway, the convoy encountered a lowered barrier gate. A tollbooth-like shelter stood alongside. Miles Wilhelm jumped from the cab of the lead truck and knocked on the booth window. "Open the gate!" he yelled. He spoke no Japanese; the Gotemba police officer inside spoke no English. "I said, 'You've got to open the gate.' I was motioning, and, of course, he didn't understand. And so I escorted him. I took him by the arm." Wilhelm yanked the Japanese officer into the rain, to a point where he could see into the back of the first truck. "Here's this idiot thirty-two-year-old Caucasian wet guy, pulling him. But when he saw that, he realized [the severity of the situation]—because he wasn't going to open the gate." The police officer raised the barrier, allowed the trucks through, then telephoned colleagues. Though firefighters from the Gotemba-Oyama station had responded much earlier to Camp Fuji, the roadblock incident marked the Gotemba police agencies' first notice of the fire. "Local authorities," a regional newspaper reported, "intervened and raced to [the camp]."

Once on the highway, drivers dispersed toward a number of separate hospitals and clinics. At the drop-off sites, efforts were made to ensure that injured Marines were not left alone. "I wanted to make sure that we had one Marine who was healthy with each Marine who was injured," Wilhelm recalled. Navy corpsmen were left at some of the clinics, as well. The Marines and Sailors would assist the local staffs—as best they could, given that none of the Americans spoke Japanese and few of the doctors and nurses spoke English.

At 4:10 p.m., fifty miles northeast of Camp Fuji, first word of the disaster arrived at the U.S. military hospital on Yokota Air Base. A major surnamed Bach from Headquarters, U.S. Forces, Japan informed the base hospital's emergency department that "a fuel tank exploded at Camp Fuji and 35–40 Marines have been injured."

The hospital commander—Air Force Colonel (Dr.) Clarence Whiteside Jr.—activated an incident control center, then ordered immediate callback of doctors, nurses, physician assistants, and medical technicians. An ambitious response plan was devised. Staffers would deep-clean the medical center's unoccupied fourth floor—fitting it with equipment and supplies. From whole cloth, as best they could, they would create a burn treatment center. Hospital work schedules would be realigned to staff the new ward. Volunteer registered nurses—many of them spouses of military members—would augment the effort.

At 4:15 that afternoon, a call from a journalist in Washington DC made it through to the BLT 2/4 duty officer. Jack Dabney, overnight news editor of the Mutual radio network, asked about rumors of calamity. He was referred to the public affairs office at Marine Corps headquarters. "All personnel," the duty officer logged, were "told to not give out any information whatsoever." News of the developing disaster did, though, move through military channels. Twenty minutes after Dabney's call, Lieutenant Colonel Redgate telephoned Okinawa, updating Colonel Charles Knowles, the Fourth Marines' regimental commander.

At NAF Atsugi, meantime, HC-3 mechanics had pieced together one of Detachment 106's Sea Knights. Under dark clouds, amid approaching dusk, it sat ready on the tarmac. As Greg Rhodes, D. C. Ray, and two Navy air crewmen rushed through preflight checklists, they noticed two figures jogging toward the helicopter. Bent against the wind as they ran, Ray recalled, Marine Captain Bob Shillito and Army Major Lewis Gold "just showed up like out of the mist." The Sailors of NAF base ops had assembled a team. In days to come, Rear Admiral Jack O'Hara, commander of naval air forces in the Western Pacific, would term the operations crew's efforts "the prime ingredient to gaining the rapid response." Dan Scandalito would accompany the second HC-3 helicopter when mechanics were able to get it flight-ready; for now, the rest of the Army medical team that had traveled from Camp Zama would wait at Atsugi to care for evacuated casualties.

As Rhodes and Ray started their helicopter's blades spinning, Shillito positioned himself uncomfortably atop a radio console between the two pilots. Everyone on board was taking a risk. Some tail-of-the-typhoon gusts exceeded fifty miles per hour. Manufacturer specifications discouraged starting up a CH-46 in such conditions. As the aircraft's twin rotors began to accelerate, an errant squall might propel a blade downward—toward the helicopter's body. If a blade struck center top, it could sever a shaft that synchronized the helicopter's rotors, or even slice into the aircraft's cabin. The group calculated its potential peril against the needs of Marines at Camp Fuji. "Realistically, we shouldn't have been doing what we were doing," Rhodes reminisced. "But what the hell do you exist for if people are dying?"

Naval helicopter 154832 launched into skies that were clearing, toward a still-storm-clouded vista in the west. The crew members' flight path grew murkier as they approached storm clouds. Power outages across the flatlands below made it difficult to discern terrain detail. To D. C. Ray, it appeared that "the complete Kanto Plain was blacked out." The Navy crew had never been to Camp Fuji and the camp offered no aids to navigation—direction signals a pilot could home in on. Getting there would require setting a general course, paying attention to visual references familiar to the Marine pilot, and keeping an eye on watches to gauge progress based on time in flight.

On their over-water aerial supply missions, Rhodes and Ray had become expert at navigating with instruments when visibility was restricted. "At sea, though," Ray observed, "one thing you don't have are towers." Power lines dotted the terrain below, as did numerous 1,500-foot broadcasting masts, many unmarked by flashing lights or other indicators. "We had to stay high enough to be over the wires," Bob Shillito said, "but low enough to stay under the clouds." That kept them some 2,000 to 3,000 feet above the ground.

Formal kits were available to configure CH-46s for medical evacuation. The crew of 154832 had not had access to one. Inflight, two HC-3 Sailors did the best they could to arrange the helicopter's cabin to carry casualties.

As the pilots' dead reckoning indicated they should be nearing the camp, they activated landing lights that illuminated the area below. "[Shillito] guided us to an approach," Ray recalled. The helicopter descended toward what appeared a long, rectangular clearing—the camp's airfield runway, they assumed. At lower altitude, though, they suddenly realized it was the expansive, metal coop of an industrial chicken farm. "We got the reflection off the top of the roof. It was long and straight," Ray remembered. "[Shillito] yelled, 'Wave off!' And started yelling, 'Power, power, power!'" As they quickly ascended, signs in the skies let them know they were quite near their destination. Marines along the Camp Fuji airfield—hearing the distinctive sound of an approaching twin-rotor helicopter—had fired up signal flares.

Amid dusk descending into night, Shillito guided Rhodes and Ray into an approach from the south. As the Sea Knight set down, Lewis Gold remembered, lights around the airfield highlighted still-falling rain. Having rushed from his quarters at Camp Zama, the doctor had not donned his uniform. "I was wearing blue jeans," Gold recalled, and "a camouflaged rain jacket." His hair was longish and unruly. The only visible sign of his profession was a stethoscope he had stuffed into his coat pocket. Radio messages to the camp had alerted the Marines that an Army doctor—a major—was onboard the helicopter. A senior enlisted Marine met Gold, saluted, and told him that he was now the senior medical officer at the camp. The thirty-two-year-old pediatrician felt a weight descend. He had expected to be working alongside more—and more seasoned—physicians. Nothing in his experience managing critically ill children from birth to adolescence had prepared him for the evolving mass casualty event. Never before, he said, had he "been as scared as I was at that moment." Still, he knew that a first important step was accurately accounting for everyone impacted. Who had been hurt? What were their specific injuries? He began collating data corpsmen had collected.

Along the flight line, injured Marines were still being loaded onto trucks for transport to clinics off base. Captain Bob Shillito joined fellow Marines in that work, then encountered a gracious John Redgate, "thanking me for bringing the guys in, asking if I needed anything. . . . He was feeling pretty bad about having his men hurt and some problems that he had had to deal with. But he was holding up pretty well." Shillito accompanied the BLT commander to the base camp offices from which Redgate was directing his unit's post-fire response.

The medical facilities in and around Gotemba had not been expecting the Marines' arrival. They were not public institutions; those tended to be located in metropolitan areas. Of the 8,580 hospitals operating in Japan during the late 1970s, nearly 70 percent were run by private practitioners or corporations. Private ownership of the nation's 75,000 clinics was even higher, at 85 percent. Few physicians practiced in rural areas. Those who did often provided specialist services. It was not uncommon for modest practices—sometimes located in a physician's home—to be handed down from father to son. In and around Gotemba—as was then still the case in the rural United States—emergency care was frequently limited to ambulance crews trying to keep patients stable while driving them to the nearest large city.

No standing agreement had arranged for the private clinics to care for American military force members. Moreover, the Marines were being brought to the clinics' doors in the midst of a death-and-destruction-dealing typhoon. Area residents injured by the storm were already stressing the facilities' nominal critical care response capacity.

In addition to the ten Marines transported just over four miles to the Fuji Sector Hospital, seventeen had been driven to Gotemba Hospital about the same distance from the camp. Four more, all described soon after arrival as "too serious to move," would be taken the not-quite-four miles to Sunto Daiichi Hospital, near the Gotemba train station. Two others would end up in a small surgical clinic, Yoshida Geka, three and a half miles distant. Farthest afield, more than twelve miles from the camp, would be five Marines transported by Jieitai drivers to Susono Nisseki—a Red Cross hospital in Susono City.

As painkilling medications ebbed, and the jostling of movement into the clinics shook them into groggy cognizance, the Marines registered their new surroundings. A *Shizuoka Shimbun* reporter witnessing relief operations at Gotemba Hospital observed Marines in "the first floor waiting room, filling the air with their groans. [They] could be heard calling out for water from their beds."

"I was laying on a gurney," Mike Cummings recalled. "They started cutting the rain suit off of me in the hallway. I wasn't in a room at the time. And then, after that, I was just kind of—in and out."

"There was a Japanese doctor talking to me," Issac Williams remembered. "I couldn't understand a word he said. And I told him that I'm tired, and that I'm going to sleep."

Glenn Roberts noticed a bowl not far from his bed, catching typhoon-driven rain. "The roof was leaking," he observed. "That's how bad the storm was."

Jon Jurgen was bandage-blinded, experiencing his circumstances only by touch and hearing. He was also deeply craving something to eat. "I asked for some food," he said, "motioned that I was hungry. I ate and I immediately threw up."

From a gurney in the hallway of one of the medical centers, Steve Neal could glimpse fellow burned Marines. Some, he was sure, he should have recognized but could not. "They were shaking," he recalled. "I'm not being morbid just for gratuitousness, but they looked like burned hot dogs on the grill—overgrilled. Their skin had split open and it was pink on the inside."

After moving the last patient from his battalion aid station, Mac McDonald had been driven to the Fuji Sector Hospital. Some of the military doctors and nurses there were bilingual. An assigned interpreter helped him communicate with those who were not. "I remember going into the operating rooms with some of the teams, and helping. I was impressed by how much everyone was so helpful. I mean, they were doing everything they could to take this up to the hospital level of care—the next level."

"The Japanese bent over backwards to help," Hospitalman John Barniea agreed. He asked a Japanese nurse where he could find a pole from which to hang an IV drip. "She didn't take time to explain," he said, "or even point to where I could find it. She literally just ran out of the room and returned seconds later with the pole."

The quality of care injured Marines received at the five Japanese clinics varied. The ten treated at the Fuji Sector Hospital were seen by doctors and nurses more deeply versed than their civilian counterparts in dealing with trauma. The military providers could also access larger stockpiles of medical supplies. The number of patients delivered to other medical centers strained the clinics in ways for which they were not prepared.

As would also have been the case in rural U.S. clinics, few of the Japanese providers were skilled in the complexities of placing intravenous lines through burned skin. As a consequence, quite a number of the Marine patients went for hours without infusion of helpful fluids. "I never had an IV," Steve Neal laughed, but "they gave us cigarettes." Still, Mike Cummings affirmed, "they were doing their best to take care of us"—in many cases exhausting both their supply stocks and themselves.

In the large base camp hangar, word was passed that, for at least the night, everyone would be moved off-camp to Japanese military bases. As October 19th's afternoon hours merged into those of the evening, scores of badly injured Marines were spread throughout Gotemba and other communities nearby. It was uncertain where they would be taken next. And weather conditions, though slowly improving, continued to keep additional helicopters at bay.

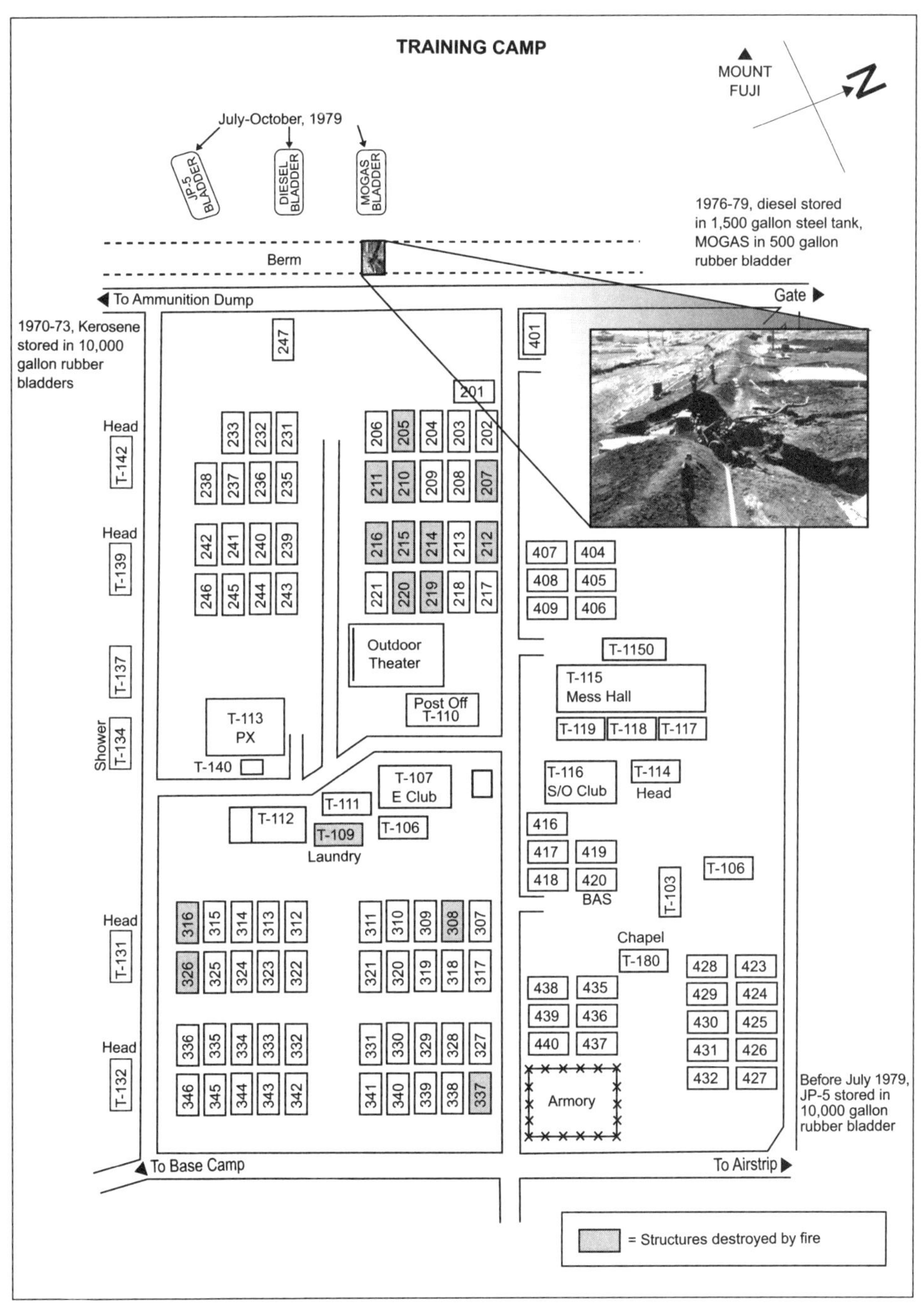

MAP. 4. Camp Fuji training camp. Created by Scott Gannon, based on materials included in the 1979 incident investigation. Map is not to scale.

9

FRIDAY, OCTOBER 19, EVENING

There was a very calm sense of, I don't want to say panic, but like surrealism. What the heck just happened?

—*Lance Corporal David Luttenberger, Weapons Company, Battalion Landing Team 2/4*

OCTOBER 19'S DAYLIGHT had been obscured first by thick rainclouds, then smoke. What remained of the natural illumination fell away with sunset at 5:05 p.m.

BLT and LSU Marines—those mostly unharmed, but displaced—began moving from the large base camp hangar toward temporary lodging spaces. Some would be ferried four or five miles by Japanese trucks to barracks and large open rooms at Fuji Gakku. Others—exiting in columns of twos through Camp Fuji's eastern-most gates—would walk the one thousand or so paces across Route 23 to a gymnasium on Camp Takigahara. With only a couple hours' notice, the Jieitai began to shelter the displaced American Marines and Sailors. The military schools complex would take in 529 of the Americans; Camp Takigahara, 619.

"We walked down the road," toward the latter destination, Rob Ahrens recalled, "and waded across where the road was washed out." A small gaggle of newspaper reporters and a TV news crew watched as they did so, documenting the disaster as best they could from outside the camp's perimeter fence.

Just inside Camp Takigahara's front gate, Ahrens recalled, stood "a lot of Japanese soldiers standing around trying to help." The hosting mission had been spun up quickly. Makato Yamamoto, then a young Jieitai enlistee, recalled that he and his barracks mates had no idea why the Marines had needed to leave their camp, nor why they were so unkempt. Looking around as they were directed through the camp, the Marines took in buildings constructed of brick and wood—more permanent than at Camp Fuji. The trek did not take long.

Inside the gymnasium Paul Verdier and others stood around—barely clothed, rain-soaked, stunned—looking for answers in each others' faces. "The mood was shock," he remembered. "Trying to figure out who was missing, what the fuck had happened."

The Marines' Japanese counterparts handed out blankets and thin foam sleeping mats. From around their base, the Japanese gathered whatever clothing they could find that might fit the Americans. For those they saw had fled without footwear, they collected and shared boots, shoes, sneakers, and slippers.

By 5:30 Gotemba firefighters, aided by the flushing effect of the day's inundating rain, had brought the blazes on Camp Fuji under control. Incinerated Quonset huts would smolder into the next morning. Some who had remained in the camp expressed appreciation. One Inno Village volunteer recalled Marines sharing canned C-ration meals with the firefighters. Not long thereafter, though, the responders were ushered out the gate. They would not be allowed to inquire into what had happened, nor prepare a damage estimate. The hurried ouster, before completion of this response routine, engendered some consternation. "While they wouldn't let us come in [under normal circumstances] . . . they would cry out for help when they had a fire," one first responder complained to the *Nikkan Shizuoka* newspaper. "They demanded that we dispatch our fire engines, but they wouldn't even give us a chance to investigate the cause of the fire."

Several exchange employees had by now made their way to the camp-adjacent home of Taeko Matsuzaki. Akira Yamada was there, as was Ms. Sato of the barber shop. Sumiko Yuasa and Kimio Hata had joined them, as well. The group watched TV newscasters describe the fire incident. One solemnly reported that Yuasa had died. They laughed at the confusion. Anxiety, though, abated their amusement. Yasuko Nakayama, they knew, had sustained worse injuries. The group headed to the medical center where she had been taken.

"It was a Japanese hospital," Matsuzaki recalled, "so we were expecting to see only Japanese patients. By the time we arrived, though, there were also many Marines who had been injured in the fire."

Making their way to the ward on which Nakayama was being treated, their shocked reaction mirrored that of a consulting physician there. A local newspaper quoted a Dr. Goto's succinct description of Nakayama's condition: "What terrible burns."

"Her face had turned kind of gray," Taeko Matsuzaki recalled, "and was swollen to the size of a basketball. She kept saying, 'I feel cold. I'm cold.'" Briefly, they offered their friend encouragement. Before they departed doctors tended to Sumiko Yuasa's less urgent injuries, then sent her on her way.

Leaving the hospital Matsuzaki glimpsed an injured Marine standing beside a hallway phone booth. "With both hands," she said, "he was ripping a phone book about an inch and a half thick—trying to take his mind off his pain. Somebody said he was the person who helped Nakayama-san."

At Camp Fuji a more formalized plan was being forged for eventual aerial evacuation of the injured. It involved establishing a helicopter landing zone just below Golf Company huts at the bottom right of the training camp. "The Marines," D. C. Ray recalled, "suggested it would cut down transit time from these clinics where the injured Marines were."

"It was a baseball field," Jacob Evans remembered, "just a rough field that we used as a makeshift LZ." Marines from Evans's platoon cleared a large rounded portion of the field, then positioned jeeps and other vehicles around the outside of the circle. Their headlights, pointed inward, illuminated the open space. Portable strobe lights were positioned to make the hasty LZ more easily discernible from above. Rhodes and Ray moved their CH-46 from the airstrip to the new landing site.

At 6 p.m. an Air Force Disaster Response Force destined for Camp Fuji departed the Yokota Air Base hospital. Led by Major Cesar Sarmiento—commander and chief surgeon of the 655th Tactical Hospital—many on the team were still in the civilian clothes they had been wearing when urgently recalled to duty. The three physicians, three nurses, two physician assistants, six medical technicians, and two Japanese drivers traveled in two ambulance buses and one "cracker box" field ambulance. All three vehicles had been packed with supplies.

By 6:30 p.m. the developing events at Camp Fuji had grabbed the complete attention of Marines at the service's command center in Arlington, Virginia, where it was 5:30 in the morning. Watch officers were forwarding still sketchy "spot reports" to the Corps' top leaders.

Inside the gymnasium at Camp Takigahara, Sergeant Major Hendrix talked with Marines and Sailors, Rob Ahrens recalled, "seeing who was all right. . . . I remember seeing the battalion commander and XO and stuff. They were all over in one group—and the sergeant major was running back and forth, giving them reports."

At Fuji Gakku Andy Bonwit surveyed barracks "pretty spartan but pretty modern." They were certainly "better than the Quonsets," he assessed—and they came with clean pillows and warm, if scratchy, blankets. What Fredric Britton Jr. appreciated most about the training command accommodations was access to showers. "The hardest thing for me was getting that gas smell off of my legs that night. I scrubbed. . . . We all had one complaint: 'Man, that gas is burning.'"

Crashed from exhaustion, some of the Marines and Sailors were able to sleep. Slumber evaded others who Britton recalled as "shell-shocked, you know—just traumatized."

"I kind of just—had a little bit of a breakdown," recalled the fuel farm's Rickey Lamon. "I don't remember a whole lot until the next morning."

Knowing that their fate had been more fortunate than that of fellow Marines was not necessarily a good thing for young men inculcated in a group-over-self ethos. Chaplain Ferguson recalled talking with them about their "survivor's guilt, there was a great deal of that."

By 7:30 p.m. it seemed clear to Greg Gregory that Marines injured at Camp Fuji would not be evacuated to the clinic at Atsugi. A plan was organized for the medical team gathered there to convoy to Camp Fuji in their respective Navy and Army ambulances. Then Gregory received word that HC-3 crews were making progress assembling a second helicopter. Two more Detachment 106 pilots stood by to fly it to the camp. Marine Captain Dan Scandalito would guide them. Gregory assigned some members of the combined Atsugi/Camp Zama team to the airlift, others to travel by road.

While most of BLT 2/4 and LSU 3/9 had been evacuated from the training camp—the injured to local hospitals, others to the Japanese bases—a number of Marines had remained. Shotgun-wielding guards, for instance, had been posted to rove designated portions of the camp. "Anybody that had a uniform," Steve Holmes recalled, "they held back and gave them a post." He was among those ensuring security of what had been left behind. Sometime into his regimen of walking around a number of Quonset huts, Holmes heard a commotion across the road. A Marine guarding another post was yelling something. One or two others had run toward him. Holmes called out, "'What's going on? What are you guys doing?' And they go, 'There's cash! There's money all over the effing place!'" Perhaps it had come from a pay officer's storm-tossed ammo can, or a similarly misplaced NEX cashbox. "I gotta think it was quite a bit," Holmes remembered, "because there were at least three of them over there stuffing money in their pockets." The cash grab did not last long, he recalled. "I don't know whether the on-duty officer or whatever came through," but soon, he said, "everything kind of calmed down and got under control."

At Camp Fuji's base camp, Lieutenant Colonel Redgate was drafting messages informing higher headquarters of the unfolding disaster. The most urgent requirement would be to file casualty reports—definitive lists of who had been hurt, and to what degree.

The effort to move injured Marines to medical clinics somewhere—anywhere—had been successful but ad hoc. As the evening wore on, a dozen or more Marines were dispatched from Camp Fuji in an attempt to account for each patient's location and condition. The battalion adjutant led one mission. Because he was days away from transferring back to the United States, he brought along his soon-to-be replacement, First Lieutenant Michael Weltsch.

"We spent probably four or five hours driving around various parts of Japan and going into the little hospitals," Weltsch recalled. "And I remember some of the Japanese faces. They looked very concerned, and they were very obliging." Determining each patient's identity was not easy, he said. Not all had been wearing dog tags. "A tremendous language barrier" further impeded documenting their health status.

Senior corpsman Murray Simpkins had similarly been tasked with helping to document who was where. An English-speaking Jieitai master sergeant by the last name of Kato was assigned to accompany him.

Also drafted into the effort were a number of junior officers—Golf Company Second Lieutenant Adolfo Martinez among them. They were driven through the dark in a minibus, then, one by one, dropped off at neighborhood clinics. Each carried a piece of paper noting the Camp Fuji telephone number to call, Martinez recalled, after having learned "how many, who they are, and what their conditions are." Delivered to the Sunto Daiichi hospital, Martinez found four Marines being treated in two upstairs rooms. All had received some measure of fluid replenishment, he believed; their bodies were swaddled in varying volumes of gauze. Nineteen-year-old Rodger Larson was bandaged head to toe; slits in the wrapping allowed him to see and breathe. "He had what appeared to be a cage over his chest," Martinez recalled. The private first class from Eau Claire, Wisconsin, was awake, but silent. "He saw me come in. Didn't say a word. And that's the way he remained for the rest of the night. Conscious, eyes open, looking around. I could tell in his eyes he was frustrated. He would occasionally pick up his arms and set them down heavily on that cage. But he didn't say a word all night." The second Marine in that room, near a window, was twenty-one-year-old Robert Turner of Cassopolis, Michigan. He was not as extensively bandaged. "I could see most of his face," Martinez said. "He was in and out of consciousness. His face was heavily burned." Coming to occasionally, Turner would ask for water. Nurses had provided the lieutenant a fluid container. "I could squeeze some water into his mouth periodically. He didn't move. But he would moan, his eyes would open up, then he would fade out of consciousness again." Two other Marines were in a second room, next to the first. "The first Marine there was completely bandaged," Martinez remembered. "His eyes were closed, and I'm not sure if he was in a coma or just simply unconscious. He didn't speak or move all night long." The officer never learned his name. The last of the four was twenty-year-old Orlando Sandoval. "He was bandaged a bit, but I could see his face. He didn't seem to be too badly burned." Among the four Marines at Sunto Daiichi, he was the most able to speak. "He would express his pain and would also ask for water," Martinez said. When the young man from Pueblo, Colorado, asked if he would be okay, and what had happened to his platoon mates, the lieutenant tried to be reassuring. "At one point," Martinez recalled, "he said, 'Sir, can you pray for me?' I did what I could; I wasn't much of a praying man at the time, but I stood beside him and I prayed for him and the others, and left the rest to God. It struck me at that point how utterly useless I was in that situation." After having initially bandaged the Marines, the clinic's medical staff seemed to have retreated. Martinez paced the two rooms into the early morning. "In case a Marine needed immediate attention," he felt, "I could run downstairs to get help."

Additionally rounding Japanese hospitals that evening was First Lieutenant John Seal. Seal had commanded Weapons Company for three and a half months. Taking charge of more than one hundred Marines and Sailors over that time, he had barely had time to associate faces with most of their names. Now he tried to identify his men through the camouflage of bandages and burned skin. By jeep he moved from one hospital to the next. Seal was not squeamish, having himself suffered and recovered from serious enemy gunfire injuries in Vietnam. What he saw in the Japanese clinics, though, gave him pause. It reminded him of "visible body" illustrations in college science texts—images in which skin had been removed to reveal muscles, organs and the circulatory system. Fortunately, many Weapons Company Marines recognized him, or the junior company officers who accompanied him on his mission.

"I remember our new lieutenant coming by," said Steve Haishuk, "and, you know, talking to some of us."

Steve Neal, "euphoric because of the morphine," remembered getting the attention of Second Lieutenant Alan Crook. "And I said, 'Hey, Lieutenant'—knowing full well we would not get Purple Hearts [which were awarded only for injuries resulting from enemy action]—I said, 'Do we get Purple Hearts?' And I vomited right in front of him. I don't think I vomited *on* him, but it was close."

At one of the Japanese clinics, likely the Fuji Sector Hospital, peace began to descend onto Mark Bedwell. His eyes wrapped with gauze, Bedwell could not see what was happening to and around him. "I started to feel very, very good and I was getting very sleepy," he recalled. Entering a dream state, pain disappeared and his body begin a slow, floating ascent. The bliss was impeded only by muffled yelling of seemingly far-off voices: "He's turning blue!" Medical team members converged around him, realizing that secretions and swelling were constricting his airway.

"Suddenly I remember being yanked up in a sitting position. And I'm still feeling good, but my body, my soul stops moving upwards. And then

I remember hearing this cutting sound. The next thing I remember was taking a huge lungful of air."

A doctor had sliced open Bedwell's throat. The rapid tracheotomy prompted the sweep of a horrible burning sensation through Bedwell's head and arms. "It was like somebody was holding a torch to me," he recalled. "And I screamed. I mean, the pain hurt so bad. And I could hear 'em, and they're happy! They're going, 'He's breathing!'"

For Bedwell it was a moment of epiphany. "It doesn't hurt to die," he said he realized. "You know what hurts? Coming back to life."

Sometime between 8:30 and 9 p.m., the Yokota disaster response force's ambulance buses—"ambuses," they called them—pulled onto Camp Fuji. "Thank God the Air Force arrived," Lewis Gold recalled. "I will take care of logistics," he promised Cesar Sarmiento. "You take care of the patients." Quickly whisked to the Fuji Sector Hospital, Dr. Sarmiento was introduced to Mac McDonald and saw the ten badly injured Marines being treated at the Fuji Gakku site.

From there DRF members moved on to other clinics holding injured Marines. Sarmiento's team—which also included Captains Andrew Hazely and Salvatore De Vincenzo, both doctors; and nurse Patty McDougall—would stabilize as many of the injured Marines as possible.

At 9 p.m. the physicians commanding the two major U.S. military hospitals in the area spoke by telephone. Navy Captain Bernett Johnson Jr. and Air Force Colonel Clarence Whiteside agreed that their respective hospitals would share responsibility for treating the injured; half of the number would be evacuated to the Air Force hospital at Yokota, half to Yokosuka—site of the Navy's principal medical center in Japan.

At Yokosuka staffers unboxed emergency equipment and supplies, preparing an empty twenty-five-bed space assigned as the hospital's disaster ward. At Yokota chief nurse Rita Gengler asked the surgical department to begin sterilizing bandage packages. It was not uncommon at the time for manufacturers to ship such wrappings non-sterile. The lieutenant colonel also began creating a roster of eight-hour staffing shifts.

Over the course of the evening, confused communication would inhibit planning at both facilities. Were patients on their way? If so, how many? Would more crews drive from the hospitals to retrieve them? "It was hard to tell what was happening," recalled Yokosuka-stationed Navy nurse Mike Monahan. "So we stood up, stood down. Stood up, stood down."

At 9:15 Cesar Sarmiento was able to get a call through to Yokota. He updated Whiteside on the apparent number of patients impacted, where they were, and the severity of their injuries. He lauded the care being provided at the Jieitai's Fuji Sector Hospital, but characterized treatment at the other clinics as "minimal."

"The Air Force proved to be lifesavers," McDonald said. Their ambuses would be key to the evolving plan to safely transport injured Marines to next-level care settings. After making his report, Sarmiento led DRF members to examine and help stabilize Marines at Gotemba Hospital.

For several hours Navy Hospitalman Third Class Leroy Dunn and other corpsmen had been caring for injured Marines at the site—less a hospital, in his estimation, than "a large aid station." Given their unannounced arrival, he had felt generously received. "I think we used up all their burn supplies"—topical creams and bandages—he said. "They really didn't have to let that happen."

From the base camp, where Lieutenant Colonel Redgate was now operating, Weapons Company platoon commander Fred Winters had been ordered to shower, don a borrowed camouflage utility uniform and head to the same medical center. Most of the seventeen injured Marines taken there were members of his company. Redgate directed him to look out for the men.

When Winters arrived, a couple of the Air Force doctors and nurses were already there. Gathered in a hospital conference room, they, and a Japanese military officer with them, seemed uncertain what to do.

Salvatore De Vincenzo had been an Air Force physician for just over a year. During his preservice internship and residency in internal medicine, he had gained significant familiarity with trauma. The "calamity, the scope of the situation" he and his colleagues encountered at the small community hospital, though, left him deflated. The burn patients' care did not seem to include resuscitation. "I do not remember any medical paraphernalia around the Marines," he recounted. "No IV poles, no IV tubes, no IV bags. I don't think there was even oxygen being given." Adding to a feeling of helplessness: at that moment, he and his colleagues "didn't have IV set-ups" to offer.

Awaiting Dr. Sarmiento's arrival, Fred Winters walked through the two rooms filled with burned Marines. Corporal Colin Miller called the lieutenant over. The Marine's uniform had been removed. With it had come a surprising thickness of charred skin. His left ear had burned away. Fire blisters covered his lips and mouth. His eyes—"barely slits," Winters recalled—were all but swollen shut. "'I think I'm really screwed up, sir,'" Miller confided, struggling to breathe.

"And then he immediately went into asking where all of his troops were," Winters said. "He was very concerned about Malveaux. Apparently, he had heard that Malveaux had died. I don't know that I confirmed it, but I said, 'He may have.' I didn't give him a definitive." Miller asked about every Marine in the mortar section he had led. In some cases corpsmen on hand were able to share that they had seen a particular Marine alive and being treated. When the corporal asked about one for whom the corpsmen could offer no status—possibly Issac Williams, Winters recalled—a voice rang from a bed in the corner of the room. "All of a sudden, we heard a Marine saying, 'I'm over here, I'm over here.' Whoever it was was not recognizable enough for anybody to have identified."

Finally, Cesar Sarmiento arrived. He gathered American and Japanese providers in the hospital conference room. "That's when he totally took charge of this," Winters said. He ordered the lieutenant and McDougall to stay with him. Other DRF members he directed to stabilize, and prepare for transport, Marines at other local clinics.

As Sarmiento, McDougall, and Winters left the conference room, the surgeon issued instructions to the nurse and the Marine. They were interrupted by a corpsman running their way. "Miller can't breathe," the Sailor said. "He's in trouble." Winters recalled Sarmiento doffing his Izod jacket, handing it to Captain McDougall, and stepping into the hospital room. In short minutes, with the help of a Japanese physician, the Air Force doctor had performed a tracheotomy on the Marine corporal. Stepping back into the corridor, Winters vividly recalled, Sarmiento completed the sentence he had started before undertaking the emergency surgical procedure.

"He became the instant hero in my eyes," Winters asserted decades later. "That man came with a plan. . . . He was going to do what he believed was best for everybody inside of there—and never lost sight of that, or wasn't rattled by it." Sarmiento's decisiveness, to Winters's mind, contrasted with what he had experienced immediately after the fire outbreak. "I realized that so many of the senior personnel in the earlier event were just so rattled," Winters said, "that nobody was coherent or focused."

As 10 p.m. approached Cesar Sarmiento again reported back to Yokota. His team had been prepared to use its ambulance buses to drive injured patients to Yokota. With skies clearing, two HC-3 helicopters would be available. Army aviation detachments were also said to be spinning up to help. The ambuses would instead retrieve the injured and return them to the training camp for aerial MEDEVAC.

At 10:15, anticipating the need to eventually transport patients Stateside, Clarence Whiteside passed word of the disaster to the Ninth Aeromedical Evacuation Squadron at Clark Air Base in the Philippines. The MEDEVAC operations unit in turn alerted the Air Force's Illinois-headquartered Military Airlift Command.

The calls initiated development of a medical evacuation plan. Two aspects required immediate attention: the large number of patients, and the significant percentage that would require oxygen and ventilators during transport. At least two aircraft would be required for the Marines' transpacific MEDEVAC. C-141A Starlifters would suit the mission best, planners determined. Before the day was out, one had been identified. The aircraft—tail numbered 40619—and its crew of reservists from the 445th Military Airlift Wing had been scheduled to depart Okinawa for their home base near San Bernardino, California. Orders changed. They were directed to gather and load medical supplies, then fly as quickly as possible to Yokota. Separate orders to assist were issued to the 9th AES.

In addition to the stethoscope Dr. Lewis Gold had snapped up before heading to Camp Fuji, he had grabbed a portable telephone. Such devices were far from common in 1979. Eight or nine inches tall and around three inches square, the phone had been loaned to him by the officer commanding all U.S. Army forces in Japan: Lieutenant General John Q. Henion. The general often hosted Japanese dignitaries on the Camp Zama golf course. Because those visitors held physicians in high regard, Henion frequently invited Gold to join them on the fairway. The phone allowed the doctor to keep in touch with the clinic as they played. Over time Gold had used the device to confer with pediatricians at other U.S. bases in Japan. It could even, he had been told, connect to numbers in the United States.

With the phone he kept an extensive list of contact numbers. Some were for acquaintances made during his 1975–77 internship and residency at Brooke Army Medical Center in San Antonio. There he had watched Institute of Surgical Research surgeons apply skin grafts to a fire-injured infant. Among numbers typed onto his portable contact list were several for the ISR. At around quarter past 11 p.m. in Japan—roughly 9:15 a.m. in San Antonio—Lewis Gold put the brick-like portable phone to its most important use yet.

"I talked to the head nurse at the burn unit," he recalled. "It was very short. I said, 'There has been a burn catastrophe at the base of Mount Fuji, with Marines.' I said, 'Somewhere between thirty and thirty-five have 50-to-100 percent burns. There needs to be communication between you and Yokota Air Base.'"

Twenty minutes later—11:35 p.m. Japan Standard Time, 9:35 a.m. Central Daylight Time—the Yokota hospital commander was on the phone with the ISR. Dr. Whiteside apprised burn specialists there of estimated casualty figures and the patients' conditions—and of the plan to treat the Marines at Yokota and Yokosuka. The surgeons in San Antonio were eager to help, they said, and implored Whiteside to gather the injured at a single location, ideally near an airfield capable of accommodating the large MEDEVAC aircraft. Whiteside quickly conferred by phone with Captain Johnson at Yokosuka.

As the storm's tail began to move beyond Central Honshu, an evacuation plan jelled. The Marines would be returned from the Japanese clinics to Camp Fuji, helicoptered to Yokota, then flown to San Antonio for admission to ISR-administered wards at Brooke Army Medical Center.

In San Antonio Army Lieutenant Colonel (Dr.) Michael J. Walters was leading a surgical procedure in a BAMC operating room dedicated to burn center use. "[Colonel William] McManus stuck his head in," he recalled, "and told me to leave the operating room. 'You're going on to retrieve these people.'"

Army nurse Robert Marchi remembered that "we were all called down to a meeting in a big conference room near Ward 13B. I remember Dr. McManus talked about 'We're going to be sending a team to Japan.'"

Gruff and sometimes irascible, McManus directed all clinical work within the ISR. "This was a disaster," ISR Chief Nurse Jean Truscott recalled the doctor making clear. "One person had to make the decisions," she said, "and it was going to be him." They would be, fellow ISR surgeon Cleon Goodwin attested, "the right decisions at the right time."

The high casualty figure at Camp Fuji would require a flight team of unprecedented size. Captain Catherine Syby was at home in bed when the call came telling her she would be part of the retrieval group. "I needed to bring very little with me," the nurse remembered being told, "but enough to get me through two days." Such deployments were not a surprise; ISR staffers rotated through "on call" status for such missions. While all were expert in burn treatment, most had not undergone specialized instruction in providing airborne care to patients requiring ventilators. That would require assistance from Air Force flight nurses and technicians. The ISR team, she was told, would fly to Japan, evaluate and stabilize the injured Marines, then oversee their MEDEVAC to San Antonio.

At NAF Atsugi Greg Gregory led a small Navy medical team across the tarmac toward a second, nearly flight-ready CH-46. The group included Lieutenant (Dr.) Susan Robertson; Rod Forrey, a chief warrant officer physician assistant; and several corpsmen. As Bob Shillito had done on the first helicopter to make it to the camp, Marine Captain Dan Scandalito would perch "up in the tunnel between the two pilots, giving them directions to get there"—guiding from a map and visual memory, referencing "towns, or roads, or terrain—and certainly Mount Fuji." By air and road, 10 Navy medical specialists were prepared to launch from Atsugi, along with an Army nurse and two Army corpsmen.

As October 19 drew to a close in Japan, sobering metrics tallied a disastrous 24 hours. Across the nation, Typhoon 20—as Japanese meteorologists described Tip—was already being called the worst storm to strike Japan in 13 years. It had left 110 dead, five missing, 543 injured.

In a single day, the storm had dumped 10.94 inches of rain on Camp Fuji—one-third of an inch more than its average *monthly* rainfall. Under spitting residual precipitation, ambulance buses had begun returning injured Marines to the camp. Those already brought back from Japanese clinics lay atop litters alongside the training camp's baseball-diamond-turned-landing-zone. Vigilant doctors, nurses and corpsmen tending to them did what they could to assuage the patients' pain.

Everyone looked to the skies. When winds subsided sufficiently, helicopters could begin transporting the injured to Yokota, and patients yet to be retrieved from Japanese hospitals could be more easily gathered and returned. At 11:10 a message from Dr. Cesar Sarmiento warned of a complication: "Problems with the Japanese medical facilities regarding release of patients, everything on hold status."

10

SATURDAY, OCTOBER 20

Somebody takes a scalpel, whoosh, and just jams an IV down in the ankle—because the arms were burned so bad they couldn't start an IV up there. That'll wake you up.

—*Corporal Glenn Roberts, U.S. Marine Corps*

It was something to see a Marine with burns over 70 percent of his body offer to help a buddy whose burns were still more severe.

—*Captain (Dr.) David Snyder, U.S. Navy (Ret.)*

THE FIRST HOURS of the day after the fire remained blustery. The worst impacts of Typhoon Tip, though, had moved beyond Shizuoka prefecture. Additional helicopter crews would soon begin making their way to Camp Fuji. They would transport injured Marines to the U.S. Air Force hospital in Yokota, fifty miles to the northeast. Six or eight hours after the Marines had been moved from Camp Fuji to medical centers in nearby communities, they would need to cover the same distance in reverse.

Earlier in the evening, Second Lieutenant Fred Winters had blocked out what he thought could be a makeshift helicopter landing zone adjacent to Gotemba Hospital. The space was tight, with overhead electrical lines nearby, but he felt it could serve the purpose. Picking up Marines at the hospital and sending them by air directly to Yokota, he reasoned, would save the jostling of a return to Camp Fuji by road. The Japanese military officer who had been assigned to liaise between the Marines and his senior officers checked on the idea. "No helicopters," Winters remembered him reporting back. Helicopter operations in the tightly packed neighborhood, it was explained, would endanger or frighten people already unnerved by the typhoon. Winters grew angry, pushing back on the edict. Major Cesar Sarmiento quietly ordered him to calm down. "It's not worth it," the doctor told the young officer. "We just have to go to Plan B.'"

Sometime later Sarmiento and his team were ready to implement the alternate stratagem. As abruptly as the Marines had been imposed upon the medical facility, they would be pulled away. The DRF's ambuses—too long and wide to negotiate some narrow Japanese roadways—had been parked as near the hospital as possible. If it was not possible for litter-bearers to move patients directly onto a bus, one or more "cracker box" ambulances would ferry them to the larger transport vehicles.

Sarmiento informed the hospital's supervising physician of his intention. The idea did not sit well with the senior doctor. The inevitable commotion, he told Sarminto, would disturb other patients in the hospital.

For a time the sides remained at an impasse. "Will you storm the hospital by force if I order you to?" Sarmiento half-joked to Winters. In the end the Japanese military liaison officer on hand convinced the hospital supervisor to allow the group's departure. Side by side Japanese doctors and nurses helped the Air Force team and Navy corpsmen move the seventeen Marines out and onto the ambuses.

After a flight Rod Forrey recalled as "a very bumpy ride," the airborne portion of the NAF Atsugi medical team landed at Camp Fuji. Its members made their way toward Marines beginning to be brought back from clinics in town. Kneeling over stretchers placed on the ground, the physician assistant tended to patients "burned so badly that their faces were almost a charcoal color appearance, and very swollen. The ones I remember talking to couldn't speak very much at all." He knew each needed an IV, but his efforts to insert them were frustrated by broad patches of burned skin.

Dr. Susan Robertson stepped in. "For a while," Greg Gregory recalled, "she was basically *the* doc" in the area where the team had begun working. "She was on her hands and knees, cleaning and bandaging, starting IVs. She was a general service physician, this was her first duty station. She did a hell of a job." Forrey recalled Robertson being "more comfortable than I was with treating these patients. I was, I think, shocked by the kind of trauma that we saw."

Soon after the Atsugi team's arrival, Lieutenant Commander Gregory went to check in with Colonel Lamb. "I told him," Gregory recalled, "'Looks like we're going to have a lot of bad casualties here, and we're probably going to have some deaths.' And he said something to the effect of 'It's not going to be that bad. You guys do your job.' My recollection is he was basically in a state of denial."

During the first seven hours of October 20, Navy and Army helicopters would ferry the injured to Yokota. As importantly, they would also fly missions replenishing the constantly depleting store of medical supplies needed to sustain those at Camp Fuji still awaiting MEDEVAC.

From Rankin Field on Camp Zama, the U.S. Army Aviation Detachment, Japan would contribute three aircraft to the relief effort, likely UH-1 Hueys. "The biggest obstacle we had that evening was getting to the Marine base itself," acknowledged the detachment's operations officer, Major Earl Dennis Jr. "Since the remnants of the storm were still hovering over the area, we had to combat winds gusting up to forty-five miles per hour."

Lifting the heaviest weight—figuratively and literally—would be the Navy crews of HC-3. Over the course of the night, the squadron's two CH-46s would transport twenty-five of the forty-three injured aerially evacuated to Yokota. Moreover, they would ferry fifty-nine additional passengers in support of the disaster relief effort—and heft three tons of cargo.

"We didn't shut down at all in the ball field LZ," D. C. Ray remembered. "We kept the bird turning and just lowered the ramp."

The first patients to be airlifted that night rose from Camp Fuji soon after 12:30.

"The weather hadn't dissipated that much," Rod Forrey recalled, so the flight to Yokota "was another pretty rocky ride."

“Bumpy as hell,” is how pilot Greg Rhodes remembered weather conditions, “but at least we had navigation aids.”

At around 1 a.m., as injured Marines were being transferred back to camp from the Jieitai Fuji Sector Hospital, Navy corpsman John Barniea glanced around the medical facility. Most of the Japanese military caregivers there were the same that had been at the facility when ten injured Marines had arrived the previous afternoon. “Many of those staffers,” the Sailor noted, “had refused to leave and continued to work.”

On Yokota Air Base, at 1:05 a.m., “Medical Evacuation Mission 1”— as it would be chronicled by Technical Sergeant Roman Rusynko in the Yokota Hospital Control Center— landed at the air base’s Delta East pad, a helicopter landing site just 2,637 feet from the hospital entrance. “There were a number of ambulances there at the flight line,” Rod Forrey recalled. After each two-minute drive to the hospital’s rear entrance, a Marine was placed onto a gurney, guided into an elevator, then lifted to the hospital’s fourth floor. As soon as the helicopter was emptied of patients, medical technicians began loading supplies to be returned to Camp Fuji.

Earlier Dr. Sarmiento had passed along an urgent request for easily portable oxygen bottles. Respiratory therapy was essential to keeping many of the burn patients alive, he had told his Yokota colleagues; it was imperative that the aid be continued during MEDEVAC flights. As Greg Rhodes and D. C. Ray piloted toward the U.S. air base, Lewis Gold, tending to patients in the back of their aircraft, expanded the catalog of requirements. “Over the intercom,” Ray remembered, “the doctor gave me a list of medical supplies that we needed to pick up at Yokota and bring back.” Rhodes recalled Silvadene being high on the list. “I had to write them down phonetically so I could transmit ’em to Yokota over the radio,” Ray said. “By the time we got there to unload the first group, everything we had asked for, and probably more, was [ready to be] loaded on the aircraft.”

At 1:15 a.m., a second group of patients lifted from the ball field LZ. “Medical Evacuation Mission 2” set down at Yokota at 1:44.

The flurry of helicopter activity on the Yokota flight line caught the attention of an Army staff sergeant who lived with his family in on-base housing. Driving quickly toward the Delta East pad, the thirty-one-year-old parked his car, threw a camera bag over his shoulder and rushed over the tarmac toward crewmen standing beside one of the aircraft. “I’m with

Stars and Stripes," Ron Hatcher yelled over the rotor noise as he lifted his press credential. "What are you guys doing?" They quickly detailed the disaster in progress and assented when he asked, "Can I go?"

It did not take long for the MEDEVAC mission to develop an operational rhythm. At Camp Fuji Air Force ambuses continued to return injured Marines from Gotemba and nearby towns. Each time a helicopter landed at the training camp, those who had been caring for Marines near the LZ peeled off to load their patients and monitor their condition in flight. Dozens of uninjured Marines stepped up to carry litters. Helicopters emptied of the injured Marines at Yokota were loaded with medical provisions there, or took on supplies at Atsugi before returning to the camp.

The supply effort, once up and running, was impressive. At one point during the night, Greg Gregory telephoned Colonel Whiteside with an update from the camp. "He said, 'What do you need?'" At that point bandages and IV kits topped the list. The resulting resupply, Gregory recalled, exceeded his hopes. "I think we could have treated another hundred after what they sent us."

Three hours into the MEDEVAC, with more helicopters involved, the evacuation pace intensified. Medical Evacuation Mission 3 touched down at Yokota at 3:10. It was followed by Mission 4 at 3:17, and Mission 5 at 3:35. The night's sixth mission landed at Yokota at 4:26.

En route D. C. Ray recalled seeing one patient covered from head to toe in white bandages. "He looked like a mummy. . . . My heart went out to the guy." Army physician Lewis Gold was not optimistic about the Marines' fate. Quite the opposite. "My assumption," he remembered decades later, "was they were all going to die."

Rod Forrey imagined that the Marines themselves might also be thinking the worst. "Beyond relief of their pain, and trying to get fluid onboard," the Navy physician assistant felt, they needed to be encouraged. He talked with those he accompanied in flight. His goal was modest: "To comfort the patients and make sure they weren't injured in the evacuation process."

"That was all night," Dan Scandalito said of the rescue cadence—"going back and forth." After guiding the second HC-3 aircraft into the camp, "Scando," as his friends called him, had remained with the CH-46, moving into the back to help ferry fellow Marines to Yokota.

At the hospital it had taken time to understand the effort the emergency would demand. Early staffing had been based on the plan to take in half of the number injured. After it was determined that all would be brought to Yokota, and the severity of their injuries became clearer, staff numbers were tripled. Shifts were extended from eight hours to twelve.

Back at Camp Fuji's base camp, Bob Shillito had remained with Lieutenant Colonel Redgate. "He was talking on the radio," the Marine pilot remembered, "giving directions, and getting information back from the people around the landing zone, and working the casualties towards that area."

In the battalion adjutant's office, the effort to account for all casualties was making progress. "We put a list together and refined it and worked through it," Michael Weltsch recalled. Creating a casualty roster they believed truly accurate and comprehensive, he said, "took all night."

Once the data had been gathered, it would be included in messages sent to higher headquarters. Lieutenant Colonel Redgate drafted the messages himself, by hand, on legal pad pages. Given the seriousness of events at the camp, he required that the text be typed—perfectly—onto the forms that would then be transmitted via the base camp communications center.

"He insisted there not be any typos," Weltsch recalled. "That was a challenge for us, because we didn't have great typists." The four or five Marines on the adjutant's staff had remained at Camp Fuji to help with the work, as had a number of the twenty-some assigned to the BLT personnel office. Their manual typewriters were not equipped with correcting mechanisms. Drafts would be typed, then delivered to Redgate—to Weltsch's mind, "a very dot-the-i-cross-the-t kind of guy." The commanding officer would "read the message traffic, would make pen changes, he would give it back to me. I would go get it retyped." While the eventually transmitted messages were highly accurate, particularly given the confusion of emergency conditions, they were not without flaw. Corporal Colin Miller, throughout much of the transmitted correspondence, would be identified as "Colim."

As BLT 2/4 officers worked to inform Marine Corps leaders about individuals who had been hurt, a Range Company radio operator was making a similar effort on behalf of those who had not. The "CHOP" (chief operator) of Station NNNOMJF had hundreds of hand-scrawled "I'm okay" messages in hand—each containing a postal address for the desired recipient. Messages were relayed to Military Affiliate Radio System (MARS) volunteers across the United States. The goal was to get the message to one living near the individuals Marines and Sailors wanted to reassure. The final volunteer in the chain would handwrite the message onto a standardized form then drop it in the mail. Tim Howell's MARSGRAM, intended for his mother in Florida, had been transmitted at 12:17 a.m. Under the word "Unclassified," it read: "Am perfectly alright. Don't worry. Timmy sends." The transmissions would continue around the clock for two or three days.

From the ball field landing zone, helicopter evacuation missions continued. Moving about quietly, camera in hand—shooting roll after roll of film—Ron Hatcher documented the life-saving efforts. Every now and again, when the *Stars and Stripes* reporter happened upon someone standing still, catching a breath, he would pull out a narrow reporter's notebook and gather an observation.

At some point during the night, Greg Gregory made his way to the base camp headquarters to provide a progress report to Colonel Lamb. "He had gone to bed," Gregory recalled, "which surprised me."

By 3:50 a.m., Japan Standard Time, planners from the Illinois-based 375th Aeromedical Airlift Wing had put into motion a complex choreography of airplanes, crews, and specialized medical equipment. If a multitude of moving pieces fell correctly into place, the effort would speed the injured Marines' return to the United States.

A C-141 from Norton Air Force Base was nearing San Antonio's Kelly Air Force Base. The Starlifter Captain George Ziegler piloted from Norton Air Force Base in Southern California carried two complete 445th Military Airlift Wing flight crews. It would pick up the Army burn center team then fly to Elmendorf, Alaska.

Because many of the Marines to be evacuated were in respiratory distress, ventilators would be required to sustain their lives in flight. The systems that helped patients breathe, however, were designed to plug into 120-volt electrical outlets in hospital rooms. Power systems onboard the cargo aircraft were not instantly compatible; adapters would be required. An effort had begun to gather every available military-owned MA-1 ventilator and adapter system on the U.S. west coast. Military Airlift Command planes began delivering them, and additional medical supplies, to Elmendorf.

By 4 a.m. JST—2 p.m. Central Daylight Time in San Antonio, where it was still October 19—the Army Institute of Surgical Research's nineteen-member flight team had arrived at Kelly Air Force Base. It included three surgeons, three nurses, a bacteriologist, inhalation therapist, and eleven burn-specializing corpsmen. Doctor Michael Walters had divided the team into three caregiving crews, each including a physician, a nurse and several of the corpsmen.

In Japan, by 4:10 a.m., twenty-seven Marines injured at Camp Fuji were under care at Yokota, where a recall order had now been issued for the entire hospital staff. At 4:26 a.m. Technical Sergeant Rusynko noted in the hospital control center log the arrival of Medical Evacuation Mission 6.

By around 5 a.m. JST—3 p.m. of October 19 in Texas—the ISR burn team and its gear had been loaded onto the 445th MAW Starlifter. Skip Zeigler took off once again, this time setting a course for Alaska.

In Japan 250 hospital staffers had returned to their posts at the Yokota Air Base hospital. When Medical Evacuation Mission 7 landed on the Delta East pad at 5:10, the total number of injured Marines transported to Yokota rose to 28. The hospital's hastily arranged fourth-floor burn ward was almost full; space had allowed set-up of just 30 beds. From wards on floors below, additional beds were brought up and positioned in hallways. An eighth group of injured Marines landed at Yokota at 5:20, a ninth at 5:54.

Through the course of the night, as telephone lines had allowed, Lieutenant Colonel Redgate and others had been updating Marine Corps leaders on Okinawa and at the Corps' command center in Washington. At 6 a.m. the BLT's overnight information-gathering, drafting, and typing came to fruition in a formal Situation Report. Transmitted as a teletype message, it provided higher headquarters the first substantive details of the typhoon, fuel spill, fire—and resulting casualties.

As operations slowed at the ball field landing zone, it struck Greg Gregory how long it had been since his team had last eaten. "My crew was hungry," he remembered, and exhausted. "I go to the [base camp officer of the day], who I seem to recall was a first lieutenant. I said, 'My crew needs some food.' And he said, 'Mess hall's closed.'" Gregory mentioned the need for nourishment in a radio report to Yokota. One of the next helicopters to return from the Air Force base, he recalled, carried "more burgers than you could shake a stick at."

After Medical Evacuation Mission 10 landed at Yokota at 6:15 a.m., a Lieutenant Commander Kline, on the staff of Commander, U.S. Naval Forces, Japan reported to the Marine Corps Command Center that thirty-nine injured Marines were now at Yokota. At 6:30 a.m. one of the HC-3 helicopters lifted the last five patients designated for aerial evacuation from the ball field LZ.

Dennis Zickefoose had spent the night helping prepare Marines for MEDEVAC. He and fellow Navy corpsmen had been told to rally some distance away. He lagged. "I was not going to leave where I was standing," he recalled, "until I saw that helicopter get out sight."

Twenty-one minutes later, the CH-46 set down at Yokota. Forty-two injured Marines and one injured Sailor had been airlifted to Yokota.

Checking his flight log decades later, former HC-3 pilot Greg Rhodes noted that "D. C. [Ray] and I flew 6.3 hours that night and into the first dawn." Ten of their MEDEVAC landings were accomplished in darkness, four during early daylight. Additional flight time had been tallied by the Navy squadron's second CH-46 and supporting Army aircraft.

In coming hours six other Marines—their injuries serious, but not critical—would be transported in ambulances to Yokosuka Naval Hospital.

After a tumultuous night of heavy winds, and the noise of near-constant flight operations, the skies above Camp Fuji were suddenly, eerily tranquil. "The thing that I remember," Mac McDonald mused, "is how absolutely beautiful the next day was." Conditions were calm. The sky overhead was a vibrant blue. "The sun was coming up," Dennis Zickefoose remembered, "and Mount Fuji stood there in the background." It did not seem right. Destroyed Quonset huts were still smoldering. Was nature trying to disavow what had just happened? "It was almost confusing," Zickefoose recalled.

Seemingly capricious wreckage was now clearly visible. "Where a building had been full of people the day before there was a burned-out husk of a place," Bill Meyers remembered, "and the building right next to it was just fine."

The quiet allowed reflection. "You sort of start processing things," McDonald said.

"I looked down," the doctor recalled, "and my boots are still untied. You know, because the Marines are very meticulous about their uniforms, I would try to emulate that. I was kind of aghast that I was walking around like some hillbilly with my boots untied. I sat on the bunk and I cried. It caught up."

Exhausted members of the Air Force DRF walked the training camp, surveying damage. It had taken them until 3 a.m. to return all the Marines from off-base clinics. Thereafter they had helped prepare patients for evacuation by air. At around 8 the group made its way to the base camp mess hall. The response was similar to that received by Lieutenant Commander Gregory's team. "We're done serving," they were told. With the same persistence that had served him well in retrieving patients from Gotemba Hospital, Dr. Sarmiento forced the kitchen's reopening. Weapons Company's Fred Winters dined with the medical team. He had only met the group the previous evening, he noted, but "you all feel like you were part of something together and you were never going to see each other again." At around 9, breakfast-fortified, the Air Force team began driving back to Yokota. In its standard ambulance rested the remains of L. C. Malveaux.

By 10:15 the Yokota Air Force hospital staff had reassembled in full. The number of people tending to the Marines on the fourth floor had grown. Beyond the ward, the hospital's laboratory, pharmacy, and X-ray center had moved to around-the-clock staffing. So had the command's medical supply center and dining facility.

Never having imagined, much less trained for, a care effort of such complexity and scale, the Yokota team made a best effort. "You don't even know where to start when that happens," Salvatore De Vincenzo conceded.

The Army burn team would be arriving within hours, they were told. "This," Chief Nurse Rita Gengler noted, "gave us an estimate of about how long we would have to sustain support of what in essence was a thirty-five-bed intensive care unit, plus the care of [at the moment, eight] other less injured men."

The Marines' injuries varied by location and severity of their burns, Gengler remembered, and the degree to which their respiratory systems had been damaged. "They [also]," she said, "varied in level of consciousness and degree of shock."

Nurses cut away patients' remaining clothing. New dressings were applied.

Glenn Roberts, eyesight obscured by bandages, lay on one of the fourth-floor beds. "I'm on my back and I hear a couple of English voices," he recalled. "I assume corpsmen, doctors, I don't know—it wasn't Japanese. And they said, 'Hey, Bud, we're gonna start an IV.'" Again, significant patches of charred skin made that work difficult. In Roberts's case an unburned ankle seemed the only option. The jab into a vein there was painful.

"Our main goal," Rita Gengler recalled—assuming quick arrival of the Institute of Surgical Research team—"was to hydrate, reinforce the dressings, and provide staffing."

"We kept being told that the 141s would arrive sooner than they actually did," recalled Chuck Merlo, an Air Force public affairs officer who had responded to help at the hospital. "At first we were told that they might be taking off [transporting the patients to the United States] as soon as Saturday night."

"We had been advised," Gengler said, "not to mess with their dressings, to reinforce those. Sometimes, there were so many dressings on them that it was almost impossible to find a location for a blood pressure." The obscuring of injuries also created confusion about how much fluid replacement each patient required. The chief nurse worried that "each individual doctor [was simply] ordering as his past experience told him to."

Nurses and medical technicians—awed, worried, and inexperienced in burn care—did their best to keep patients comfortable as they awaited transport. One Marine—"missing features from his face, his ears and so forth," Chuck Merlo recalled, "was shoving the doctors and nurses away from himself, saying, 'Work on my buddy.' I guess one of his closest friends was in a bed close by to him. He was more concerned about him than he was about himself."

"Some of the men were big and agitated," Rita Gengler remembered. "I often saw as many as six people guiding them around their beds." Others, laying stock-still, would stop breathing. "Had they just died?" she recalled asking herself. "Or were they apneic—in other words, not breathing for a little bit?" She intentionally startled one to ensure he was alive.

When it became apparent that the ISR team would not arrive as quickly as originally anticipated, hospital leaders initiated more thorough resuscitation and wound treatment. Nurses were assigned to watch over groups of six patients. At each bedside a dedicated technician ensured that Marines were breathing easily, and that their IVs were dripping at the proper rate. After Foley catheters were inserted in the worst burned, the technicians began measuring and recording the Marines' urine output. As best they could, they measured blood pressure, working around burns that sometimes precluded application of upper arm cuffs. Checking for circulation loss, they verified pulses on each of their patients' four limbs.

Across the air base, word slowly spread about what was happening at the hospital. Some who heard made their way to the medical center. "We had scores of people in the lobby," remembered Merlo, at the time a first lieutenant. The gathered crowd, he said, was "begging for anything that they could do. Any kind of errand. Anything that the Marines might need. Anything that they could do to help people at the hospital."

Much of the BLT and LSU—1,148 Marines and Sailors—had awakened that Saturday on a Japanese military base—displaced, dispossessed. At least twenty-nine with minor injuries were still being cared for by unit corpsmen.

At Camp Takigahara Richard DesLauriers marveled at how quickly and efficiently the Jieitai had provided refuge. "Hell, they had people working" around the clock, he noted, "keeping the restrooms clean the whole time we were there."

Because most of the Marines and Sailors had not eaten since before the previous day's fire, they welcomed being ushered into the Jieitai chow line for breakfast. Cuisine available in the cafeteria-style line was distinctly Japanese. Andy Bonwit remembered it as "some of the best canned fish I ever ate in my life. And rice, hot steamed rice, and some kind of greens."

"I was not much of a fish-eater," Tim Howell conceded, "but I ate whatever they put before me, trust me."

Other activities were arranged to keep the displaced Marines and Sailors occupied. Michael Bendt recalled martial arts demonstrations at a dojo in the Camp Takigahara gymnasium. "We would watch the old sensei out there whoop up on the Japanese army guys," Bendt remembered. "He'd tap that stick, and about twelve guys would come at him. And the next thing you know, he's got twelve guys flying away from him." Volleyball games were organized, as well, pitting teams of Marines and Sailors against Jieitai members. By Saturday morning, Makato Yamamoto recalled, he and his friends understood the tragedy from which their unexpected guests had escaped. Though a language barrier prevented most verbal connection, the groups played hard. Japanese soldiers brought out cameras and the young men took photos together. "The hospitality was great," Tim Howell declared. "I mean, for them to open up their base for us. The two countries working together, that was awesome."

Robert Hendrix remained a visible presence to enlisted Marines at the Japanese camps. "I was impressed by the sergeant major," Rob Ahrens recalled. It struck Ahrens that Hendrix had a plan. "The sergeant major," he said, "really kind of took charge."

Officers, Sam Sanders remembered, found themselves in "tons of meetings." Many involved Lieutenant Colonel Redgate, Major Woodburn, or Major Brosnan. "Every time you looked around," the disbursing officer recalled, "you had to go to a meeting. We were trying to game plan what we were going to do next."

The eventual decision: while some of the BLT and LSU Marines would spend two or three days on one of the Japanese military facilities, most would be returning to Camp Fuji before the day was out.

At Camp Fuji orders were prepared to send Lance Corporal Terrence Stokes "for duty as body escort." His year of overseas service almost completed, the Weapons Company Marine would have rotated back to the United States anyway. Now, en route to his next duty station, Stokes would accompany L. C. Malveaux home to Texas. At Yokota Marine Colonel Bruce Truesdale, a senior officer on the U.S. Forces Japan staff, had posted himself at the hospital to help fellow Marines. Because Stoke's possessions had been destroyed in the fire, Truesdale arranged purchase and tailoring of a new dress uniform. As the Marine's payday proceeds had similarly gone up in smoke, service members at Yokota took up a collection; the donated cash would allow the lance corporal to afford food and lodging as he safeguarded Malveaux on the Marine's final journey home.

Six thousand miles away—in Dell Rapids, South Dakota—sixteen-year-old Lori Brees happened to catch something about Typhoon Tip on a Friday evening newscast. Two American TV networks had made brief mention of damage caused by the storm. CBS anchor Walter Cronkite reported that "the most destructive typhoon to hit Japan in more than ten years has claimed at least twenty-five lives, including two U.S. Marines. One Marine was swept out to sea from a beach on Okinawa. The other was killed at a Marine base at the base of Mount Fuji, when high winds collapsed a fuel storage platform. The fuel exploded and at least forty-six others—most of them Marines—were burned, seven of them critically." On ABC Peter Jennings announced that, "at a U.S. military base, [the storm] caused a fuel tank to explode. One Marine was killed and forty-six others injured."

"My brother's hurt," Lori Brees told her father. "I just felt it. And my dad said, 'No, they would call us if something happened.'"

Robert Brees was thirteen months older than his sister Lori. The two were close. Born in Northern California, they had been raised by their father after their mother left the family when Rob was five and Lori four. In 1976 Bill Brees, finding work in Dell Rapids, had moved there with his children. At their new schools, Rob and Lori began skipping classes. Over time the rebellious behavior led their father to tell Rob: "Keep *that* up and you're going into the service." The son's truancy continued. Dad said, "Join." Rob picked the Marines. On his seventeenth birthday, the young man and his father signed the enlistment papers. A few days later, Rob was off to Marine Corps Recruit Depot, San Diego. The older brother who returned three months later, Lori recalled, had changed: "He had muscles, and had lost all his boyhood fat. He was a grown man." Neighbors were impressed by the handsome young man in uniform. "He had lots of girlfriends," his sister beamed. "He was very attractive."

Three days after the TV news reports had left Lori chilled, Marines *would* show up at the family's door. When they did Lori bolted. "There was three feet of snow outside," she said, "and I took off running—barefooted. I didn't know where I was going. But I didn't want to be there." The Marines told Bill Brees that Private First Class Robert Brees—six months into his service as a Marine—had been hurt, badly. When she finally came in from the cold, Brees's sister recalled, "I looked at my dad and told him it was all his fault."

By 9:30, at Camp Takigahara, it appeared to Lieutenant Fred Winters that—after more than twenty-four stressful hours without sleep—he was going to be able to close his eyes and rest. Back with the remaining portion of Weapons Company, now housed in the Jieitai gymnasium, he gathered something to use as a pillow and reclined.

"I was lying down," he remembered. "I had my feet flat on the floor, my knees up, when somebody kicked my foot and said, 'Sir!'"

A group of Weapons Company Marines stood around him. Among them was Lance Corporal Jesse Lugo. "And Lugo was just—he was moving weird," Winters recalled. Though the Marine from Chicago claimed to be okay, one of the others turned him away from Winters, exposing the Marine's seared upper torso. "It's like Lugo had a blister that *was* his back," the officer recalled. "I said, 'Go find a doc. He's got to go someplace.'" At 10:30 an ambulance left the training camp, shuttling Lugo to Yokota.

At Camp Fuji a stream of BLT and LSU Marines began returning from the nearby Japanese bases. Most had been sent to assess damage and do what could be done to ensure postfire safety.

"They come and got me," Lance Corporal Rickey Lemon remembered. "They said, 'We need a couple of volunteers'—quote, unquote—'to go offload the rest of the fuel that was up there.'" He and two other bulk fuel Marines jeeped over. "They brought in tankers and we pumped the bladders empty, into the tankers—if I remember right. I was pretty much in shock for a day or two after that."

Some of those arriving came from farther afield. Notes made on October 20 suggest that two arrived from the U.S. Navy installation at Yokosuka: the facility's fire chief, John J. Simpson, and its director of safety, Glen Mosman. The officer overseeing facilities maintenance at the Marine Corps' principal base in Japan—Camp S. D. Butler, Okinawa—flew in. Lieutenant Colonel John G. Fitzgerald was accompanied by the Camp Butler Public Works officer, Navy Lieutenant Commander John N. Rever. Whereas Fitgerald's post carried with it certain accountability for the maintenance of Camp Fuji, Rever's did not. His position at Camp Butler dealt solely with overseeing new construction. As a credentialed civil engineer, though, Rever could help assess damage.

Confusingly, Fitzgerald would later state that "during the period 18–19 September 1979, I visited Camp Fuji," and that on October 19 [the day before their October 20 flight to the camp], he and Rever had "visited the fuel farm located in the Training Camp. I conducted an inspection of the berms for the specific purpose of looking for evidence of erosion or deterioration." Fitzgerald's statement remains bewildering beyond its apparent confusion of the inspection dates. The fuel farm area he and the Navy civil engineer would have viewed on October 20 was marred by rain-flattened berms around fuel bladders and the precipitation-provoked 15- to 20-foot rupture in the large berm. Yet, the lieutenant colonel continued, "both Cmdr. Rever and I agreed that there was no evidence of erosion that might jeopardize the ability of the berms to contain the fuel in the event of a leak or a rupture of the fuel cells. In my opinion, the berms appeared in satisfactory condition." Decades later retired Navy Captain John Rever would note the belief that he had visited Camp Fuji just once in his life, and that had been on October 20, 1979, when typhoon-wrought erosion of the fuel farm area was quite evident.

The Americans were not the only individuals surveying damage at the camp that day. "The local Japanese were all over the place," as well, Rever remembered. "An awful lot of them were wearing uniforms." These latter had been dispatched from Japan's Defense Facilities Administration Office. The contingent gathered interviews, measurements, and photos for a DFAO incident report.

In the early afternoon, an executive jet landed on the Camp Fuji airstrip. It carried the one-star general second in command of the 3rd Marine Division. Based on Okinawa the division was the Fourth Marine Regiment's next higher headquarters. Brigadier General James J. McMonagle—"Joe" to friends—stepped out of the aircraft, followed by Sergeant Major Robert Cleary, the division's top enlisted Marine. The two walked into the charred training camp. They examined the breached berm. Along the way McMonagle and Cleary spoke with several clusters of young men. "A lot of the Marines were asking, 'When are we going to get out of here?'" the general would recall decades later. "I told them, 'Nobody's leaving until this mess is cleaned up. And, even if we wanted to, we don't have enough transportation to move everybody right now.'"

He made the same case to the BLT commander, who he remembered "seemed relatively calm" the day after the fire. Decades later McMonagle expressed regret regarding the tenor of his day-after-the-fire interaction with the lieutenant colonel. "I might have been a little tough on John Redgate," he conceded. "Some people think he wasn't active enough. I thought he did all that could be expected."

To subordinates Redgate continued to display a measured and encouraging demeanor—"which must have been incredibly difficult for him," concluded then-Captain Richard DesLauriers. "He had lost Marines, and had a horrible accident happen on his watch." The artillery officer remembered Redgate's "pleasant, deep voice. He was still asking people, 'How are you doing? What's going on in your area? Is there anything you need?'"

McMonagle would hear more questions about the camp's safety when he later spoke to a large assembly of BLT Marines. "He came to give us a pep talk," Weapons Company's Paul Verdier recalled. "'Chin up' kind of crap. They talked about us going back to the camp. And I remember Mark Tipton just lit this guy up. . . . You know: 'The camp's safe, and we're going to go back and start cleaning up.' And Mark was just 'How do you know it's safe?' He was just right back at him. And Mark was absolutely making points. But, you know, I mean, the guy's a general officer. But we were pissed . . . because we weren't getting answers. . . . What the hell had happened? Where are our guys?"

A handful of uninjured Marines, seeking to reassure loved ones in the United States, sought out pay phones on the Japanese bases. Their calls were costly. Mike Burbo remembered toll charges at the time averaging "$22 for the first minute, and $17 for each additional minute." In time MARS station "phone patches" would allow free audio connections with loved ones. While it was good to hear the voices of those closest in their lives, the Marines were disheartened to learn that few back home were aware of what they had been through. "I just kind of went, 'Wow,'" Louis Sanford remembered. "You just went through this. People lost their lives, and people were injured for life, disfigured and so forth."

As 1 p.m. neared at Yokota, Colonel Whiteside showed Navy Captains Bernett Johnson and Joseph Smyth around the hospital's makeshift fourth-floor burn center. Johnson commanded the Naval hospital at Yokosuka; Smyth was chief of Johnson's medical staff. Gauging the need for additional assistance, Johnson promised to augment the Yokota staff with a Navy team of fifteen.

At 1:10 Jesse Lugo arrived at the medical center. Doctors there assessed his injuries: second-degree burns over 30 percent of his body. The Marines who had driven the late-arriving casualty to Yokota fell into conversation with Ron Hatcher. The *Pacific Stars and Stripes* reporter had returned to

Yokota onboard an early morning MEDEVAC flight. In an article on October 23, the Army journalist reported that "one of the ambulance attendants said the victim was found 'wandering around' the rubble in shock and badly burned." Lugo's postfire wanderings had mostly been alongside fellow Marines at Camp Takigahara. In that time he had even been among several asked to handwrite short statements about the disaster's first moments. His many hours of untreated injury and shock would finally get the urgent attention they required.

On Hatcher's heels a second *Stars and Stripes* reporter sought out the ambulance crew that had ferried Lugo. From a second-floor apartment across from the hospital, Marine Staff Sergeant Bill Pederson and his wife, Yvette, had been following the activity below. Seeing uninjured Marines milling about the medical center parking lot, Yvette Pederson told her husband, "Let's get them inside." In the family's living room, she said, the young men seemed "shell-shocked, sort of." Many at Camp Fuji, they told the Pedersons, had been left with only the clothes on their back. As the Marines ate a meal the couple prepared for them, and were entertained by the Pederson's kindergarten-aged daughter, the two—and their good friend Emily Dabney, an Air Force wife—began calling friends and knocking on doors of nearby apartments. Within two hours military families at Yokota had donated boxes full of jackets, trousers, and sweat gear. Some made quick stops at the base exchange, then contributed underwear and socks. Others filled bags with soap, toothpaste, razor blades, and combs. The hasty effort netted sufficient clothing and toiletries to help 150 or so. The eclectic wardrobe and hygiene products were packed into the returning ambulance. At Camp Fuji, thinking longer term, Captain Roger Mauer, the BLT 2/4 logistics officer, would later in the afternoon telephone the 3rd Marine Division headquarters to request complete basic uniform issue for 300.

At Yokosuka the group Captain Johnson had ordered to Yokota was ready to go. Three physicians, five nurses, and seven corpsmen had been assembled. Several had provided frontline medical care in Vietnam. At its core the team led by Lieutenant Commander David Snyder, a general surgeon, consisted of individuals competent in surgery and intensive care. It was augmented by an internist and an ear, nose, and throat specialist, Snyder recalled, because with serious burns came "problems with renal failure, metabolic issues, and airway access."

On a Yokosuka flight line, awaiting the helicopter that would carry them to Yokota, the team gathered around Snyder and took a knee on the tarmac. "He pulled out this card," recalled Navy nurse and former combat corpsman Richard Fink, "and said, 'This is what our plan is when we arrive.' There were probably eight or ten things on that list."

As soon as they arrived, Snyder recalled telling the team, they would check that the Marines' airways were cleared and that they were getting oxygen. Then they would ensure that blood was circulating to their limbs. Each patient would be weighed, and an estimation made of his burn percentage. Nurse and former corpsman Mike Monahan recalled the surgeon instructing the team to insert Foley catheters into each Marine's bladder. "If they didn't need it, eight hours later, or twenty-four hours later, we could take it out. What we didn't want is someone to not be making urine, and we didn't know about it for some period of time." Snyder explained the formula team members would use to determine how much fluid they would infuse if a patient's urine output fell below 30 to 50 milliliters per hour. It was the same protocol Mac McDonald had attempted to follow—developed at the institute whose burn specialists would soon arrive from Texas. Because the Marines had been operating in field conditions at the camp, Snyder also ordered that each be immunized with a Tetanus shot booster. Finally, keen to avoid patients' developing antibiotic resistance—given the heightened infection threat they would face in days ahead—Snyder instructed his team to provide antibiotics only to patients exhibiting infection symptoms.

By the time the Yokosuka group arrived, twenty-three patients had been placed in rooms. Twelve were on gurneys in hallways. Nine in less serious condition had been sent to rest at a far end of the ward.

"We were assigned to the north end of the nurses station," Richard Fink recalled, "and the Air Force was assigned to the south end." The Navy team assumed primary responsibility for eighteen of the most critically injured. Some of their burns, ENT specialist Dr. Cameron Gillespie thought, resembled "the dense bark of an old oak tree."

The hospital's chief nurse noticed the value added by a team that had been afforded time to plan. They were "organized as a group," Rita Gengler observed, and "knew a lot better how to deal with burns." A fluid replenishment standard was adopted ward-wide, as was a plan for more easily and safely controlling patients' pain.

Across the ward providers were struck by the Marines' stoicism and selflessness. "Do you hear that?" Cesar Sarmiento asked Chuck Merlo. "And I said, 'I don't hear anything,'" Merlo recalled. "And he says, 'Exactly. If we were in a civilian burn ward right now, the screaming would be unbelievable.'" Mike Monahan wondered at the apparent absence of self-pity. "These guys are so sick, so wounded, so thrust-upon in their lives," he said. They were able to understand the fire's destructive impact to their physical appearance, yet "not a one of them ever moaned or groaned. . . . It was all, 'How's so-and-so doing?'" When a Marine had to be wheeled away for an X-ray or lab work, the nurse recalled, "the other Marine in the room was just a wreck until they got back. That degree of caring about each other, it was just so evident that I'll never forget."

Patients who were able stepped up to help with the care effort, sometimes surprisingly. "I was doing a procedure on one of the really badly burned wounds," David Snyder recalled, "and just accepting tools as I asked for the equipment. It was sort of frantic. When I was done, I turned around." His assistant had not, as he had assumed, been a corpsman. "One of the Marines is standing there," Snyder recalled. "He had on a pair of rubber gloves, he was wearing a sheet and nothing else—very badly burned. He just says, 'My buddy going to be okay, Doc?'"

At 3 p.m. large groups of BLT and LSU Marines began departing the refuge of Japanese bases. Camp Fuji had been declared safe for habitation, they were told. It is difficult to understand who made that determination. Decades later retired Navy Captain John Rever, the then-Camp Butler-based civil engineer who accompanied Lieutenant Colonel John Fitzgerald from Okinawa, noted that it would not have been within his professional capacity to make such a decision. It seems likely to have been the judgment of Range Company commander Allan Lamb, guided by advice from Fitgerald and perhaps the Yokosuka fire chief and safety director.

Many in the BLT and LSU shared the concerns Corporal Tipton had raised with Brigadier General McMonagle. Fox Company Marine Roger Miller returned to a camp "with no electricity, heat, or drinking water—and no smoking because of vapor and more fuel that could erupt." A prevailing stench of gasoline did not inspire confidence. Lieutenant Fred Winters watched Marines engage in a macabre form of entertainment. "You dug your heel in the volcanic ash," he explained, "you threw a match on the ground, and you watched the ground around you go 'whoof!' because it was still soaked full of gas."

"The sheen left over from fuel, just there in the sand, came right up to the edge of our huts," Richard DesLauriers remembered. He and other Hotel Battery Marines marveled at the role a bit less erosion had played in keeping their area safe. "If the water had been two inches deeper," DesLauriers mused—as it was near Weapons Company huts on the same tier—"we would have gotten it, too."

Those returning to buildings destroyed in the fire, Jacob Evans recalled, stepped into sobering scenes: "They were in a daze."

In the lower-tiered Headquarters and Service Company spaces. Rob Ahrens kicked at the pile of ashes that had been his seabag. Little remained, he said: "I had an iron, and the metal parts of the iron were laying on the floor, surrounded by all these half-burnt clothes and stuff." Mike Burbo was unable to look inside his nearby hut; it had collapsed into a pile of rubble "about four feet high."

With fourteen huts destroyed, the camp's already crowded conditions tightened further still. Some platoons consolidated from two huts into one; in this way Echo Company made space for some Weapons Company survivors. Others shoehorned cots into already packed barracks. At least one platoon erected a tent, flooring it with wooden pallets on which they laid out sleeping bags.

Lieutenant Fred Winters listened as staff NCOs told him they were finding it difficult to counter Marines' concerns about the wisdom of reoccupying the camp so quickly. "I'm not a firefighter," Winters told them. "If [senior leaders] tell me it's good, I guess we're okay. I don't know. But I do know that we're playing this 'light the ground' trick."

Made anxious by the previous day's events, Louis Sanford remembered, "we took the doors off the building . . . or we blocked them open, one or the other—so nobody could close 'em." It was cold inside. Use of the camp's kerosene heaters had been banned. Temperatures outside were colder still, yet some Marines, particularly from Weapons Company, insisted on situating their cots in the open air. Some staff NCOs wanted to order the Marines inside. Lieutenant Duane Schattle, days away from taking command of

Weapons Company, suggested they let the Marines be. Cold temperatures, he said, would sooner or later cause the Marines to seek indoor shelter. "Fortunately," Schattle recalled, "the very next night, freezing rain forced everyone inside voluntarily."

Eleven nurses and technicians from the 9th Aeromedical Evacuation Squadron arrived at Yokota at 4 p.m. Medical supplies they brought with them from the Philippines were trucked to the hospital. Thirty minutes later, additional supplies arrived by helicopter from Yokosuka.

By 6:10 p.m., Japan Standard Time, Air Force fueling teams in Anchorage, Alaska, were topping off the 445th Military Air Wing C-141 that had traveled from San Bernardino, by way of San Antonio. From hangars where multiple aircraft had deposited them over the course of the day, loadmasters wrangled ventilators and electrical conversion kits into the aircraft. As they did so, Dr. Michael Walters called the Yokota hospital via a radio-telephone patch. Colonel Whiteside confirmed that all the burned Marines had been gathered at Yokota. Captain Skip Ziegler and his crew left the plane. A new pilot, Captain Ron Wilhelmsen of the 14th Military Airlift Squadron, would take command of the second 445th MAW aircrew and lead the team's flight to Yokota.

Medical supplies at the hospital continued to be quickly consumed. Military commands across the Pacific responded. At 6:30 p.m., a helicopter landed at the air base carrying bandages, Silvadene, and other supplies, as well as an MA-1 ventilator. At 8:15 clinicians at U.S. Marine Corps Air Station Iwakuni called to ask what they could provide. Navy doctors and nurses on Okinawa had made a similar query earlier in the day. At 8:30 a Navy P-3 Orion—from Misawa Air Base in northern Honshu—set down at Yokota, packed with burn treatment staples. At 10:15 another C-141 Starlifter from Clark Air Base arrived full of medical provisions. American military units at Atsugi and Camp Zama would continue to contribute. In the end supplies valued at $93,000 would be exhausted during what would be the Marines' comparatively short weekend at Yokota—$31,000-worth from stocks held at Yokota, the remainder shared by other U.S. bases in Japan.

At Camp Fuji, administrators continued forwarding casualty updates to higher headquarters. One was transmitted at 7 p.m., another at 9:22.

Incoming adjutant Michael Weltsch recalled the battalion commander then beginning to draft a letter of condolence to the family of Lance Corporal Malveaux.

Navy Lieutenant Mel Ferguson continued his rounds of the BLT and LSU area. Fox Company commanding officer Jeffrey Bearor recalled the chaplain as a ubiquitous presence in days after the fire. "I credit his force of will with helping us all get through that," Bearor affirmed decades later, "to include the battalion commander, who was a Vietnam vet himself, a great leader, who, even himself, I mean, we were all pretty well shocked by this."

In the evening Lieutenant Fred Winters was called to the BLT 2/4 headquarters hut. Someone there wanted to talk with him. As he walked toward the "head shed," a young Marine who Winters did not recognize walked up to him. "Hey, sir," he said, "watch yourself in there. They're trying to blame you." Winters walked on. "The young hard-charger must be confused," he thought. Before arriving at the headquarters, a passing staff NCO—perhaps a gunnery sergeant or first sergeant—drew him aside with a similar warning: "Do not relax with these people." The lieutenant, who had had little sleep since the fire began, entered Hut D-417. He was told to sit across a table from two senior officers he had never seen before. One was likely the Range Company executive officer, Major Richard M. Reilly. The base camp officer had begun gathering notes and statements about the recent events. One officer sat across the table from Winters, the other stood off to the side. They began formally asking his name and position. "Then I was asked why I had told [my Marines] to nail the doors shut. And I said, 'I don't know of any . . .' I'm sure I was respectful when I started. I said, 'Sir, that's not correct.'"

Over time there would be no indication of blocked passageways in any Weapons Company hut except D-220. On the ground outside that hut, which housed Marines from a platoon other than Winters's, someone had spotted a "U" bolt. It was assumed to have been part of a padlock.

The two did not seem to accept the lieutenant's answer. "The person who was antagonizing me was standing to my left," Winters recalled. "He kept pushing it, to the point where I told him to go 'F' himself. And they tried to remind me what their rank was. And I told them, 'I don't care who you are, but I don't know what you're talking about.'" He yelled that, even as the fire continued to burn, he had been pulling doors open to look for survivors. The weary-turned-angry lieutenant felt he had been pulled into a "we've got to hang this on somebody" spotlight. "And my answer to 'em was—and I remember having this fight—'The fuel farm is above the living quarters! . . . And I was threatened," Winters recalled: "'You understand that you could be . . .' And I said, 'I don't give a crap what you do.' And then I was pulled out of there." He did not remember by whom. "But that confrontation," confessed the officer who went on to retire as a lieutenant colonel, "left a bad taste in my mouth for twenty-two years in the Marine Corps."

Later that evening Winters was called back to the same building, though brought in through a back door to the room where the BLT commanding officer worked and slept. John Redgate was not inside. Rather, Brigadier General Joe McMonagle welcomed the young lieutenant and told him to take a seat. The conversation was calm, "like talking to your grandfather, the wise sage," Winters remembered. "He asked me what I thought, and I said, 'Well, sir . . .' I blamed the Marine Corps. I said, 'We need to take responsibility for the fact that, look, you can't claim it's an expeditionary camp and pat yourself on the back because you built it halfway.'" The lieutenant bemoaned having lost half of his platoon to the fire and wondered out loud how his platoon, even if replacements brought it up to strength, would be ready for a combat readiness test one month hence. "He asked me if we should stay. And I said, 'The answer is no.'" The general promised that he would pass the lieutenant's remarks to every senior officer he briefed, but that the BLT would likely end up remaining at the camp. "His exact quote was, 'If you fall off a horse, you get right back on it,'" Winters recalled. "And I said, 'So long as the horse isn't defective.'"

By 10:20 that evening, planners at Yokota were anticipating that two Starlifters carrying the injured Marines to Texas would take off the following morning at 9 and 9:30. As Marines and Sailors back at the training camp laid down in their racks, safety-related anxieties restrained rest. Among the Marines and Sailors of Weapons Company, ghosts of the missing forestalled slumber. "You know, them being there one moment," Mike Tuttle recalled, "the members of the platoon—and then the very next moment they're gone."

Across the United States word of the disaster began making its way to those whose loved ones had been hurt. In Detroit, Corrine Davis's clock radio was set to a radio station in Canada. Waking on Friday morning, she had heard a newscaster mention a fire in Japan. It had happened, he reported, at a camp near Mount Fuji. She was sure her son had written about heading to the area. "I got up and I got the letter," she recalled. "It was where he was." TV newscasts she watched after work that day made no mention of the incident. No one was talking about it as she spent time downtown Saturday. That evening, she joined three good friends who met once a week to relax and catch up over shared wine. She was distracted, though. "Something just told me," she said, "'You shouldn't be here. You should go home.'" She did. Approaching her house, she encountered a uniformed Marine stepping down from the porch. He had been about to walk away. Inside he informed her that Willie Davis Jr. had been injured in the fire. At the moment, he said, there were few additional details to pass on. "He asked if I had anyone there with me," Davis remembered. She called her mother, who came and spent the night. They pondered next steps. "I was thinking I was going to have to go to Japan, and I'm wondering how." On Sunday a cousin joined them. As a social worker, she understood bureaucracies. Making a series of phone calls, she learned that the Marines were being flown to Texas.

In Indianapolis a Friday morning radio newscast had also caught the attention of Lloyd Neal as he drove to work. "He knew that was right at the place where Steve was," remembered his wife, Freida Neal. Their son served in BLT 2/4's Weapons Company. Friends who worked at a nearby Army base made inquiries with the handful of Marines stationed there. The following day a government sedan pulled up outside their home. "Of course, when you see that car, it does do something to you," Freida Neal laughed nervously. Two uniformed Marines told them what they knew of the incident. "They were very nice and courteous. We didn't know for sure yet how Steve was, as far as that goes, and we knew we had to get there. So we got on a plane that night and flew to San Antonio."

In Applewood, Colorado, that Saturday evening, Sam du Pont was watching TV in the basement of a home he rented with a couple friends. "It came on the news that there had been this fire in Japan, in the Marine base," he recalled. "And I'm telling you, it was literally like the newscast reached out of the TV and grabbed me by my collar." His brother Phil was there. In Richmond, Virginia, Victor du Pont, their father, took the phone call apprising him that his son was among the injured. He and the mother of the young men were amicably separated. Joan Moore du Pont was in Bluemont, Virginia, when she learned of the disaster. Father and mother spoke by phone; each then quickly headed to an airport, on their way to Texas.

In Oakland, California, Orwin Miller and some family members were pushing a grocery-loaded shopping cart uphill toward their apartment when a friend came running up. "Something happened to your brother," he told Orwin. "Call New York." He rang sisters on the East Coast. Someone from the Marine Corps had called, they said, asking to speak with their mother, Enid Miller, about her son Colin. Just weeks earlier Enid had moved to Oakland, settling in with Orwin and his wife. The children worried how bad news might impact their mother. "She's in California with me," Orwin told a Marine casualty assistance officer when he called the number his sisters had taken, "but you can't talk to her. It will kill her." His brother Colin was badly burned, they told him. It was difficult to digest, Orwin said. "When we heard 'second and third degree' of course, that was foreign to us. . . . We couldn't think. It was that serious. The phone started ringing a lot."

11

SUNDAY, OCTOBER 21

I don't remember taking off, I don't remember landing, I don't remember en route—except for that brief period where I'm fighting somebody that's trying to shove something down my throat.

—Lance Corporal Steve Neal, U.S. Marine Corps

AT 1:15 A.M., on Camp Fuji, the BLT 2/4 sergeant of the guard responded to a report of flames in a burnt-out area previously occupied by Weapons Company's 81 mm mortar platoon. "Fire was quickly put out," logged the BLT duty officer. "XO notified."

At 4:20 the C-141 that had journeyed from California to Texas to Alaska landed at Yokota Air Base. Dr. Michael Walters headed immediately for the hospital, bringing with him the group's bacteriologist.

Walters would assess the burned Marines' readiness for airlift, Navy Nurse Mike Monahan recalled. The accompanying scientist "was going to take cultures of all the patients." Understanding the germs to which they had been exposed could help counter infection threats.

The rest of the Army burn team—sweaty and groggy after a twenty-four-hour flight—would be directed toward rooms where they could sleep for three or four hours, then shower before undertaking fourteen hours of caregiving during return flights to Texas.

That plan changed soon after the Army surgeon glimpsed the ward.

"He walked around and looked at maybe ten people," Monahan recalled, "then said, 'Excuse me. A phone?' The next thing you know, he's calling that team: 'Get up. Get in here as soon as you can!'"

The Soldiers quickly showered. Those who had headed to the hospital dining hall scarfed down the nourishment on their plates. Scrubbed and in fresh uniforms, they rushed upstairs. The scale of the mass casualty event was worse than the burn specialists had imagined.

"It was astronomical," Dr. Roger Yurt remembered. The ISR surgeon had never seen so many acutely burned people in one place. "We rarely had this many patients even on a busy day back in San Antonio."

The Air Force and Navy teams had been working tirelessly to stabilize the Marines. There were just so many, though, so badly hurt. "This is why," Salvatore De Vincenzo affirmed, "the people from Brooke were a godsend."

Preparing the patients for transport became a nearly all-day ordeal. "Even for this fast moving group of people," Rita Gengler observed, "the sheer volume of work just about swamped them."

"We had to get 'em ready for transport and continue their resuscitation," Walters recalled, "whether it meant establishing secure airways, or central veinous access or IV support."

The effort would require more people. In a hospital conference room, additional Yokota staffers queued up to help. A member of the Army burn team thanked them for volunteering. Before they moved to the fourth floor, though, he had each look through a folder of photos depicting severe thermal injuries previously treated by the ISR. "This," he told them, "is what is up there." He accepted those volunteers who felt they could work without distraction.

By mid-morning Sunday, some forty hours had passed since Typhoon Tip had precipitated the fuel spill and fire at Camp Fuji. To more precisely assess wounds, the team from San Antonio removed dressings and scraped away layered Silvadene. Laboratory studies were ordered. Tubes delivering gas-soothing Maalox were inserted into patients' stomachs.

Mike Monahan recalled watching the ISR team measure each Marine's arterial blood flow by pressing doppler devices to each of their arms and legs. When the devices did not detect sufficient circulation, he remembered, ISR surgeons would reach for a cutting tool—"a Number 11 scalpel blade," he recalled. "They didn't even have it in a handle. Just a Number 11 scalpel blade. They would pull it out, open it up and just slice them open." The incisions—"from calf to hip, from elbow to wrists," Richard Fink remembered—slit through leathery burned skin but did not sink into the patient's layer of subcutaneous fat. Most of the Air Force and Navy medical team members had never before witnessed an escharotomy.

"*Eschar*," Dr. Walters explained, "a piece of dead tissue, and you're opening it, *-otomy*."

Tight, fire-consumed skin separated along the incision lines. Its constricting pressure released, capillaries beneath could again circulate blood, nutrients, and oxygen. Had the eschar remained taut, it could have collapsed such underlying circulatory vessels, leading to the destruction of tissue they nourished.

The necessary procedures were quick and not particularly bloody, but performed without application of an anesthetic. "I had never [before heard] anyone screaming with an endotracheal tube in place," Richard Fink said. "It was right down the line, no questions asked, just done."

"I thought that we were being very aggressive in our treatment of these patients," Mike Monahan would later observe. "When the real specialists come in, that's when you see what they've learned."

At 5:35 a.m. Tyrone Chris Elem died. The nineteen-year-old Weapons Company private first class had been living in Alexandria, Virginia when he joined the Marines—soon after his 1978 graduation from the city's T. C. Williams High School. He had been born, though, in Arlington, Virginia. Too soon he would be laid to rest in the national cemetery there. Among those mourning the Marine on the fourth floor of the U.S. Air Force hospital was Craig Jackson. In Hut D-215 he had watched Elem try to save the life of their friend L. C. Malveaux. Back home those enduring Elem's loss would include his parents Lloyd and Marie, four sisters, and three brothers.

Elem's passing made the work of the thrown-together Army, Air Force, and Navy team that much more urgent. Further stabilizing the forty-some remaining patients would greatly increase *their* chances of survival.

During immediate emergency treatment, medical teams had inserted intravenous lines into the Marines' hands, wrists or elsewhere on their bodies. Over the coming days, it was likely that these "peripheral lines" would not be sufficient to deliver the steady stream of fluids and liquid medications each patient would need. "Most of these Marines required anywhere from five to ten liters of fluids," Salvatore De Vincenzo remembered. "That's how far behind they were." The ISR team set out to install more reliable "central lines" into veins returning to each patient's heart. In most instances,

Roger Yurt recalled, the IV lines were inserted "around the collarbone or in the neck, where you can put large catheters into large veins." The ISR team members tried to avoid burned skin as they pushed catheters through dermal layers and into veins. It was not always possible.

With patients nearing readiness to move, lung function checks were undertaken for each breathing with the aid of a ventilator. All were reslathered with Silvadene, then again swaddled in gauze Kerlix bandage rolls. The multilayer wrapping, Dr. Walters explained—"almost making them look like a mummy with bandages"—would aid in preventing the Marines from slipping into hypothermia.

Back on the flight line, aircrew members and the embarked 9th AES team had began fitting out cabins of two C-141s to accommodate rows of litters. End to end they would stretch from front to back.

Aluminum poles were vertically hoisted in the center portion of the plane's cargo cabin. Litters would be snapped into place between the poles. Captain Deanna Cox, a 9th AES nurse, noted that "big metal brackets and prongs" extending from the vertical stanchions made the process efficient. "The litters stacked up," she observed, "just like you were putting up shelves."

"We had three high on the left," estimated loadmaster Charles Brown, then a twenty-four-year-old airman first class, "and then three high on the right."

In theory up to eighty litter-borne patients could be packed into each Starlifter's just-over-ninety-three-feet-long, nine-feet-tall cabin. Space, though, was quickly taken up by the numerous medical devices that would be necessary to care for each badly-burned Marine. This was particularly true at positions near the front of cabin of the first C-141. That's where they would place patients not able to breathe on their own.

"Ventilators then were as big as me," Deanna Cox remembered. It took time to maneuver them into place and connect air compressors. "There are tracks in the plane that you have to lock the equipment into," she continued. "You had to get IVs ready, you had to get all of your suction equipment ready. You had to get your oxygen ready. Everything had to be attached."

Large plastic boxes of medical supplies were hefted onboard the aircraft. The work would take nearly twelve hours.

Meantime, Private First Class Charlie Dickerson and five other Marines were being treated at the Yokosuka Naval Hospital. "I couldn't see very good," he remembered. "Everything was just a big blur." He had no memory of his hand sustaining cuts or his face and ears being burned when he punched his fist through a window in Hut D-214. His only recollection was of having been thrown to the floor by a blast, then being picked up by his friend Charles Degnim. "Why is my face wrapped?" he asked himself. "And then I remember thinking, 'Hey, what am I going to look like when these bandages come off?'" Within a month he and the other five would heal sufficiently to return to the camp, though on light duty.

At Camp Fuji 8 a.m. brought a moment of normalcy. The BLT sergeant major had made it happen.

"Sergeant Major Hendrix is my hero," professed retired Major General Joe McMonagle decades later. "On [that] Sunday morning, he somehow found a flag and organized a morning colors ceremony. Everything he did was very positive."

The day commenced a full-scale effort to pull down and get rid of structures destroyed by the fire, wind, and flood. Marine working parties pulled sheets of metal siding from the frames of damaged huts. "The engineers came down with a couple loaders," Rob Ahrens recalled, "and they started just pushing the burned-up barracks into piles." Mike Tuttle took part in "loading burnt racks on trucks, and making dump runs." Fox Company Marine Roger Miller remembered being ordered to search for salvageable furnishings, then "carrying everything outside and scrubbing it."

To some, particularly surviving Marines of Weapons Company, the effort seemed a destruction of evidence. "It's like they were up there already bulldozing every trace of that freakin' fuel farm," Paul Verdier recalled, "cleaning it out and bulldozing it. By the time anybody [would have later looked at it] that would have been just a flat patch of bulldozed ground."

Beyond pushing away the rubble of destroyed huts, bulldozers had been put to use filling the breach in the long berm. They had also—following Masao Satoh's August suggestion—been used to begin constructing a drainage ditch significantly uphill of the now-deconstructed fuel farm. The project was being undertaken by LSU commanding officer John Brosnan, acting on orders from Range Company officers.

"They told me," Brosnan said, "'We want a trench dug. Dig a trench,' to divert anything from coming back down into the camp if it rained some more. Well, I happened to know how to run the [Terex] 82–30, so I got the bulldozer, and went and just started a trench." LSU engineers would finish the project, digging out two deep and wide culverts.

Plans were being made for Chaplain Ferguson to lead a memorial service on the camp runway early the following morning. "Everyone will be squared away," Captain Leon Craig wrote in his notes from a meeting of battalion officers—that is, in clean uniforms, boots shined. After having encountered difficulties identifying some Marines severely burned in the fire, the uniform edict included an order that "all personnel will wear dog tags ASAP."

Lieutenant Colonel Redgate and Major Woodburn were concerned that their Marines' military discipline was lapsing. After a couple postfire days wearing civilian clothes or mismatched uniform pieces, unit members needed to—as quickly as possible, they ordered—again be properly uniformed and return to displaying such military courtesies as saluting officers.

Calls went out for Marines and Sailors to forward suggestions for individuals they believed should be presented awards for lifesaving actions during the fire. Companies E, F, and G were told to offer up names of 60 mm mortar gunners they would give up in order to fill the injury-depleted ranks of Weapons Company; those selected would retrain to employ 81 mm mortars.

Another payday was scheduled. On Friday, October 26, the Marines and Sailors were told, they would receive eleven days' worth of pay and be allowed a weekend off. In the meantime many would spend days tearing down destroyed buildings and hauling away detritus. Others, as early as the following day, would return to training in the camp's maneuver area and on its ranges.

Reflecting concern that camp water supplies had been fouled by gasoline seeping deep into porous volcanic soil, Captain Craig made a note to warn his men, "Don't drink the H2O yet, not until further notice."

In the afternoon Brigadier General McMonagle and Sergeant Major Cleary flew from Camp Fuji to the Yokota Air Base hospital. "There," the general recalled, they saw "some really sad cases." The two talked with those who were able to communicate. They were awed by the medical teams. "They have been working so hard for so long that I don't see how they are still on their feet," McMonagle marveled.

By early afternoon at Yokota, crews were making good progress creating cramped but functional treatment facilities inside each of the C-141s. The two cargo planes had taxied to an edge of the airfield very near the base hospital. It was rare for aircraft to use that portion of the tarmac. At more than 168 feet long, with a wing span of more than 160 feet, the Starlifters stretched oddly close to a nearby cluster of high-rise military family housing. The placement would shrink the distance over which Marines would have to be driven to be loaded onto the planes.

Still, though, no patients had made their way out. Aboard the first C-141, Major Jim Sehorn and his crew stood by—then stood by some more. On several occasions they were provided manifests listing patients about to board. "Then," the aircraft commander recalled, "just prior to bringing them to the flight line, they would go through and check them again, and there would be men on that list no longer safe to put on an airplane."

A Marine who, moments before, Mike Monahan recalled, was speaking cogently about his family back home, would be "suddenly out of it. Their blood pressure's dropped. They're in shock, they're spiking a fever, or they're having trouble breathing."

"One would stabilize," Rita Gengler remembered, "one would lapse."

Two patients presented a particularly troubling triage dilemma. Corporal Colin Miller and Lance Corporal Robert V. Smith Jr. were in perilously critical condition. "Moving them," ISR surgeon Roger Yurt recalled, "would probably have led to their demise almost immediately." At 2:20 p.m. burn team leader Michael Walters determined that the two would remain at Yokota.

Finally, by late afternoon, more of the others seemed ready for transport. On the ISR team, nurse Catherine Syby worked alongside Dr. Walters. Her colleague, Major Judy Terry, assisted Dr. Robert Fanning. They checked patient's airways. "Did they need an endotracheal tube? Were they on a ventilator?" Those who did would be among the first evacuated. They again checked the sturdiness of each patient's multiple IV lines. "The worst thing to happen," Syby knew from experience, "is to have to start an IV in the air."

Burn-covering ointments were refreshed, bandaging secured, and full IV bags attached. Each Marine was wrapped, Roger Yurt recalled, "in what we called, like, 'astronaut suits'—it's an aluminized plastic wrap that you put around to keep patients warm."

To ensure that movement across time zones did not create dangerous confusion, clocks on the ward were adjusted to reflect U.S. Central Daylight Time. Doctors, nurses, and technicians who would travel with the patients similarly adjusted the time displayed on their watches. Notes of patient's vital signs, medicine intake, and urine output were recorded in CDT. Providers at the Army burn center in San Antonio would face challenge enough when the Marines arrived for admission. When referring to the Marines' care charts, they would at least be saved having to factor for time zone difference.

As they waited to be moved, Mark Bedwell was struck by how medical team members were addressing him. "They're calling me by my first name: 'Mark, you're going to San Antonio, Texas.'" Still in the group of three lowest ranks Marines referred to as "non-rates," he was used to being referred to only as "Bedwell." If people were being this nice to him, he thought, his condition must be bad.

Another of the patients, likely Jesse Lugo, received a phone call just before being delivered to the flight line. "His mother called all the way from Chicago," Chuck Merlo recounted not long after. "She had been notified her son had been hurt, but not how bad." The Marine's back and feet had been burned. Bandages inhibited his movement, so the Air Force lieutenant held the telephone receiver to the young Marine's ear. "He told his mother, 'Don't worry, Mom. I just got burned a little.'"

By 4 p.m. a steady parade of gurneys was making its way to elevators in the Yokota hospital. The momentum whipped up a second wind among the weary hospital staff. Watching Cesar Sarmiento prepare patients for transport, a Navy corpsman asked, "How does that man move so fast?" The surgeon had slept just three hours since having departed for Camp Fuji Friday evening.

Thirty-eight Marines had been designated for evacuation. The seventeen most grievously injured would be placed on the first of two Starlifters. One or two at a time, they were brought to the ground floor, loaded onto litters, then carefully maneuvered into ambulances well heated to prevent drops in body temperature.

“Those on respirators,” Dr. Yurt remembered, “had to have a temporary respirator.” If an electric machine was not available on an ambulance, someone would hand-pump oxygen into the patients’ lungs using manual resuscitators.

Arriving at the C-141, Marines were carried up the aircraft’s rear ramp. The Starlifters’ low-to-the-ground fuselage, just over four feet above the ground, simplified the transfer.

“The critical people got on,” Deanna Cox recalled, and were moved to the front of the cabin. “We got them hooked up to the ventilation, got them stable, had their ventilators going. Then we could bring in the other patients and get them hooked into the back end.”

As loading proceeded Joe McMonagle climbed into the cabin. Moving from litter to litter, the general spoke with those Marines who were able. “I got into a friendly argument with one of the guys,” he would later recall.

Finally, it was time to raise the rear ramp, pull in the petal doors, and seal the interior pressure door. At around 6 p.m., nine hours after Jim Sehorn’s Starlifter 40619 had landed at Yokota, it again took to the air. Mission-titled “Air Evac One”—it set a course that would carry the injured onboard to Kelly Air Force Base in San Antonio.

The sound and vibration of four turbofan engines—each generating twenty-one thousand pounds of thrust—agitated Marines already impacted by varying degrees of pain and anesthesia. Caregivers realized that a significant measure of their work would entail helping their patients remain calm. On the Yokota airfield, the stream of ambulances and litters continued to flow, depositing twenty-one more patients into the second Starlifter.

The flight plan Jim Sehorn filed for “Air Evac One” did not include a customary fueling stop in Alaska. In theory it was conceivable that a C-141 could fly nonstop from Yokota to San Antonio. “With fingers crossed,” Sehorn recalled, “that was the game plan of the day.” He had ensured fuel tanks were filled to the 24,000-gallon limit, and ordered a modified cruise profile. Instead of flying the entire mission at a consistent speed of roughly 548 miles per hour (.74 mach), the crew would begin at around 563 miles per hour (.76 mach). As the aircraft expended fuel, reducing its weight, the crew would progressively reduce its flight speed. “Even though you were flying slower as you got lighter,” Sehorn explained, “you ended up flying further, with the same fuel load.” The diminishing pace could get the Starlifter to Texas more quickly than if it flew an itinerary including a typical 2-hour, 15-minute ground stop. Slower, in this scenario, would be faster.

Beyond calculating impacts of flight speed, fuel consumption, and weather conditions, Sehorn also had to take into account the physics of providing medical care in the air. Altitude mattered. Cruising at thirty-five thousand feet, for instance, in-cabin air pressure would have been equivalent to that experienced at seven thousand or eight thousand feet above sea level—not a problem for most humans. For individuals burned as badly as those onboard, however, pressure beyond that experienced at four thousand or five thousand feet could be perilous. Dangerous tissue swelling was more likely at higher altitudes. Patients on ventilators could be harmed by pressure changes affecting air pockets trapped inside injuries. In addition, medical equipment designed for ground-based operation would sometimes malfunction when used in higher-pressure environments. The solution often involved flying at lower altitudes.

For this oceanic crossing, Sehorn and the onboard medical teams decided, the aircraft would remain twenty-nine thousand feet above the Pacific. That kept them low enough to avoid pressure problems, but not so low as to risk the possibility of icing that came with flying inside cloud layers. A significant downside: The aircraft would be more susceptible to buffeting winds. Unit historians would later note how much would ride on the aircrews' innovative reckoning. Protecting the Marines' health, they wrote, required flying "at altitudes and speeds not covered by available planning charts."

Because it had been participating in an international military exercise, Starlifter 40619 had been deployed from Southern California with more than the usual number of pilots, flight engineers, and loadmasters. Beside Sehorn, Captain Dale Hartikka, and First Lieutenant Denis Tarrin could take turns piloting. Lieutenant Colonel Neil Madden would serve as navigator. The flight engineer complement was made up of Technical Sergeant Tony Fontanez, Staff Sergeant Cindy Gorcenski, and Sergeant Rob Ruiz—while Master Sergeant J. J. Warren led fellow loadmasters Sergeant Pete Dominguez and Airman First Class Bob Scarborough.

Safety regulations allowed the augmented crew to operate the Starlifter for twenty-four continuous hours. After such a full-day period, though, rules required rest on the ground for the entire crew. Because it had taken so long to configure and load the aircraft, and the transpacific journey ahead would itself require a half-day's flying, it became clear that the Air Evac One mission would extend beyond the approved flight time. Before taking off Sehorn had gathered his crew and offered to find a replacement for anyone who felt uncomfortable working beyond the authorized limits. No hands went up. "Not one member of the crew," Sehorn recalled, "was ready to give up their opportunity to save these lives." On the flight deck, the thirty-nine-year-old aircraft commander settled into executing his flight plan.

To warm Marines who had lost skin cover, the cabin's temperature and humidity had both been raised. While that helped patients, it challenged caregivers. "You have heat and humidity," Deanna Cox recalled, "the smell of burn patients—and turbulence."

For members of the Army burn center team, all but the bouncing airframe was typical of a day's work. Such was not the case for the Air Force evacuation specialists. "They were so talented at taking care of patients in flight," Catherine Syby said, but most had not dealt with critical burn care. The burn team encouraged frequent checks of airway function and—explaining that patients' "blood vessels and everything else are now like a sieve"— offered quick tutorials on infusing sufficient fluids to ensure optimal urine output.

Thermal injury cases Air Force Staff Sergeant Lewis Pleasant had treated in years past paled when compared to the three patients he was assigned to monitor that Sunday afternoon. "The main one was totally burned," he recalled. "You couldn't tell if he was white, Black—you know, what his race was. All he was was just scabs. Just big, black scabs." Charcoal, he thought. Pleasant worried as he took the young man's blood pressure. "You didn't want to put the cuff too tightly on him." He tried hard to affect an encouraging outlook. "You can't get down," he said. Patients needed to be encouraged.

While the combined medical team monitored vital signs—and kept patients warm and well-coated with Silvadene—their most important job, to Michael Walters's mind, was preventing the injured from "sinking into shock from loss of body plasma."

Based on how much urine was passing through each patient, Roger Yurt explained, team members would "every hour readjust how much fluid you're giving them. . . . In addition, you're always trying to do all you can to treat the pain and we usually used intravenous morphine. But you have to be careful, because high doses of pain medication can cause patients to drop their blood pressure and go into shock, as well."

Early in the flight, nurse Deanna Cox found herself helping situate Lance Corporal Tom Breunig, one of the three Marines being monitored by her colleague Lewis Pleasant. "He had a trach[eotomy]," she recalled. "Because of the smoke [they had inhaled,] these patients had copious secretions, lots of suctioning was required. He was conscious, but I think he was not really lucid, or aware of all the things that were going on. But he wanted to hold my hands, a lot. When you're suctioning and taking care of a patient, it's always a challenge, because they are coughing a lot. At the time they didn't have built-in suction catheters to the tubes like they do now. So he was off the ventilator and I had been suctioning him. He coughed, and when it comes out of a trach it goes everywhere, and it got into my eye. And I was holding his hand and I had reached down to get it out of my eye."

It was at that instant that Technical Sergeant Curt Eddings snapped his shutter. The gifted Air Force photographer had been assigned by his combat camera squadron at Yokota to accompany the C-141 MEDEVAC. Discretely moving about the cabin, he documented the plight of the Marines in that moment and the lifesaving work being done by Soldiers and Airmen onboard. Within a week Eddings's image of Breunig and Cox would be published worldwide. Interpreted poignantly if not precisely—most assumed the nurse was wiping away tears—it seemed to encapsulate the grief resulting from what had happened at Camp Fuji. Within minutes of the image being captured, its significance would grow even more heartrending.

Cox moved on to other patients. Lewis Pleasant continued to tend to Breunig and his two other patients.

Some thirty minutes after the Starlifter's wheels had lifted at Yokota, Tom Breunig—who had celebrated his nineteenth birthday just thirteen days beforehand—succumbed to his injuries. It was around 6:30 p.m. Japan Standard Time; 4:30 in the morning in his hometown: St. Paul, Minnesota.

Rambunctious and rowdy, Breunig had played football at Brady High School in West St. Paul, but struggled in the classroom. He enjoyed working on cars and street-raced his blue Monte Carlo convertible. After briefly attending South St. Paul High School—and likely influenced by the example of his father, a state court judge who had done wartime service in the Navy—he and a good friend enlisted in the Marine Corps. The two young men had arrived at the Corps' San Diego recruit depot in the spring of 1979. "He really did come home a man," his sister Patty Thornton would recall decades later. "Physically, he looked different." His short hair contrasted sharply with previously flowing locks. She admired the badge on his uniform affirming his expertise with the M-16 rifle. The change, though, Thornton said, went beyond the visually apparent. "He also apologized to my parents. . . . He asked their forgiveness for all the sadness he caused them, or nervousness, for staying out." Around August or September, Breunig had reported to Okinawa and joined 2/4—seemingly unaware that a former girlfriend back home was pregnant with his child.

The weight of the loss, so early in their effort to *save* lives, could be seen on faces throughout the plane. "There was a lot of crying going on," Cox recalled, "even among the crew." A conscious effort was made to prevent news of Breunig's death from spreading. Awareness would raise the anxiety of his fellow Marines. It could also demoralize caregivers. "There were so many others who needed us at the time," Cox noted, "and the entire flight was such a challenge, so we just—we kept going."

In the cockpit Jim Sehorn logged Breunig's death in Greenwich Mean Time, as well as "place of death" in latitude and longitude. He continued on, "hoping and praying that we would lose no more."

Sehorn had not always flown cargo aircraft. At twenty-seven the Forest Grove, Oregon, native had been piloting fighter missions over North Vietnam. On December 14, 1967, enemy fire disabled an F-105 Thunderchief he was flying. Forced to eject from the aircraft, he fell into enemy hands and more than five years of brutal captivity as a prisoner of war. Finally freed at age thirty-two, his bearing during 1,917 days of imprisonment in Hanoi had earned him a Silver Star Medal. Six months after reuniting with his family, he had thrown himself back into his work, transitioning from flying fighters to piloting C-141s.

At the Yokota hospital, a few minutes before 7 p.m., the stress of loss was catching up with Terrence Stokes, set soon to escort home the remains of L. C. Malveaux. Colonel Bruce Truesdale spent time encouraging the Marine who, a hospital log noted, was "getting nervous about his buddies dying."

By 7:30 p.m. twenty-one additional badly burned Marines determined fit to fly had been loaded into Air Evac Two. All had been declared "very seriously or seriously" injured. The jet would ascend fifteen minutes later.

Loading the aircraft had taken time, Roger Yurt recalled—a couple hours, perhaps. Given all that had to be accomplished before takeoff, though, the surgeon emphasized, "it was amazingly quick because of all the assistance that we were getting from the local people there." Yurt would be one of two physicians accompanying the second group and overseeing the combined team of Army and Air Force nurses and medics. He would be joined by Air Force Dr. Cesar Sarmiento.

On the Yokota tarmac, the Third Marine Division's Brigadier General Joe McMonagle and Sergeant Major Robert Cleary watched the second C-141 get smaller in the sky. Hustling back to the CT-39A Sabreliner that had on Saturday carried them up from Okinawa, they boarded for the flight back. On arrival that Sunday evening, they would brief their division commander, Major General Calhoun J. Killeen. First, though, the two would undertake a MEDEVAC of their own. Three less seriously injured individuals had also been shepherded into the executive jet. They would receive further treatment at Okinawa's Camp Kuwae. Taking off from Yokota at 7:50 p.m., the entire party would, quite soon that Sunday evening, be back on the Rock.

On the two C-141s now headed over the Pacific, many of the injured Marines were being kept in medically induced comas. Ventilators breathed for them. From time to time, patients would stir. Doctors and nurses at their side would have to determine whether a rise in blood pressure and increased pulse indicated movement into shock—or simply recognition of their plight.

"You could hear the engines and everything," Frank Huerta recalled. "You could feel the bounce." The dreamy drone of jet engines blended with snippets of conversation, even occasional laughter. Floating voices were speaking English, some with discernible Southern accents. In Huerta's case burns on his neck kept him from looking around. His mind drifted back into murky shadows.

Arising cognizance in some induced claustrophobia. "Of course, you're on your back, on a stretcher," Glenn Roberts recalled. "You can't move. There's no way to get comfortable."

For others waking brought horror. "Clearly," Roger Yurt observed, "there were times when these patients would wake up and sense, and really feel, the dire straits that they were in."

On Air Evac One—heavily bandaged and enclosed in an insulated "space bag" to keep him warm—Mark Bedwell felt encased in "almost a hellish nightmare. . . . I've got a catheter, and I've got a tracheotomy, and I've got an IV. I mean, I just remember tubes running in and out of my body. And I'm in this cocoon. I'd reach up, like, 'How do I get out of this cocoon?' And my hands were so sore. I couldn't touch anything, it hurt. And so I just would have to stay in like almost a fetal position, and stretch out."

Issac Williams's airborne fever dream involved his being trapped inside a body bag, on his way home to Louisiana. Rising from his body, he engaged in a conversation with Jesus. Floating back into his earthly self, he began tapping from inside the body bag. "And a dude came by," he recalled, "and said, 'Someone's alive in this bag.'" Steve Neal, whose morphine-induced sleep obscured most every other aspect of the evacuation flight, did remember "fighting somebody that's trying to shove something down my throat."

Every one of the Marines, on awakening, craved liquid. Glenn Roberts heard others begging for water, even as the nurse looking after him told him it wasn't possible. "'We cannot risk you guys vomiting,'" he remembered her explaining, "because fluid was so precious." He was allowed to suck on a damp washcloth.

Jon Jurgen recalled, the couple times he awoke during the flight, being allowed bits of ice. Mike Cummings was parsed ice chips by a nurse who seemed never to leave his side. "Every time I come back around, she was right there. I don't remember which one she was. I wish I knew."

Somewhere in the middle of the Pacific, Jim Sehorn had handed over command on the flight deck, and laid down for a couple hours' sleep. He woke refreshed, in good spirits until he asked the flight engineer for an updated estimate on how far the Starlifter could fly with remaining fuel. "The response," he frowned, "was not what I would have hoped for." Had the pilot who relieved him not observed the "max range" flight plan? Had turbulence interfered? Whatever the case, it became apparent that the C-141 would need to refuel somewhere before continuing on to Texas. Sehorn worried. One of his passengers had already died. Additional delay added risk of more fatality. Refueling, even if not to the tank's full capacity, would take time. The major diverted the Starlifter to Travis Air Force Base in Northern California's Sacramento valley.

Ten miles from Travis, anxiety escalated further still. With Captain Hartikka at the controls, and the aircraft descending, control panel sensors began warning of overheating in the third of the C-141's four engines. Sehorn and his crew worked their way through a malfunction response checklist. In the end they shut down Engine Three. The plane's weight—comparatively light, carrying people, not tons of cargo, and with depleted fuel tanks—helped Hartikka land the craft safely.

Would the engine complication, Jim Sehorn worried, force the plane to be grounded for maintenance? If so his passengers' risk would be ratcheted by another order of magnitude. It would take countless hours to move everyone to another aircraft. Could patients clinging to life survive such a forced transfer?

As the plane taxied toward the terminal on its three remaining engines, Sehorn noticed that the same engine overheat light flashed on, then off, each time the plane crossed a seam or bump in the runway. Almost certainly a short in the sensor, he surmised. As soon as the Starlifter was shut down and chocked, the aircraft commander dropped the cowls encasing Engine Three. He dispatched one of the airmen from his crew to inspect the engine closely. Nothing indicated overheating. To Sehorn's mind the problem should not inhibit completing the mission. That decision, though, would not be his alone. And it would not be the only concern added because of the stop.

International protocols required formal declaration of the death on board. Sehorn considered what could result from reporting Tom Breunig's passing: more delay as a medical examiner was called to investigate. Conferring with Dr. Walters, he decided to hold off on reporting Breunig's death until the aircraft reached San Antonio.

Because the crew of Air Evac One had radioed ahead, ground crews at Travis understood the critical nature of their mission. With extra Airmen and intense motivation, they set about fueling the C-141 and cleaning its exterior.

During a routine stop—because of the fire risk associated with fueling—all electrical systems on the plane would have been shut down, and passengers required to disembark. "We could not do that," Lewis Pleasant recalled, "only the people who were ambulatory. The serious patients stayed on, and I remember staying on the plane with them. . . . The patients who were on respirators had to stay on the plane. You had to keep the respirators on electricity."

Given that the flight was arriving from abroad, U.S. customs agents made their way toward the plane. As was their routine, they intended to inspect for contraband potentially contained in baggage, or stashed in the C-141's myriad nooks and crannies. They had not anticipated the sights and smells they encountered. Plans to scrutinize the space fell away. "I remember them going up the front opening to the aircraft," Michael Walters recalled. "Their faces blanched. They left."

The only upside to having landed before completing the mission was that it allowed restocking of fast-diminishing medical supplies. The Marines' dire condition had required use of so much oxygen and IV-delivered fluid that supplies on board had been running low. Additional Silvadene and bandages could also be immediately helpful. Medical supply specialists at Travis speeded it on board, along with other materials team members wished they had packed more of—including nebulizers and Y-tube connectors. "They really were rushing," recalled Captain Dolly Velasquez, medical coordinator of the 9th AES team.

As refueling continued Jim Sehorn made his way to the airfield command post. His goal: to as quickly as possible file a flight plan to San Antonio—and obtain the one-time waiver he would need to put off examining the intermittently flashing "overheating engine" indicator.

When the duty officer overseeing flight operations balked at his entreaty, the conversation became heated. Doing his best to explain the life-or-death gravity of the mission, Sehorn pledged to assign a crew member to keep constant watch on Engine Three; should any sign of overheating appear, he swore, he would shut it down and continue to Kelly Air Force Base using the three remaining engines only.

The duty officer's response: "I'm not in a pay grade to make that decision."

Feeling at that moment personally responsible for sixteen lives hanging in the balance, Sehorn lost his composure.

"You may not be in a pay grade to make that decision," he yelled, "but *I am*, and I'll be airborne within the next hour with or without your [expletive] waiver."

The pilot stormed away from the command post to get a weather update necessary for planning the remainder of the flight. While waiting for the meteorologists' report, he felt a tap on his shoulder. "I turned around," he recalled, "and was eyeball to eyeball with a full bird colonel. He said, 'I overheard your conversation with the duty officer.'" Now Sehorn second-guessed his outburst. Had it compromised his accomplishing the mission? Perhaps done in his career? "'You get your weather brief and get ready for departure,' the colonel instructed. 'I'll bring your [expletive] waiver to you myself.'"

Sehorn grabbed the weather data and ran back toward his plane. Far earlier than he had expected, it was ready to go. The Travis ground crew had fueled, cleaned and resupplied the C-141 in one hour, ten minutes. Sehorn situated himself on the flight deck. He would pilot the remainder of the journey. As he and his crew began running through preflight checklists, he again felt a tap on his shoulder. Again it was the colonel. "He handed me the waiver," Sehorn recalled, "and with a smile said, 'Have a good flight.' I thanked him, cranked the Starlifter, and headed for Kelly." In the cabin Mark Bedwell heard the astounded reaction to the speed of the refueling operation. "You could hear 'em all bragging," he recalled. "And we were back, those jet engines going again." When the second of the two C-141s would stop at Travis, a bit less than two hours later, it would be fueled, resupplied, and sent on its way in one hour, thirty minutes.

By the time each of the Starlifters embarked on the last, continental U.S. segment of the flight to San Antonio, everyone onboard was tiring. Some two and a half hours remained before their arrival at Kelly Air Force Base. Catherine Syby remembered "the ride from California to San Antonio as being very bumpy."

"Patients were getting very restless," Deana Cox recalled. "Not the ventilator patients, they were mostly sedated—but the ones who were in the back end on the litter stanchions. The closer we got, I think the harder it got for them. If you've ever laid on a litter for any period of time, it is not very comfortable."

Along the way a special routing dispensation allowed both aircraft to complete the trip more quickly. The Federal Aviation Administration, having received word of the Marines' plight, allowed the two C-141s to fly through usually restricted air space—directly over the Grand Canyon.

At 5:30 p.m., Central Daylight Time, after an approximately thirteen-hour, thirty-minute flight, Starlifter 40619 landed at Kelly Air Force Base. Heavily bandaged from head to toe, Mark Bedwell weakly lifted his head and asked: "Are we here? Are we in Texas? That's my home, you know." Finally weaned from his anesthetic coma, Steve Neal heard how he had apparently struggled during insertion of an airway tube. "They said, 'Yeah, you put up a good fight.'"

The landing, Jim Sehorn would recall decades later, "ended what was, and is, for me one of the two most memorable flights that I've ever had in an aircraft." Neither, noted the by-then-retired brigadier general, involved dropping bombs or firing airborne weapons. Both had been on C-141s. The first occurred March 14, 1973, when Sehorn and other U.S. prisoners of war were evacuated from Hanoi to a U.S. air base in the Philippines; the second entailed his transporting seventeen burn-injured Marines from Yokota to San Antonio.

Soon after taxiing into place, the aircraft was surrounded by ambulances. Groups of journalists were on the flight line, as well; word of the Marines' arrival had spread. Also on the tarmac: several Fort Sam Houston-based UH-1 helicopters—engines turned up, rotors spinning.

With the Starlifter's engines now shut down, the helicopters' distinctive clamor blared into the cabin through the jet's rear petal doors. The sound shook some patients from their morphine slumber. Deanna Cox and others had worried that the din would trigger post-traumatic stress, "with the patients remembering the night on Mount Fuji when the choppers took them out of the fire." Some patients began screaming, she said.

Army corpsmen stepped off the tarmac into the plane and began off-loading the burned Marines. Those on litters could be moved fairly quickly; it took longer to extricate patients on ventilators. Disembarking the critically injured Marines struck a tired Catherine Syby as a "kind of chaos." In less than an hour, though, all sixteen living patients onboard Air Evac One—and the remains of Tom Breunig—were moved off the C-141.

On the Kelly Air Force Base tarmac, Dr. William McManus praised those who had brought the Marines from Japan. For many of the injured, he contended "the airlift will mean the difference between life and death." Army Specialist 6 Richard Hodge, one of the ISR corpsman who cared for patients in flight, deflected praise to military colleagues in Japan. "Our work was easy compared to what they had to do over there," he maintained.

Six of the most critically injured were carried to awaiting Army helicopters. One patient on each, they were airlifted the six or eight miles to Fort Sam Houston. Doctor Walters flew with one of the first. Ten patients were carried or walked off Air Evac One, then placed into ambulance buses. Soldiers lifted Tom Breunig's body onto a bus, as well. A police escort preceded the vehicles as they made their way through city streets from one base to the other. "We were going through San Antonio," Jon Jurgen recalled, "and I tried to sit up to see outside." Little was discernible; in addition to charring his skin, he realized, the fire had harmed his eyes.

Shortly after 6 p.m. the first of the helicopters carrying burn-injured Marines touched down on the parade field fronting Brooke Army Medical Center. Reporters witnessed "waiting attendants rush the victims, strapped into litters and covered with gauze and antiseptic foam, into ambulances for the block-long trip to BAMC."

By 6:40 p.m. the first ambulance bus had arrived at the medical center's rear entrance. Many onboard were conscious, Cecil Clift and Wade Roberts would write on the front page of the *San Antonio Express*. Though "their partially bandaged faces contorted in pain," the reporters observed, the Marines "made little noise."

At 7:35 p.m. the second Starlifter landed at Kelly Air Force Base. It had taken Air Evac Two a bit longer than nine hours to get from Yokota to Travis. After its rapid refueling stop, it had also transited the Grand Canyon during a final, three-hour, twenty-minute flight from Northern California to San Antonio.

Fifty-seven hours after the U.S. Army Institute of Surgical Research had been notified of the incident in Japan, it had admitted the first of the fire-injured Marines to its burn wards.

"We got as many of them back alive as possible," Michael Walters avowed.

12

BROOKE

Severe burns are best treated in a specialized burn center because of the high risk of mortality.

—*Principles and Practice of Emergency Medicine, 1978*

The time in the hospital was strange and hard. I had so many surgeries, it was uncountable. Every day they would scrape me, and that was unbearable.

—*Lance Corporal Issac Williams, U.S. Marine Corps*

AMERICANS TUNING INTO the *CBS Evening News* on Monday, October 22, heard a somewhat clearer, if terse, update on the status of Marines injured at Camp Fuji. "Today it turns out that the tragedy was greater than at first reported," Walter Cronkite intoned. "The Army now says that, of thirty-seven badly burned Marines, nineteen have less than a fifty-fifty chance of survival."

The increasingly evident gravity of the situation weighed on the Marine Corps commandant. Early that morning he had sent a globally transmitted teletype message to all 185,000 U.S. Marines. Its subject line: *Service of Prayer for Camp Fuji Casualties.*

"The prayers of all members of our Navy/Marine Corps family," Robert Barrow wrote, "are earnestly solicited on behalf of the victims of the tragic fire which took place at Camp Fuji. . . . Some 71 persons including a Navy corpsman, a Japanese national and Marines from BLT 2/4 were injured during the fire which resulted from a fuel bladder rupture during typhoon conditions. Of that number, there have been 3 fatalities, and 39 Marines are seriously injured with 2nd and 3rd Degree burns.

"I believe the fraternity which binds our Navy/Marine Corps team together, when given expression," the general continued, "becomes a powerful spiritual force for the well being of all in a circumstance such as this." He encouraged commanders of Marine units around the globe to have their chaplains conduct prayer services for the men and women hurt at Camp Fuji.

Marines reading the message, particularly those who had trained at the camp, were taken aback. The scale of injury, in peacetime, was unexpected. Among those shocked was Colonel Warren Wiedhahn, recent commanding officer of the Fourth Marines. Weidhahn recalled "trying to remember where the fuel bladders were, and how that could have happened. But the main thing that we all talked about was the horror—the dead and wounded."

General Barrow had drafted and transmitted his message from California. "I was on the West Coast on a trip," he remembered during an interview in 1991. "Patty [his wife, Patricia Ann Barrow] was with me. A couple of aides." The general quickly directed an itinerary shift. "We go right now," he ordered. "Break off and go to San Antonio." His message had concluded with the announcement that, on Friday, October 26, he would visit the injured Marines at Brooke Army Medical Center.

In 1943 the Army had gathered a handful of medical scientists on New York's Staten Island. At the service's Halloran General Hospital, the Surgical Research Unit evaluated trauma treatments and how newly discovered antibiotics could save lives on global battlefields. Four years after the organization's inauguration, its modest staff—just twelve strong—was transferred to San Antonio, Texas.

On the north end of Fort Sam Houston, an Army post dating to the mid-1870s, the researchers were provided clinical space within Brooke General Hospital. While their headquarters and laboratories would be elsewhere on the base, they would treat patients in dedicated wards of the eight-story, 418-bed care center. Opened in 1937, the hospital edifice—numbered as the post's Building 1000—was architecturally impressive. Its walls were made of brick and cast stone, its flooring constructed of tile and terrazzo. Aspirational Latin was etched above its ornate entryway: *Non Sibi Sed Proximo* and *Salutem Hominibus Dando*—translated as *Not for Himself, but for His Neighbor* and *Giving Health to Their Fellow Men.*

In San Antonio, the unit's staff grew. Its mission expanded to include improving treatment of burn injuries.

In the summer of 1968, the organization's rise to prominence began with the arrival of a new commander. Within a year of taking charge, Colonel (Dr.) Basil Pruitt had refashioned the SRU into the U.S. Army Institute of Surgical Research. He took advantage of a program that allowed some physicians to defer then-obligatory military conscription until they had completed residencies. Developing relationships with directors of the nation's top medical schools, Pruitt identified the most promising young surgeons. He then ensured that a significant number, postresidency, would perform their two years of mandatory service at the ISR. Rotating surgeons between clinical practice and research, he expanded the number of studies undertaken by the Institute, and ensured they were widely published.

To yield useful findings, the ISR would need to treat and study a great many burn patients. Mishaps in military settings would provide some. Typically, though—and fortunately—the number of such patients available each year was relatively small. To increase its patient pool, arrangements were made for the institute to accept military veterans and their family members—then people with no military connection. Many of the latter were individuals lacking wealth. "Burn units around the country really didn't want to keep them," noted Sandra Nee, an ISR nurse during the 1970s, "because it's expensive care and they would have to foot the bill." Whenever possible the institute collected reimbursement from civilian patients' insurance coverage. Ability to pay, though, would not preclude their admission. The rationale was both altruistic and practical. Every patient contributed to the ISR's ongoing studies.

From the genesis of the Army's burn research effort, its scientists assumed that early treatment was key to better treatment. In 1951, to ensure more rapid admission of critically burned patients, the Surgical Research Unit established partnerships with companion U.S. Air Force wings. Patient retrieval teams they created traveled to pick up the injured—most often within the continental United States. In 1977 an ISR team flew to the Canary Islands to retrieve fourteen people burned in an airliner crash there.

By the time the Camp Fuji Marines arrived, the ISR's exhaustive and prolific burn treatment studies had placed it at the forefront of international scientific inquiry into such injury. No organization in the world was conducting or sharing more research regarding the specialized area of medical care. With each study generated, best-care practices were refined.

Most of the 250 to 400 patients admitted annually arrived individually or in small groups. Never before in the institute's history had numbers of casualties anywhere close to those from Camp Fuji been simultaneously transported and admitted. Indeed, affirmed Basil Pruitt, the Marines constituted "the largest number of acutely burned patients that has ever been moved that quickly anywhere in the world."

Such an influx would inevitably be complex. Adding degrees of difficulty: just days before, burn center beds had already been mostly filled.

On the day the Marines were injured, the ISR occupied two wards in Brooke General Hospital: 14A and 13B. The first numeral of each ward number indicated that it was placed within the principal building of Brooke Army Medical Center; the second signified its floor placement.

Ward 14A—in Building 1000, on the fourth floor—was where treatment was provided to the most critically-injured. It included an enclosed sixteen-bed intensive care unit called "the cube," and an open area containing twenty-some beds. "The back of 14A was a large clinical research area," Dr. Cleon Goodwin recalled, "with a lot of instrumentation and this and that." Just beyond was the "tank room" containing large stainless steel tubs called Hubbard tanks. Patients were washed in those tubs, their burns firmly scrubbed. Ward 13B, one floor down, was where patients were moved when their stabilized conditions allowed ongoing skin-grafting surgeries and physical therapy.

Even before the ISR team departed for Japan, the BAMC commander—Brigadier General (Dr.) Andre J. Ognibene—ordered several hospital departments to cede additional space. The ISR would expand into Wards 14B and 13A. That required moving scores of individuals currently under treatment.

"They didn't want the patients coming from Japan to be intermingled with the patients we already had," burn center nurse Sandra Nee recalled. The Marines, fresh from foreign soil, might carry dangerous organisms against which other vulnerable patients mustered no immunity. Because some being treated on Ward 14A required intensive care, ISR chief nurse Jean Truscott recalled, "we needed two ICUs immediately."

Unbeckoned, and on the cusp of a weekend, Fort Sam Houston maintenance engineers—electricians, plumbers, carpenters—appeared at the lieutenant colonel's door. "I couldn't have felt more supported," Truscott remembered. "Not to have to call anybody and ask, but have people just show up. . . . All I had to do was say, 'We need this,' and it was done. People wanted to help."

Working day and night throughout the weekend, construction crews expanded the burn care space. Wards 14A and 14B were cleared of patients. Those receiving intensive care for burns were moved into a cube newly fashioned on Ward 13A. Research equipment in the rear of 14A was pushed aside; more beds were added. "They did like a terminal cleaning," recalled Ron Hilliard, a BAMC nurse who augmented the ISR staff. "We completely restocked and got prepared to start receiving the Marines."

When the Marines had been triaged on arrival, "all the critical ones went to the [14]A side," Nee remembered. "The less critical went to the 14B side." Nurses and corpsmen began removing patients' bandages, cleaning their wounds, and intubating any who still required the procedure. Each Marine was weighed. Photos were taken to document the state of their injuries.

Caring for the Marines would require many of the institute's 15 Army surgeons. Most of its 17 full-time registered nurses would be caught up in the effort, as well. So would the ISR's 30 enlisted corpsmen, all of whom were qualified as licensed practical nurses. Ezequiel Cortez, the Army sergeant whose job it was to keep an ISR-dedicated operating room constantly ready for burn care operations, remembered vacation plans being tossed aside: "All leave cancelled." An additional 53 Army nurses would eventually join the effort. The augmentation swelled the burn center staff by one-third, to 150.

Everyone involved in clinical care would work twelve-hour shifts, six days a week. Many put in longer hours. Corpsman Maurice Jenkins recalled being "home [only] long enough to eat, sleep and go back." The twenty-six-year-old Soldier's ISR assignment had begun just three months before the daunting arrival of so many casualties. He closed his eyes in a moment of focus at the beginning of each shift. "Please," he prayed, "don't let me be the cause of anyone dying."

In 1979 two rules of thumb floated constantly in the consciousness of health care workers treating burn patients. The first was called a Baux score. It calculated the likelihood patients would die from thermal injury. A patient's Baux score was determined by adding the individual's age to the percentage of body surface that had been burned. Twenty-year-olds who suffered 50 percent burns, for instance, faced a 70 percent mortality risk. The second rule suggested that patients would require one day of hospitalization for every single percentage of scorched body surface.

As Walter Cronkite had reported, ISR specialists' Baux score calculations had not yielded an optimistic tally. Of the nineteen Marines in critical condition, four had suffered greater than 81 percent total body surface burns. Another seven, more than 60 percent. The condition of seven other Marines was listed as serious; eleven were said to be satisfactory.

Finally ensconced in an expertly staffed hospital setting, the Marines' survival odds had improved. The functioning of most every organ inside their bodies, though, was under immense stress because of the damage suffered by their bodies' largest organ—the one wrapping their exterior. The burn center's iconoclastic director was blunt: "We anticipate more deaths."

Early on sixteen of the thirty-seven Marines were provided intensive care in the cube on Ward 14A. "You did not know how bad you were," Glenn Roberts remembered. "They told you, 'Your arms are burned. Some of your back. Ears. Feet.' In fact, I think it was my right foot was burned like almost down to the bone. Of course, the beauty of a third degree—you can't feel it."

Outside the hospital temperatures hovered near 90 degrees Fahrenheit. Inside ISR wards room temperature rarely dipped below 80. Reflective curtains around each bed helped contain the torridity around bodies left without natural casing. Warming mattresses and bedside heat lamps kept patients' temperatures between 99 and 101.9. "This prevents calories from being wasted by shivering," a visitor handbook explained. The warmth sapped medical teams. "You felt good if you only had one heat lamp" at a bedside, Maurice Jenkins said. There could be two or three. "It gets to the point sometimes," Jenkins remembered, "that you actually have to change scrubs, because they're soaking wet." Hydration became important not just for patients, but for the medical staff, as well.

Lighting was kept intentionally dim to reduce patients' stimulation. Given their pain any sleep the Marines might luck into was fitful. Frequent interruptions by corpsmen and nurses providing care further interrupted prolonged rest.

In the 14A cube, a corpsman was assigned to each Marine. A registered nurse would track one or two patients, depending on their health status. A surgeon was always on hand. The work was nonstop. Fluids were replenished, urine output measured. At half-hour intervals corpsmen and nurses would suction the airways of patients on ventilators, checking for carbon in their sputum. Every hour or two, patients were turned; the seemingly simple task could take fifteen to twenty minutes.

Those Marines in the ICU space who could speak, did. They learned which of their fellow Marines were nearby. Issac Williams—severely burned and cinched tightly into a Stryker bed, Ron Hilliard remembered—"was always the positive one, giving these guys support, encouragement."

The greatest danger the Marines faced at that moment was infection, which research had shown became a particular risk seventy-two to ninety-six hours postburn. "You need to do everything you possibly can," Dr. Roger Yurt explained, "to keep any invasive organisms from getting into the body."

Key to the preventive effort were the antibiotic creams constantly smeared over the Marines' wounds as they lay unclothed in what doctors described as "open treatment." BAMC spokesperson Audrey Urbancyzk explained: "The patients are completely naked and covered with just the cream," Though gauze was still placed over some burn wounds, the practice of constant, heavy bandaging, she understood, had been abandoned because "bacteria can accumulate in them." A small cloth—"their fig leaf," one visiting Marine officer called it—covered their genitals. Steve Haishuk recalled that he and others able to walk the ward, "wore just a towel around our waist."

From the day they were injured, the Camp Fuji Marines had become familiar with Silvadene. At Brooke they encountered another, quite different, medicated ointment. While Silvadene exemplified the definition of a salve—it smoothed, mollified, and relieved—the second ointment did not. "It should be noted," a medical text of the time cautioned, "that Sulfamylon causes pain on application."

While both topical agents fought infection, Silvadene's effectiveness remained primarily on the skin surface. Sulfamylon could penetrate thick-as-leather eschar—battling infectious agents below and softening the hard tissue.

"I remember it was in a little white round tube," Mike Cummings said. "When you put it on, it was like they was sticking you with a hot poker." He would ask for pain medication before it was applied. "Oh! It hurt like for half an hour, like unbelievable," Jon Jurgen declared. "You'd just sit there and moan."

Twice daily ISR nurses and corpsmen would remove gauze dressings that lay over not skin, but deeper tissue with exposed nerve endings. Sulfamylon was applied after the day's first change. Usually it was rubbed on as a cream. Sometimes a powdered form would be diluted in sterile water; gauze dressings would be soaked in the milky chemotherapeutic, then affixed over wounds. "At least for the evening," Glenn Roberts remembered, "you got a little relief—they used to put on Silvadene, which I always likened to Noxema. . . . Then you got the morphine. I mean, this was every frickin' day, I forget for how long."

The major effort to remove patients' dead skin tissue occurred in an operating room. Excising the hard-cooked eschar, in which no fatty tissue remained, was a fundamental first step in facilitating a burn patient's recovery. Until all such debridement was completed, surgeons could not begin grafting skin to permanently heal in place over the Marines' wounds.

The work was different from other types of surgery. "In any standard operating room," ISR surgical nurse David Berry explained, "the patient comes in, hopefully you fix what's wrong with them, they go out and you never see them again. In the burn unit, they come back. Depending on how acute their burns are, they come back many times over a period of months."

The debridements—surgical removal of burned skin—were intricate and bloody. Hard charred tissue was excised to the greatest extent possible at that moment in the patient's healing. While harsh the cutting away was far from indiscriminate. "We were fanatical about protecting the good skin," Berry emphasized. Later, a thin layer of skin surgically harvested from nonburned areas would be needed to graft over each patient's own wounds.

Initially, the increasingly uncovered wounds—until they could withstand further debridement—would be cloaked with gauze. As healing continued surgeons would begin overlaying other materials.

Some of the temporary coverings applied were synthetic, infused with honey ointments or impregnated with antiseptic silver. Others were such "biological dressings" as sterile pigskin or human skin harvested from deceased donors. A sizable stock of the latter was shipped to San Antonio from the Navy Tissue Bank in Bethesda, Maryland. There surgically trained corpsmen routinely retrieved transplantable skin from cadavers. The skin had been freeze dried, a process the Navy had pioneered. That allowed it to be stored and transported at room temperature. Its collagen and scaffolding made it an effective natural bandage. All that was necessary before its surgical application was to soak the freeze-dried skin for thirty minutes in sterile saline. "You literally add water," Basil Pruitt explained to reporters, displaying a rolled sheet of the stretchable biologic material in a small glass tube. "It's kind of like instant skin." The delivery to San Antonio, recalled Commander Michael Strong, the Bethesda tissue bank director, "used up our entire inventory." The temporary dressings helped patients retain heat and curb fluid loss. They would be replaced five to thirty days after application—before provoking immune system rejection in patients' bodies, or beginning to fuse with healthy tissue.

Patients undergoing surgery in the ISR operating room were provided anesthesia unlike that used for most patients in surgery. Ketamine, a hallucinogen, was the agent of choice. Under its influence, ISR surgeon Hani Mansour maintained, patients "were still breathing on their own, but not in pain." They did not need to be intubated, they could react to instructions during a procedure, and they could be returned to wards after surgery without layover in a recovery room. Calibrating ketamine levels was both science and art. "Sometimes [patients] would start getting light," surgical nurse David Berry remembered, "and we'd know it right away because they'd start screaming because they *would* feel it. That always gave me a case of the horrors. 'What are they going to remember?'" On the whole the Marines' hallucinogenic experiences seemed "good trips." One Marine told Berry that the drug had caused him to be "fixated on the lights, and he was part of the lights."

Frequently, Dr. Anton Jirka would be at the head of the operating table monitoring the patient's breathing and administering the hallucinogen. Dr. Mansour regarded the career Army physician "a genius in anesthesia," and remembered Jirka frequently showing up without prompting when a seriously injured patient arrived at the BAMC ambulance entrance. If the receiving surgeon perceived an immediate need to operate, Jirka was ready.

Operating room schedules were fluid. Urgent procedures moved front of line when infections took hold. About a week after the Marines' arrival, surgeons amputated one of Lance Corporal Willie Davis Jr.'s arms. Germs had penetrated burns on the limb; their spread could prove fatal. Chunks of tissue were cut from other Marines for similar reasons.

On Wards 14A and 14B, daily care began each morning with the cleaning of patient's teeth and mouths. The young men would then be weighed. Morphine or Percocet was administered. Those who could get out of bed were then taken to shower stalls to be washed—or to the tank room at the rear of Ward 14A.

Mark Bedwell remembered the two warm-water Hubbard tanks as being "about two feet deep, in the shape of a large cross. . . . You're spread out like Jesus." A lifting device was used to lower patients into the tubs. The maneuvering was not easy for those on ventilators and bearing intrusive IV tubing and catheters. Sunlamps would be pulled close to try to keep patients warm.

While skin impacted by third-degree burns had been completely consumed, tissue burned to the second degree remained living, if raw, flesh. It leaked a protein-rich blood serum. The gelatin-like film—attractive to deadly bacteria—adhered to the Marines' wounds, hardening into a dense, waxy crust. In the tanks nurses and corpsmen had to pull, cut, and scrub the scabs away.

Patients were administered painkillers before each tank session. "They would give you whatever the maximum [safe] dose of morphine was at the time," Glenn Roberts recalled. "Pffft. Didn't matter. Oh my God, didn't matter. A lot of times, you'd go in there, two of them would hold the arm down, pour the Hibiclens"—an antiseptic Roberts thought looked like red dish soap. Abrasive washcloths would be used to scrub away the protein scabs. "They'd take that towel, and—you couldn't be gentle about it." The removed substance—"a sickening green and yellow," he recalled, "had to come off every day." The process was messy; at times blood weeped into the tub water. "You felt," Roberts cringed, "like you were being skinned alive."

"A lot of them would buck on the ventilator," then-corpsman Robert Marchi recalled.

Water from hoses in the tanks flushed away the grisly runoff. Tanks were drained, sterilized, and made ready for the next patient in queue.

The obvious misery borne by those undergoing daily scrubbing wore on those whose job it was to carry out the ultimately beneficial procedures. "The nurses," Issac Williams remembered, "were scared to touch me. They knew they was hurting people when they took them to that tub." Glenn Roberts recalled an older medical staff member decamping to a nurses' station after assisting with such a session. "You could hear him sob in the next room."

Nurses watched, impressed, as Marines would walk as far as they could alongside buddies headed to the tank room. "Until you see it, and experience it firsthand," Ron Hilliard said, "you don't really understand what that Marine esprit de corps is all about."

After Issac Williams found his first tank sessions unbearable, he racked his brain. How could he divert his attention from the scrubbing and cutting? As a child he had constantly serenaded his mother; music still brought him joy. In the ward spaces, shared with fellow patients in agony or trying to sleep, it was generally not allowed. "I just decided I needed a radio," he said. Williams's mother, Joan, brought him one. In the tank room, nurses tuned it to San Antonio hit music stations. "If I started singing first—before they started scraping me, before I knew it, they'd been scraping me, I'm still singing and it wasn't bothering me," he remembered. Irrespective of what song came on, he added loud vocals. In lyrical irony, hits airing frequently at the time included Michael Jackson's "Don't Stop 'Til You Get Enough" and Nick Lowe's "[You've Gotta Be] Cruel to Be Kind." Williams attested: "I started looking forward to going to the tub, you know, because I had the music."

The fortitude of the young man from Alexandria, Louisiana, astonished his fellow Marines. "For me, Issac was courage itself," affirmed Gust Miller, who spent three weeks alongside him in the cube. "He suffered worse than the rest of us," Mark Bedwell remembered, "but he did it with a dignity that—it was remarkable."

Williams's stamina was buoyed by a strong spiritual faith and the constant presence of a loving mother. He admitted, though, having "had the strength and the willpower to do certain things for myself." That seemingly included selecting his own surgeon. Soon after arriving in San Antonio, the lance corporal heard the doctor first assigned his case talking with someone else: "He made a comment that he didn't think I was going to make it." Williams did not share that view. Soon after, he encountered another, younger physician at the foot of his bed: Issac Williams met Isaac William Goldfarb. "It just so happened," Williams laughed, "his first two names the same as my name."

The two clicked.

"You know, I had a good interaction with my surgeon," Mark Bedwell remembered, "but the interaction with Dr. Goldfarb and Issac was a tremendously personal thing. There was something about saving Issac—nothing else mattered more to Dr. Goldfarb. In the middle of the night, here comes Dr. Goldfarb looking at Issac. In the morning. In the middle of the day, there's Dr. Goldfarb checking Issac."

Bill Goldfarb, thirty-three years old at the time, could not turn away from the Marine who displayed such determination. "Anywhere along the line," the surgeon said, "it would have been easy for him to quit, and die. But he would not quit."

Similarly close relationships developed between other patients who persevered and the surgeons assigned their care. Mark Bedwell and his family developed a friendship with Dr. Hector Benitez.

Surgeon Hani Mansour bonded with Steve Dye, and Steve's father, James. Even decades later Mansour could close his eyes and picture the location of Steve's bed in the cube: "He was next to the exit door on the right." The cutoff jeans Dye had been wearing when he rushed from his hut, the doctor remembered, had prevented burns "from the waist to the upper third of the thighs." The rest of his body, however—82 percent was the estimate—had been scorched. "I kept him very sedated," related the doctor who had treated combat burn casualties in his native Lebanon before migrating and being commissioned into the U.S. Army. The procedure was the thirty-two-year-old's norm. "It was always my fear that the patient would be in pain." Over time Dye's treatment would involve a good deal of skin grafting. "I operated on him maybe six, seven times," Mansour recalled. For months and months, the Marine's survival was not a foregone conclusion. "He fought very hard," Mansour said.

In some respects, the young men of BLT 2/4 and LSU 3/9 differed from most burn patients. Roger Yurt recalled seeing first evidence of that soon after their admission. He watched as two young men, burns over 80 percent of their bodies, climbed out of their ICU beds and began to exercise. "They were doing push-ups," he remembered. "It was something I had just never seen and didn't think was possible. It made me really wonder whether people who are in extremely good shape, and take care of themselves and so forth, can survive these injuries and do so much more than the normal patients can."

He would learn, over the next several months, that the answer was sometimes yes, sometimes no. To a then-young surgeon, the latter instances were "sort of devastating," Yurt revealed—when "those Marines, even though they were really fighting the battle very strong, didn't survive their injuries."

Back in Japan Captain Salvatore De Vincenzo had spent nearly five days caring for Corporal Colin Miller and Lance Corporal Robert Vinson Smith Jr. The Marines had been moved into the Yokota hospital's rarely used critical care suite.

"I had two patients," Dr. De Vincenzo recalled, "one twenty-one and one nineteen. They were left because someone made a decision that they would not survive. But I did not have any direction as to what to do." Chief Nurse Rita Gengler recalled staffing the suite with "one nurse and one corpsman around the clock, minimum. And then the doctor didn't much go home."

The Fourth Marines commanding officer and sergeant major visited the sealed-off area containing Miller's and Smith's side-by-side beds. "We had to wear these white suits—masks, gloves, and everything," Sergeant Major Valdemar Vasquez recalled, "just to go to the room next to it." Looking through a window, he said, "I could see their hair and their faces, but that's all I could see. The rest of them must have been covered up." Dr. De Vincenzo and a scrum of nurses and technicians actively tended to the two, Vasquez remembered decades later. "It looked to me," he said, his voice choked, “that they were making their best effort to try to bring them back to life.” As a company gunnery sergeant and acting company commander during combat in Vietnam, Vasquez had dealt with a good deal of close-at-hand injury and death. To his mind, “it would have been kinder to just let them die.”

De Vincenzo understood the sentiment. “The word ‘alive’ obviously has a lot of meaning in this situation,” he conceded. With arrangements being made for Miller’s and Smith’s families to fly to Japan, though, the physician wanted relatives to “see them while they were still alive.”

“We all knew these men were perilously near death,” Rita Gengler remembered. De Vincenzo’s attitude, though, she confirmed, was, “We will not give up.” To keep Miller and Smith as comfortable as possible, the doctor ordered alternating doses of morphine and valium. The first blocked pain, the second offered anxiety-reducing sedation.

In the event Colin Miller’s injuries would preclude the sort of reunion for which De Vincenzo had hoped. At 4:30 p.m. on Wednesday, October 24, the twenty-one-year-old corporal died from impacts of the second and third degree burns covering more than 85 percent of his surface skin.

Five hours later, inside a small apartment in Oakland, California, Orwin Miller and his sister Bridgette Miller were up and dressed. Marines had arranged for the two to fly to Japan to be with their brother. By now everyone in their family except Enid Miller, Colin’s mother, knew what was happening. Concerned that hearing of her son’s injury could prompt a heart attack, they had shielded her from the bad news. The Marines had said they would be there at 6 a.m. By 7:30 there was still no indication of their arrival. Orwin stepped downstairs, leaving the house at the time he typically departed for work. Bridgette discreetly followed. On the sidewalk, Orwin remembered, they were met by four or five “larger-than-life figures, some in white, green, and so forth. . . . I thought I was leaving with them. And then they pulled me aside, and said, ‘I’m sorry. Your brother didn’t make it . . .’” The sounds of multiple bodies entering the apartment alarmed Enid Miller. “Orwin! Orwin!,” she called out from her bed. “What happened?” Besides a chaplain, the Marine casualty assistance officer had also brought along a Navy corpsman. “I had the medic walk ahead of me,” Orwin Miller recalled. “The minute she saw them, she started screaming. By that time, there was not a dry eye in the house. If I remember correctly, they tried to console her. I was outside. It was a small room. She's hollering and crying. I feel helpless as a son."

The six Miller children had been born in Guyana. Orwin, about three years older than Colin, remembered his brother as serious: "He didn't party and do a lot of things." In 1969 Enid Miller visited the United States on a single-year visa and applied for residency. After returning to Guyana for a year, she emigrated to the United States and filed immigration petitions on behalf of her children. As the children awaited approval, they imagined opportunities in a new country. Chief among them, Orwin recalled, was buying their mother a house. "We wanted to make sure she was happy. Because she had a lot of stress, raising us kids." In August 1974—when Colin was sixteen—the children had been able to join their mother in New York City. After a couple of years, concerned about his family's safety in the Bedford-Stuyvesant neighborhood, Colin decided to join the Marines. His rationale, Orwin remembered, echoed their long-held aspiration: "We can help buy a house and get out of here." Military service would eventually make Colin eligible for a veterans home loan. After an assignment in North Carolina, then Christmas 1978 at home with his family in New York, he had reported for duty on Okinawa. While there he had taken advantage of deals available to military people serving overseas—buying high-end stereo components and shipping them to the northern California apartment Orwin had secured, and to which they had moved their mother. "I think she kind of blamed herself," Orwin remembered of Enid Miller, "because she felt he did it for her, and he lost his life in the process."

Already ordered to accompany L. C. Malveaux's body to the Marine's home in Beaumont, Texas, Terrence Stokes's escort mission was expanded to also oversee transport of Corporal Miller's remains to the West Coast. Caskets containing both his fellow Weapons Company Marines were stowed in the cargo hold of a Delta 747. Landing in Northern California, Stokes stood watch on the tarmac as the body-length metal cases were off-loaded. Colin Miller's casket was placed in a hearse. Someone else would escort the corporal's remains on for burial in New York.

Accompanying Malveaux's body onto another jetliner, Stokes flew to Beaumont, where he met the lance corporal's family. When he asked about affordable nearby lodging, they were firm. "No!" he remembered them insisting. "You ain't going to no hotel." The family would put him up. "I stayed at one of his relatives' house until the funeral." From Beaumont Stokes traveled home to St. Louis. During a week at his mother's place, he tried to relax both his mind and voice. Since escaping the fire, he had had difficulty speaking; it was all he could do to muster a husky whisper. "It took me like three months before my lungs was cleared," he remembered, "before I could talk again."

A handful of the injured Marines' family members had made their way to Fort Sam Houston even before their loved ones had themselves arrived. So had Lieutenant Colonel Gerald Reczek, the active-duty "Inspector-Instructor" in charge of the Marines' San Antonio reserve center. When Reczek returned to the hospital Monday morning at 6:30, he encountered Victor du Pont. "He had flown in on his own personal aircraft," Reczek remembered. Donning the same sort of gowns, masks, and sterile gloves worn by medical staff, the two stood beside Lance Corporal du Pont. The young Marine was "covered up in all the bandages, and muzzled." He did not seem responsive. Phil's mother, Joan, arrived soon after. Care in the cube struck her as impressive, though provided in cramped space: "There was hardly room to turn around from one bed to the next."

"I was able to talk to Philip," Joan Turner Moore, the former Joan du Pont, later recalled. "Knowing I don't drink, he said, 'Oh, Mom, go have a good beer for me.' He was—arms, face—tremendously burned. I knew he would be blind." Inexplicably, "there was a space over his heart which didn't burn. . . . I was able to touch him at that spot.

"I asked him if he was scared," she remembered, "and he said yes."

More family members arriving at "Fort Sam" made their way to Building 1000. Soon—like most everyone else on post—they were referring to the Brooke Army Medical Center site as "bam-see." In time their injured sons, brothers, husbands, and boyfriends would further trim descriptions of their location to simply "Brooke."

The relatives' arrival had taken Gerald Reczek somewhat aback. "I didn't really expect that families of the injured Marines would be coming down there," he recalled. "My understanding in the past had been, if you're a family member, you're notified by the Marine Corps that your son is injured, or a casualty, and you stay home." That would not be the case in this instance. Within hours caring for *them*, as well as their injured loved ones, would become Reczek's full-time job. A first goal was to see that Marines met every arriving family member—at the airport, if they traveled by air, or at the hospital, if they drove to San Antonio. As often as possible, he would greet them personally.

When Corrine Davis flew into the city to see her son, she remembered, "there was two Marines waiting at the airport and they carried me to the hospital there where he was." Nurses on Ward 14A helped Davis don gown, mask, and gloves, then ushered her to Willie Davis Jr.'s bed in the cube. "He wasn't in a good condition," she said. "He couldn't even talk to me."

Reczek's role was formalized on the evening of Monday, October 22. Brigadier General Bain McClintock—deputy commanding general of the Corps' recruit training center in San Diego—flew to San Antonio. Robert Barrow had assigned him to oversee the support effort. McClintock gathered senior-ranking Marines from the area. "We met in the recruiters' office," Gerald Reczek remembered. "The topic came up of who was going to take charge in San Antonio. And they looked at me and said, 'Do you think you can do it?' And I said, 'Yes. Yes, sir.'" For an extended period, the lieutenant colonel's assistant, a captain, would take up most duties related to training reservists in the area. With several members of his administrative staff, Reczek would focus full-time on seeing to it that the injured Marines and their families had what they needed. Area recruiters would help out as necessary.

The officer's wife stepped up, as well. In following months Lisa Reczek would invest hundreds upon hundreds of hours at the hospital helping the young men and their families. "They were there a lot," remembered Phyllis Stensgaard, president of a charitable organization that would also provide assistance. "Him and his wife, both. They were really terrific."

Driving family members from the airport—or greeting them at the hospital—Reczek would calmly but fully describe the physical harm their loved one had suffered. He encouraged them, when visiting, to show strength rather than despair. As they showed him photos of handsome young men, often their recruit training portraits in the dress blue uniform, he knew it would not be easy.

Jon Jurgen, after a time, had recognized Reczek. The two had crossed paths some years before. At Camp Pendleton, California, Jurgen had served in 3rd Battalion, Fifth Marines, a unit Reczek then commanded. "My first meeting with Lieutenant Colonel Reczek was battalion office hours," Jurgen recalled—"office hours" being the term used when Marines appeared before their commanding officers to be punished for minor offenses. Jurgen's infraction: "I got busted with weed." Reczek reduced him in rank from lance corporal to private first class. While Jurgen remembered the encounter, it seemed his former commanding officer did not. The Marine from Connecticut, whose subsequent performance had earned him corporal chevrons, did not push the point. "Never asked him," he said. "Never brought it up."

In short order, an exceptional effort was organized to make space for arriving families. Fort Sam Houston leaders arranged their easy access onto the gated post. If the visitors chose, they could check into an Army guest house: Davison Hall in Building 1002. It offered modest rooms and suites for between five and ten dollars daily. The lodging was just 350 anxious paces east of the hospital's front steps. "It was quite nice," Corrine Davis recalled. When a cousin who lived in Houston came to stay with her, they put the two up in one of the suites. "My mom and dad came down to be with us," Freida Neal remembered. "They stayed a couple weeks. And they gave them a room, too." Staying near one another allowed family members to share information and, frequently, offer each other support. Most of the visitors were extended temporary shopping privileges at a small nearby post exchange (PX)—and relatives of Marines deemed "seriously ill" or "very seriously ill" would be allowed to eat in the hospital's first-floor dining facility.

Accommodating the influx of visitors in and around the burn wards was an even greater challenge. The burn unit had no waiting area. That left patients' families hovering near elevators and the unit's front door, waiting to query staffers about their loved ones. General Ognibene set aside a significant portion of the medical facility's uppermost seventh floor as a site where families could congregate. Less than a decade before, it had been the facility's presidential suite. Former President Lyndon Johnson had been treated there. In subsequent years it had served as the BAMC commanding general's conference and entertaining venue. A small chapel on the floor afforded room for quiet reflection. ISR Chief Nurse Jean Truscott was more than pleased when a volunteer group, "the Marine Corps League Auxiliary from San Antonio showed up and said, 'We'll take this.'" They would organize the space into a site of solace and more.

The Marine Corps League veterans organization traced its roots to 1922. Principally made up of men who had served as Marines, the group in 1937 created an associated women's organization. Most in the "Auxiliary" were wives of league members. In San Antonio during the 1970s, Auxiliary member Carole Darlington had convinced her good friend Phyllis Stensgaard—mother of an active-duty Marine—to join in the group's efforts to aid the Corps community. Stensgaard had eventually become president of the Auxiliary associated with the league's "Alamo Detachment." Darlington served as its treasurer. To raise funds for their philanthropic projects, the Auxiliary sold fabric remnants donated by area department stores. Their business was brisk. Member Elaine Liddell recalled encountering lines "of over twenty people fighting to be checked out with their mountains of drapes." In October 1979 the nonprofit's bank balance sat at thirteen thousand dollars.

Immediately they began providing food and drink for families on the seventh floor. "I remember having cream of chicken soup," recalled Lori Corsaut, sister of injured Marine Mark Bedwell. "They would have rolls and doughnuts and cereal." Soon Auxiliary members made room in the lounge's kitchen for volunteers to set up a MARS radio station. The radio-transmitted telephone calls it offered saved family members then-expensive long-distance fees as they kept others informed of their Marine's recovery progress.

A dilemma arose when transportation costs prevented some families from rapidly traveling to San Antonio. In general, Gerald Reczek explained, "the Marine Corps doesn't pay for that." The Auxiliary began covering individuals' sometimes multiple round-trip flights. "The ones that drove in," Phyllis Stensgaard added, "we paid for their gas and everything."

The Auxiliary's transportation subsidies were more than simply kind, doctors and chaplains attested. They were potentially lifesaving. The bedside presence of encouraging loved ones would be essential to some Marines' survival. Family members' understanding could also help mitigate patients' periods of pain-induced self-pity and anger.

Over time, records indicate, most all of the Marines evacuated to Texas would be comforted by extended visits from loved ones. Not all, however.

"My dad never come to see me," Mike Cummings mulled. "I grew up in Texas, you know, four hours away. My mother came one day, and then went back home." Embarking on the complex, painful path of recovery would be particularly difficult for the handful unaccompanied.

As family aid efforts jelled, the positive impact on Marines and their families became clear. "There was always someone asking us, 'Is there anything that you need? What can we do?'" family member Carrie Beth Hogan remembered. Two young volunteers "very quietly" told Joan du Pont, "We can do anything. Get you a toothbrush, get your clothes washed. Whatever you want. We're here . . ."

"You can't believe the comfort that is," affirmed Robert Turner's mother Joan Pompey, "when all you can think about is your child."

At the guest house, Auxiliary members stocked food in common spaces near the families' block of rooms. Sometimes they cooked meals for them on site. When long stays began pushing lodging costs beyond a family's budget, the Auxiliary paid the tab.

The aid impressed ISR staffers and allowed them to focus on their patients' medical crises. "That was somewhat different than with other patients," Dr. Bill Goldfarb observed. "You really saw the Marine family concept kick in." Maurice Jenkins remembered Auxiliary members helping families "gown up" before visits. They would also make the food they brought into the hospital available to hard-working burn ward staffers. "If I remember correctly," Jean Truscott added, "they somehow got [families] beepers, as well"—allowing them to be more quickly contacted by medical teams.

When Antonia Perez Reyes arrived at the San Antonio airport, her son Frank Huerta professed, "they treated her like a queen. My sisters told me they picked her up in a limousine, took 'em to Brooke Army Medical Center. And then Colonel Reczek and his wife were really lovely to her." Huerta's mother had left the Los Angeles garment factory she owned to be at her son's bedside.

Jon Jurgen, his eyes bandaged, listened as his mother Joanne Jurgen stepped over to a nursing station. "She asked how I was," he remembered. "They said I had a fifty-fifty chance." Jurgen's parents would remain with their son for much of the time he was hospitalized. A twin sister would visit, as well. "Just them being there was good."

When Mark Bedwell heard his father's voice in the cube, communication efforts were inhibited by his bandaging, and the family's protective clothing and face masks. Mack Bedwell and his daughters, Carrie Beth Hogan and Lori Bedwell, had not immediately recognized the bloated young man in a bed before them—his head so large, unnaturally white, his arms both sliced open from shoulder to hand. "My dad said, 'Son, if you can hear me, wiggle your right toe,'" Bedwell remembered. "So I wiggled my right toe." Watching his son struggle to breathe was difficult for Mack Bedwell. He had to step into a hallway outside.

"Hmmm. I'm in ICU," Steve Neal remembered realizing just before his parents walked in and caught a first glimpse of their only child. He heard Freida Neal, in quiet desperation, call out to his father. "She goes, 'Oh, Lloyd.' So I took my oxygen mask off. 'Oh, Mom, I'm fine.' I wasn't fine, but I didn't want her to see that."

"My dad came down for a week," Glenn Roberts remembered, "then he had to go back. My mom stayed there until we actually went home" more than two months later.

Over time many family members would help each other, as well—in practical matters, sharing of medical information, and on occasion in grief. Carrie Beth Hogan saw her father's difficulty dealing with his son's injury abate when the family began "trying to help others around us. That seemed to soften the blow."

A small diary into which Issac Williams's mother chronicled events at the hospital evidenced the collegiality that developed among many family members. "She had this little notepad that she kept," the Marine veteran marveled decades later, flipping through its pages. The notations recorded far more than just what was happening with her own son. "I'm talking about people that I didn't even know were there," he said. "And the dudes that died, and those one's that went home—that were hurt with me."

At 5:38 a.m. on Thursday, October 25, a fifth Marine died of injuries sustained at Camp Fuji. Infectious parasites had breached the 69 percent of Philip Everett du Pont's skin ravaged in the fire. They were consuming the Marine's body—not the portion burned, his mother remembered, but healthy flesh. "It didn't seem fair," she said. Trying to stop the spread, doctors had been cutting away the tainted tissue. "Every day we go in there," Sam du Pont recalled his father Victor telling him, "they've taken another piece of him." Just the day prior, doctors had detected a fungus infection. Simultaneously weakened by severe inhalation injury, the Marine's body had surrendered.

Phil du Pont had grown up on a thousand-acre farm in Bluemont, Virginia—the second-born of eight children and scion of one of the nation's wealthiest families. "There was three farm hands, four hundred calving cows, or thereabouts," recalled the Marine's next younger brother Sam du Pont. "My mother would have had forty horses, four or five brood mares, twenty ponies." Phil began driving tractors at age eight. Adventurous in adolescence, Phil and Sam motorcycled together: "'Hey, man, let's go thirty-five miles an hour and see if we can touch handlebars!' On gravel roads," Sam du Pont remembered. "Stuff like that all the time."

Graduating in 1976 from the South Kent School, a prep school in Connecticut, where he had been a football standout, du Pont had worked for a year or two before enlisting and making his way to Parris Island, South Carolina. In BLT 2/4 the twenty-one-year-old had been hard to miss. "He was a tall guy," Mike Cummings remembered. Six feet six, his brother Sam estimated, weighing 220 pounds. "Your family got all the money," Terrence Stokes recalled asking his fellow Marine, "What are you doing in here? He said he wanted to get away and do something different." Not long before his transfer to Japan, Phil had become engaged. He kept a picture of his fiancée, Janice Lind, near his rack in the barracks. "He was always talking about her," Mike Cummings remembered. Serving in Japan the young Marine had followed in family footsteps that dated to the mid-1850s, when U.S. warships were dispatched to coerce Japan to open trade ties. His fourth great-uncle, naval officer Samuel Francis du Pont, had sailed on multiple occasions into Japanese ports. The gunboat diplomacy had been successful. In 1860 President James Buchanan selected Captain du Pont to host the first-ever U.S. visit by Japanese diplomats.

In the cube no one was speaking. Death had that impact, nurse Ron Hilliard recalled: "Everybody gets quiet. Usually it's not until the next day that the feelings of the other Marines would come out. . . . They'll wake up and they'll ask: 'Well, how's so-and-so doing?' And we'd have to tell 'em."

Mike Cummings had been in an anesthetic coma when Phil du Pont was lost. "We were pretty good friends on Okinawa," he said. Comprehending, after regaining consciousness, that du Pont and a number of other fellow Marines had died, he recalled, was "a hard pill to swallow."

Just after noon on Friday, October 26, the commandant of the Marine Corps visited Wards 14A and B. He was joined by the Corps' top enlisted Marine, Sergeant Major of the Marine Corps Leland Crawford. More than a decade later, Barrow remembered it as "a terrible sight."

"I went into this one room," he told an interviewer in 1991, "and this rather strong voice in all these bandages said, 'It's a pleasure to see you, sir.' I said, 'I'm sorry it's under these circumstances.' To which he said, 'It would be a pleasure to see you under any circumstances.'" The general remembered being told that the Marine had died not long after their exchange.

As General Barrow was sobered, the Marines were in awe. The Defense Department's smallest service had developed a tradition of revering the individual who held the Corps' senior-most post. The admiration might wax or wane based on the degree to which Marines felt a commandant exemplified courage, physical fitness, and strong character. As the Marine Corps rebuilt from its post-Vietnam nadir, though, Barrow—a combat veteran of World War II, Korea and Vietnam—was well regarded.

Dr. Cleon Goodwin remembered that, to the shock of the doctors and nurses caring for them, "two Marines on ventilators climbed out of bed to stand at attention for the commandant." Goodwin had never witnessed anything like it: actions, he surmised, "too fast and too genuine to be a thought-out process."

Barrow and Crawford paused to speak at the bedside of each injured Marine.

"I mean, one-on-one visits," Mike Cummings recalled. "It wasn't a group visit. They came and visited with each of us individually. I'll never forget that."

Ron Hilliard summarized the conversations he overheard as promises "that they were taking care of their families. That they just wanted them to get better, to focus all their energy on getting through this. Very supportive. Very encouraging."

Steve Neal was wonderstruck at meeting Barrow, "you know, a Korean War hero," and tried to stand. "The general said, 'No,' and I reached out my hand—my left hand, because my right hand was burnt—and I shook his left hand, too." Neal exchanged handshakes with Crawford, as well. The two were "badass dudes," in Neal's estimation. "That's why we went into the Marine Corps to begin with, you know. We just idolized people like that. And they were just so kind and generous. They didn't have to do that."

The commandant asked each Marine how he was doing. Mark Bedwell loudly intoned the answer he thought appropriate for a Marine: "'I feel just fine, sir!' And he could tell I was hurting like hell. And you know what? He wiped a tear out of his eye."

Barrow also asked each Marine if there was anything he could do for them.

"And, of course," Cummings observed, "we're going to tell him, 'No, sir. We're fine. We don't need anything.' But I remember him asking, 'If you need anything, just let me know.' I do believe if I would have asked him for *anything*, he would have tried to get it. That's how sincere he was."

The commandant presented each Marine with a plaque commemorating the young man's fighting spirit. The etching on Cummings's read, "To PFC Michael Cummings." Private First Class was the rank he had held before being promoted. As Barrow was moving on to meet another of the injured Marines, Cummings whispered, "'I'm a lance corporal.' And he heard it," Cummings recalled. "He turned around, and he goes, 'You're a lance corporal?' I said, 'Yes, sir. It's no big deal.' He goes, 'No, no, no. You're a lance corporal. We're going to have this thing redone." The general retrieved the memento, he said, "and I had a new plaque that same day. He made sure that everything was right."

After spending time beside each of the hospitalized Marines, even those unable to speak, Barrow addressed reporters gathered at the hospital. He promised a thorough investigation into what he termed "the most serious peacetime disaster we've had in the Marine Corps in my time. Our concern is not just that we had a tragedy and how it happened, but who it happened to and what they mean to us."

Steve Neal was wheeled out to answer reporter's questions, as well—the only one of the Marines who had answered affirmatively when offered the chance. "They dressed me in that goofy little gown, and that sheet over me," he recalled. Neal shared memories of "throwing water on myself and trying to keep the fire off."

After the news conference, Barrow, with his wife, Patty, at his side, made his way to a BAMC auditorium to meet with more than sixty parents and other relatives of the injured. The gathering would be private and contentious. Standing in the back, Gerald Reczek felt a tension in the room unlike anything he had ever experienced—"like a firecracker ready to explode."

"Someone has to talk to these people," Barrow recalled twelve years later, "and if I end up becoming the target, that's all right. I tried to piece together the best I could—nothing like what finally came out—to try to describe the situation, how it happened in some detail, and expressed my deep sorrow on behalf of myself personally and the Marine Corps, and all that, and I would be happy to try to answer any questions."

James Dye Jr., seated beside his wife, Irene, was particularly heated in expressing anger and frustration about the circumstances behind his son Steve's horrific injuries. "His first question," Barrow recalled, "was, 'I want to know who is responsible for this. Who is responsible for my son up there dying?' Well, I'm not sure you could ever find any one individual on the scene that could say who is responsible. Neither do you want to tell this guy nobody is responsible. There were too many manmade factors involved. It wasn't just the typhoon. So I guess somewhere in the back of my head, I said, 'They can have at me.' So, I said, 'I guess I'm responsible. I guess I'm responsible. I'm as responsible as anyone, so I'm responsible.' Well, that became an open invitation and they let me have it. It was probably good for them to get it off their chest, and it was almost like one by one they stood up to attack me, the Marine Corps . . ."

A family member remembered tears streaming down the face of Barrow's wife, who sat in the front row of the chairs assembled for the meeting. Finally, Mack Bedwell, Mark Bedwell's father, spoke up. The senior Bedwell—whose son, like Dye's, was among the worst injured—had pursued legal studies later in life. The commandant remembered the Texas attorney as a "rather older man with a strong voice and sort of reassuring demeanor about him. He stood up and talked to them. 'I'm amazed at all of you for doing what you're doing to that man up there who has come to us to try to explain what happened and has said they were like his sons, too.' And it was like a piece of magic. They just quieted down."

The experience of speaking one-on-one with the Marines at BAMC, and engaging with their loved ones, made a strong impression on Barrow. Soon after he returned to Marine Corps headquarters in Arlington, Virginia, he ordered every Marine general who traveled cross country to stop off at BAMC. Their visits would, of course, display continued Marine Corps concern for the injured. More importantly, the commandant wanted the generals to "have to think about what might have gone wrong that permitted something like that to happen." In addition, he began thinking about how to provide more detailed answers to family members' questions about what had happened at the camp.

Visiting her brother later in the day, Carrie Beth Hogan tried to appear upbeat. Army surgeon Hector Benitez had been candid in describing Mark Bedwell's chances for survival: they were unpredictable. His eyes bandaged, she remembered, Mark "couldn't see. He looked like just this big mass." Through the small hole Carrie now realized was her brother's mouth, Bedwell struggled to speak: "The commandant came to see me!"

At Yokota one patient remained in the critical care unit that had been set up for the two Marines left behind. Two of Robert Vinson Smith Jr.'s aunts—Ann Page and Martha Henderson—had made their way to Yokota from Spartanburg, South Carolina, their travels paid for by the Marine Corps League Auxiliary. As a child Smith had been adopted by his grandparents, Thomas and Uris Garland. He had been a little brother to Page and her sister. Seeing the young man they knew as Robbie—as Page recalled, "wrapped in bandages and gauze from head to toe"—was not easy. Dr. De Vincenzo remembered, "trying to comfort them, trying to explain what happened." The two remained at Smith's bedside until life ebbed from the nineteen-year-old at 1:20 on the morning of Saturday, October 27. Given the severity of Smith's injuries, Page reflected, "I know that was God's Blessing that He kept Robbie alive for us." Back in Spartanburg, when Smith's family would receive guests at a funeral home, they asked that visitors not bring flowers, but rather make donations to a Shriners Hospital burn unit. "I know that mere words can do little to ease the grief you must feel at this time," General Barrow would write in a letter to Thomas Garland, "but perhaps knowing that your loss is shared by your son's many friends in the Marine Corps will be a source of comfort to you in the days ahead."

Smith had lived three days longer than Colin Miller. His passing brought an end to a mission that, for Salvatore De Vincenzo, had begun nine days beforehand. The sudden quiet yielded sorrow, relief, and fatigue. "I was pretty much overwhelmed at the enormity of the tragedy," the doctor reflected decades later. "We knew that we had done everything that we could." Memories, though, would remain. "Occasionally," he admitted many years later, "out of the blue, I will think about that very visual thing—going out to the hospitals, and taking care of these two young Marines."

By late October 1979, PFC Robert Brees was not doing well. His father was at BAMC, spending as much time as was allowed by the Marine's bedside. Unable to quickly book a flight after having been told of his son's injury, Bill Brees had packed his truck and driven from South Dakota to Texas.

Though the seventeen-year-old had always been close to his younger sister, Rob Brees insisted that she remain at home. "He really didn't want me to see him that way," Lori Beesley recalled many years later. "I wish you could hold my hand and not look at me," he told her in one of their daily twenty-to-thirty-minute telephone conversations.

The Marine told his sister that a helmet had protected the very top of his scalp, and underwear his loins. Doctors, though, had calculated his body 85 percent burned. He assured her that he was being well cared for. "The nurses would sit and hold Rob's hand," Lori said, "so he wasn't by himself."

When her brother imagined his life journey ahead, though, she could hear depression in his voice. "They said it would be years and years of skin-grafting," Beesley remembered her brother telling her. "He would never look normal again. And he kind of, just, didn't want to be like that."

As the two spoke on the evening of Tuesday, October 30, Rob seemed in good spirits. "We were reminiscing about some of the times when we went out and drank Strawberry Hill [wine]," she laughed. "He was talking about those being some of the best times that he could remember. And he had a couple very serious girlfriends. He asked me to talk to them, you know, tell them what happened, and that he would always love them. And his voice, you know—it was still him!" Lieutenant Colonel Reczek watched Brees that night climb out of bed and walk the ward—"talking about how good he felt."

On Halloween morning in South Dakota, Lori awoke at 5:30. She began writing a poem for her brother. At 6:40, in San Antonio, Dr. Roger Yurt declared Robert Brees dead. Twelve hours beforehand doctors and nurses had begun treating an evident bacterial infection. Even as brother and sister had spoken the evening prior, the Marine's body had been descending into septic shock.

"My brother and I were just really close," Beesley said. Even before her father called with the news, "I just kind of had a feeling of what had happened."

In the burn wards, news of Marines dying spread quickly. "It was shocking," Lance Corporal Gust Miller noted not long after. "I'd see them one day, and then the next day they just wouldn't be there."

Auxiliary members paid for Bill Brees to return home with his son's casket, Phyllis Stensgaard remembered. "We flew them back, and somebody else drove the truck to South Dakota for him."

In time family members staying on or near Fort Sam Houston developed routines. Corrine Davis would visit her son each morning, then retreat to the seventh-floor lounge. There she could use the MARS telephone, spend time in the small chapel, or speak with a Marine who had been provided a desk in the chaplain services office. Most evenings, she recalled, "the [Auxiliary] ladies would cook a nice dinner and bring it to us." Another ward visit could be made thereafter. Families whose Marines had been less seriously injured began to feel confident in leaving for short periods of time.

In Davison Hall guest house life was often tranquil, occasionally terrifying. "You don't sleep very well for a while," Freida Neal said, "until you know for sure things are going to be okay." During evenings she and her mother sometimes sat outside. Looking toward Building 1000, "we'd see the hearse come up. That was very upsetting. We knew some more boys had died."

Foreboding was unmistakable in every ring of a lobby telephone, or knock on a guest's door. Even the clunking of dress shoes along a nearby hallway evoked fears of impending bad news. "We began to associate that with death," Lori Bedwell Corsaut remembered decades later. Too often, early on, a knock would be followed by "wails, and people crying out in screams. It was just awful." The anxiety left her stomach, and her sister's, in constant distress.

Gerald Reczek tried to ensure that, if a Marine died and his loved ones were not on the ward at the time, he would be the first person contacted. That would allow him to find family members and escort them to the doctor who would formally bestow the bad news.

In his meeting with families of the injured Marines, General Robert Barrow had found himself able to offer only the barest, secondhand details of what had happened at Camp Fuji. Feeling they were owed what information *could* be shared, the commandant ordered the BLT 2/4 commanding officer, sergeant major and chaplain to San Antonio. Halloween 1979 found the three sitting together on the airliner that carried them from Japan. Someone had told the battalion commander, Chaplain Mel Ferguson remembered, "that this would be the first time in Marine Corps history that a commanding officer was called back to answer to, or meet with, the families of the deceased."

When Redgate, Ferguson, and Sergeant Major Robert Hendrix arrived in San Antonio, Marine Corps–appointed investigators looking into the tragedy were only one week into their work. Redgate and his team could provide certain specifics, but were not in a position to confirm conclusions. "On the flight, there was just some trepidation about how this was going to go," the chaplain remembered. Redgate, he said, "was certainly not hesitant to meet with families or to see his Marines. What was on his mind was: What could he say?"

On landing the three had been surprised and pleased to learn that General Barrow, at the urging of Patricia Barrow, had arranged for each of their wives to meet them in San Antonio. The spouses would bolster their husbands' efforts—and spirits.

Mark Bedwell remembered Sergeant Major Hendrix visiting. He introduced him to his mother, he said, "and he gave my mom a hug." Ferguson noted: "Those Marines knew their sergeant major. He had access, and he had entrée with them, that I couldn't have, that Colonel Redgate couldn't have." While the chaplain's offering of spiritual comfort was of help, he knew, the enthusiasm of the "wiry, short, and unflappable" sergeant major "was instrumental." Ferguson watched Hendrix "saunter into those rooms and just light up the room, bringing all kinds of positivity."

Sixty or seventy family members were by that time keeping vigil at BAMC. The BLT 2/4 commander's early conversations with them centered on events surrounding their loved ones' injuries. Some of the questioning was pointed. "There was anger in the room," Ferguson remembered, as some questioned Redgate's reticence to affirm things he did not really know, or felt were best left to investigators' ongoing work. When some suggested, "Well, if you can't answer that, you're covering something up," the chaplain observed its impact on the commanding officer he knew as "a very empathetic person."

"It stung him," Ferguson recognized. "He wasn't reticent—he was a Marine Corps colonel. But with these grieving parents, and worried parents, and spouses, and so forth, when they had a harsh word, it was hard for him."

Over the course of their stay, the three divided up, ensuring that one of them spent daily time with each Marine. Many, Ferguson remembered, "were in pain or anguish." Sometimes, so as to not disrupt family visits, they would nap after dinner, then return to the wards at 10 p.m. or after midnight. In addition to listening to and advocating for their Marines, Redgate, Ferguson, and Hendrix updated the young men on events at Camp Fuji. They jotted notes about how each was doing to share with the Marines' friends still in Japan. Some of the news was disheartening. Their visit coincided with what Roger Yurt recalled as a spike of infection. "We started seeing some of the Marines deteriorate," the surgeon said, even a number who had early on appeared strong.

Two days into the BLT leaders' San Antonio stay, Stephan Ray Turner became the eighth Marine to die of injuries incurred at Camp Fuji two weeks beforehand. The lance corporal passed away at 1:15 on the afternoon of Friday, November 2. Doctor Hani Mansour signed the death certificate, noting that the twenty-two-year-old from Tipp City, Ohio, had arrived at the burn ward in critical condition, having suffered severe inhalation injury and with 93 percent of his body covered by second- and third-degree burns. At three o'clock the following morning, the Marine's parents—Burman Turner, who friends called "Bud," and Dorothy Turner—returned to Ohio to share the sad news with Stephan's sisters, Berna and Cecelia, and his brother, Paul. Bud Turner's work as a helicopter-flying Dayton police officer had inspired his son, a 1978 graduate of Tippecanoe High School, to dream of one day becoming a pilot himself. "We hoped by some miracle, that he would survive," Bud Turner told a newspaper reporter. "But the hospital said from the beginning that his chances were very slim. With his injury, maybe he is better off where he is." Stephan Turner's passing, after three years' military service, weighed heavily on Jon Jurgen. He recalled their somewhat unusual path to amiability. In Japan one evening, the two had ended up at the same nightclub. "He started harassing a friend of mine. And I told him, 'Hey, cut it out.' And we got in a fight. And I could never fight, so I got my ass kicked. But we became really good friends." After arriving in San Antonio, their gurneys had at one point been placed side by side. Though Turner had often seemed unconscious, on this occasion he had perked up, recognizing his buddy. "And I remember him saying, 'Hey, Corporal Jurgen! How ya doin'? How ya, doin'?'" When Stephan Turner's parents returned home from his November 6 burial, a letter from the Marine Corps commandant sat in their mailbox. "I was deeply saddened," Robert Barrow had written, "to receive the distressing news of the untimely death of your brave young son as a result of the tragedy at Camp Fuji, Japan." Bud Turner, who during the 1950s had served as a Sailor on the aircraft carrier USS Ticonderoga (CV-14), immediately sat down to draft a reply. His handwritten note lauded the Marines who, he said, had "carried out every detail of the duties they performed with absolute perfection, from the escort of our son's body home, all the way through the impressive graveside services." Through anxious hours shared at BAMC, the mothers of Stephan Turner and Jon Jurgen had themselves developed a friendship. "I remember my mother kept in touch with Lance Corporal Turner's mother," Jurgen recalled, "afterwards."

After receiving daily briefings from ISR surgeons, Lieutenant Colonel Redgate and his team would gather family members to pass on what they had learned. Doing so, the three soon realized, would not be as straightforward a task as it seemed. Several of the Marines' parents had divorced. A few had remarried. "In some cases, the divorce was somewhat cordial," Mel Ferguson remembered. "They could still talk. In other cases, they would not be in the same room. And so we would give a briefing for the mother, and then wait, and then give a separate briefing for the father, and perhaps his new spouse." That was a circumstance Mark Bedwell faced, twice over. He had not seen his parents since their divorce. "Here they are," he remembered, "married to two strangers I had never met." Phyllis Stensgaard of the Marine Corps League Auxiliary remembered such situations impacting her group's work, as well: "We had to be real careful what we said, because we didn't want to start no trouble. We just wanted to help."

The experience taught Ferguson, he said, that hospital chaplaincy meant more than simply helping families through the health crisis at hand. "You're having to sort through all the other stuff," as well, he discovered; "a financial situation, or an unwanted pregnancy, or a divorce, or something else going on." The addition of angst upon angst could be heartbreaking.

The young fiancée of one of the burned Marines had been shocked by how fire had consumed her intended's nose, ears, eyelids and lips. "I love him," the chaplain remembered the young woman telling him, "but I can't stay with this." On the rare occasions when the Marine was able to speak, he would proudly introduce the young woman to anyone nearby: "We're getting married soon." Ferguson encouraged the young woman to, for the time, remain supportive, not voicing her concerns. The young man died, the chaplain recalled, before he, Redgate, and Hendrix completed their brief visit.

Another Marine asked Ferguson and his wife, Linda, about his mother. She had come to San Antonio, he told them, but a day or more would go by between her visits. Having promised to see if they could find her, the Fergusons made their way to the motel where the woman was staying. They knocked on her door. "We could hear stumbling around inside the room," the chaplain recalled. "Finally we coaxed her to open the door. She thought she was dressed, but she wasn't. It was clear that she was inebriated." Linda Ferguson convinced the woman to allow her in. As the chaplain waited outside, his wife helped the Marine's mother dress and style her hair. "We took her back to the medical center," Mel Ferguson remembered, "where she could then spend the rest of the day with her son."

While Issac Williams had described singing along with music in the Hubbard tanks as "*kind of* hypnotizing," a longtime burn center nurse pursued the idea of reducing burn patients' pain through intentional hypnosis, or something like it.

Captain Clarence Wooten Jr.'s years in military medicine had taken him from enlisted "aid man" to "ward master" corpsman, to duty as a commissioned registered nurse. Amid assignments to Germany, Japan, and Guatemala, three of his tours had been in the ISR burn wards. Early in his career, he observed a psychiatric nurse colonel who spent time speaking quietly with patients. When she left, he noticed, "they were very calm and peaceful, even when it was time for them to have a treatment." He asked the colonel to coach him. "Basically all she was doing was talking to them. Some people classify that as a form of hypnosis." He began employing the treatment tack.

Jon Jurgen remembered that when Wooten "was applying the cream or something, he'd hypnotize you. And that actually helped." Fellow nurse Bryan Stephen Jordan respected Wooten and remembered the captain's conviction in the utility of such "soft treatment modalities" as humming or singing softly.

Mark Bedwell recalled being told to "'take several deep breaths and relax.'" He followed instructions to close his eyes, roll them up into his head, breathe slowly. "Then he would talk in this quiet, soothing voice. Very quiet. And he'd say, 'Now, Mark, imagine the happiest time in your life, a very happy time, that you loved.'" In his mind the Marine from Texas retreated to a pecan orchard behind his grandparents' house. There, as a child, he walked along with a shotgun, hunting squirrels. For up to thirty minutes, the Marine contended, "all the pain would stop."

The patients were not truly sleeping, Wooten said, "because they were listening to me and they were acknowledging what I was saying to them." Having seen positive results of the effort, "Go get Clarence" became the not uncommon refrain of colleagues encountering difficulties with a patient. Because the term "hypnosis" raised red flags among doctors and some others, Wooten began calling what he did "alertrax"— for "alert relaxation."

Most of the Marines evacuated from Camp Fuji would require permanent skin grafts. The procedures would be performed over areas in which third degree burns had destroyed all dermatological layers. In most cases the tissue to be transplanted would be autografts, skin surgically removed from portions of the Marines' bodies that had escaped burning. It would be placed over an open wound from which all dead tissue had been cut and cleaned away.

The process was invasive and messy. The tissue was razed down to a healthy wound bed. Surgical teams knew they had reached it when blood began oozing; that indicated the area was receiving circulation. Sometimes resultant bleeding would reach a point that required replenishing transfusions.

If the piece of harvested skin was not large enough to cover the wound over which it was being applied, it could be run through a device that embossed the skin with a diamond pattern. That made it stretchable. "You could expand it and it would cover more tissue," surgical nurse David Berry said. "Skin would grow into the gaps" left by the embossing.

Grafting procedures early in a patient's recovery were not yet primarily focused on cosmetic smoothing. Rather, they served utilitarian purposes—reestablishing functional eyelids, for instance.

Soon after surgery grafts would crust over. In time they could be trimmed. At patients' bedsides nurse Sandra Nee found that work rewarding; each procedure in some measure improved patients' appearance and their ability to perform activities necessary to independent daily life.

Scarring, though, would almost certainly remain visible. The impact would be particularly notable in individuals with darker skin. Their residual scars were more likely to be thick, raised, and more noticeably of a pinkish hue. Patients would need to wait a year for more effective aesthetic procedures; they were more likely to achieve best possible result if done after wounds had softened and matured. Meantime, in cases where a burn patient had little unburned skin, surgeons might—over time, more than once—need to harvest healthy tissue from the same portion of the patient's body.

At 9:15 p.m. on Sunday, November 4, Lance Corporal Orlando Eloy Sandoval died on the burn ward. The Marine's father, Jose Sandoval, had just recently left the twenty-year-old's bedside. "He had some skin grafts, and the doctor said he'd be all right," the elder Sandoval noted, "so I went home"—to Pueblo, Colorado, where he and his wife Maria Sandoval had raised Orlando and his four brothers. After graduating in 1977 from South High School, the eighteen-year-old, unable to find desirable work in his hometown, headed to the Marine Corps Recruit Depot in San Diego. During two years in uniform, Orlando's service had become more than just a job; his father could see that he enjoyed being a Marine. "I was proud of him that he was trying his best to be a man," his dad said. "The Marine Corps—put a little experience on him." Around lunchtime on Monday, November 5, a car pulled up in front of the Sandoval home on Pueblo's East First Street. Two Marines in uniform got out. "When I saw them comin' in," Jose Sandoval told a newspaper reporter, "I said, 'Here comes the bad news.'" Word that his twenty-year-old son had died the evening before was difficult for him to comprehend. During four days at Brooke just the week prior, he had seen Marines seeming to recover from burns covering 80 percent or more of their bodies. Orlando's had covered 64 percent.

The day Orlando Sandoval died also marked a signal moment in U.S. history. Amid violent political revolution in Iran, fifty-two American diplomats and citizens—including thirteen Marine security guards—were seized inside the U.S. embassy there. With national attention focused on the hostages, what little had been pinpointed on the incident at Camp Fuji dwindled.

On Tuesday, November 6—as John Redgate, Mel Ferguson, and Robert Hendrix prepared to return to Japan—another BLT 2/4 Marine succumbed to fire injury. Private First Class Gregory Lawrence Hassel died at 8:40 a.m., eighteen days after fire had scorched 62 percent of his body surface. Ten days prior the twenty-year-old's kidneys had failed; he had also begun to exhibit serious heart problems. On November 2, doctors had begun treating him for probable burn wound sepsis. Though not at first understanding, Lieutenant Colonel Gerald Reczek had observed the infection's impact. "I think he was delirious," Reczek remembered. "He was using a lot of profanity. His parents were shocked that he was speaking that way. So was I." The Marine died soon after.

From Washington DC two condolence letters were mailed to Chicago. Greg Hassel's parents lived apart. Both, though, had remained by their son's side throughout his weeks in the burn ward. "May God give you added strength in the days ahead," General Robert Barrow wrote to Lawrence Hassel and Lois Hassel. Early the next year, Lawrence Hassel, who had served as an Air Force officer, replied to the Marine commandant's note. He thanked Barrow for having taken a personal interest in those who had been hurt at Camp Fuji, then at length praised Gerald Reczek, who, he wrote, "was instrumental in lifting and easing some of the burden and daily agony we parents carried while witnessing the slow death of our son." The lieutenant colonel, he attested—personally, and in coordinating Marine Corps League Auxiliary support—"gave of himself in heart, spirit and in meeting any material needs that we may have had." His efforts, along with those of Lisa Reczek and other volunteers, Hassel attested, had "succeeded in many ways in taking the shock, grief, bitterness, as well as hatred that was built up by some of the parents as a result of the burning and death of their sons." Reczek, Hassel wanted the commandant to know, was "the Officer who was on the firing line, easing a catastrophe which I believe should have never happened."

To augment support Gerald Reczek and his administrative staff were providing, the casualty assistance office at Marine Corps Headquarters activated a young reserve officer. First Lieutenant Carolyn Nelson had completed active duty not long before, one of the first-ever women assigned as a Marine Corps combat engineer. In Texas she and her husband had settled in Austin, where Carolyn joined the city's Department of Parks and Recreation. Both had affiliated with the San Antonio reserve unit. Almost before she could begin her new civilian job, the Marine Corps ordered her to begin assisting the Camp Fuji Marines and their families and to make twice-daily reports to Washington on each Marine's condition.

Arriving at Fort Sam Houston on November 6, she moved into the guest house. A telephone was installed in her room to facilitate calls to Marine headquarters. Rising early she would visit or call the burn wards, check on any upgrading or downgrading of conditions, then make a morning call to Washington. The remainder of her day, until making an afternoon report, was spent seeking out ways to be of help. She introduced herself to the Marines. "They were a little distant, at first," he remembered, "like 'Who is she?' And, 'Oh, she's an officer.' So they don't talk to you. They answered direct questions."

Nelson learned of the Marines' circuitous, morphine-clouded journey from a burning Camp Fuji to the fourth floor of Building 1000. "They needed a sense of themself and their location," she felt. Grabbing a camera, she took photos of the hospital exterior, and of the quarters next door where parents and others were staying. Sitting beside Marines' beds, she shared the resulting prints. "I would show them pictures of the hospital. 'Your window is right here.' To give them an exact feel for where they were." Postcards she purchased showing sites around San Antonio helped orient the young men to their wider environs.

Though in conversation she was always "Lieutenant Nelson" to the Marines, Carolyn addressed each of the injured by first name. As a woman, ISR surgeons explained, her behavior would be of particular import. "They're terrified about what they're going to look like," she recalled doctors saying. "It's important, essential that they not feel rejection." As they interacted Nelson looked patients in the eye. If a spot of unburned skin allowed, she would rest her hand on it while speaking with them. "People don't want to touch them," ISR staffers had made plain. "They need human touch."

Some Marines asked Nelson to accompany them to the tank room. Employing a Lamaze technique she had learned prior to having given birth fifteen months earlier, she taught Mark Bedwell to synchronize his breathing with hers. They locked eyes and breathed during some of his sessions in the Hubbard tank.

"I was desperate," Nelson recalled, "to feel that I could do something."

Before it was all over, the lieutenant's portfolio would also include emptying bed pans and, once or twice, measuring the inseam of Marine who had died—ensuring provision of a perfectly-fitted dress blue uniform in which he could be buried.

Like Lieutenant Colonel Reczek, Nelson was occasionally called on to retrieve relatives when a patient's condition changed. "I had one or two family members faint when they saw me," she remembered, "because they felt they knew why I was there." Eventually, Nelson told nurses to avoid specifics when they paged her. "I said, 'Don't tell me. From now on, just tell me, 'Go get so-and-so . . .' And sometimes make it good news: 'Oh, the surgery worked, the grafts took.'"

While the treatment the Marines were receiving was widely considered the best available in the world, it was being provided in a building forty-two years old. "Appearances, I think, were sometimes shocking to patients or their families who heard so much about the burn unit," David Berry observed, "and then came into this old and tired building that really needed to be replaced."

One indication: the building was susceptible to infestation by what Berry learned "were seven types of ants that lived around BAMC." When they did, the nurse remembered, "they got into everything. They got onto the patients in the ICU. That created quite an uproar. One day in the OR, a sugar ant had somehow gotten into a bag of IV solution. We discarded that, but we had to check carefully." Part of the antidote, Berry remembered: "They put out pieces of liver that had been treated with hormone, held in place by numbered pieces of masking tape."

In early November Carole Darlington reconciled the Auxiliary's books. Five thousand dollars had been expended to help relatives of the Camp Fuji Marines. While most initial transportation expenses had been covered, other needs arose. They were manifold and varied.

In order for a single mother to remain by her injured son's bedside, for instance, she needed to pay a babysitter to care for another child. Families whose breadwinner was at the hospital were having difficulty paying rent and utilities back home. A Marine, critically fighting for his life, asked to see his girlfriend; the Auxiliary paid the young woman's round trip airfare and expenses. As temperatures dropped a plumber had to be called to turn off the water at a home left vacant in the midwest. Even in Texas some family members needed warmer clothing. Families whose Marine would be hospitalized into or beyond December wanted to send Christmas gifts to loved ones back home. All continued to run up food and lodging expenses.

The Auxiliary members' goal was to remove every distraction from family members' singular focus on their Marine's recovery. Doing so, they could see, would very quickly exhaust their fabric sales proceeds. They began to solicit additional donations from Marine Corps League members in San Antonio. Word was spread, as well, to other Marine Corps League detachments across the nation. Within its own ranks, the Marine Corps publicized the address to which donations could be sent.

Among the first to respond was Alamo Detachment member and World War I veteran Steve Schwebke. In France during the summer of 1918,

Schwebke had been injured while fighting in the Battle of Belleau Wood. After recovering sufficiently to rejoin his unit that autumn, he was wounded a second time engaging enemy forces in the Argonne Forest. The Camp Fuji Marines' difficult path to healing reminded Schwebke of the road he had trod. He and his wife Sylvia contributed a check for $1,000. Groups of Army noncommissioned officers at Fort Sam Houston added to the fund. So did military wives clubs on the post, which also joined in serving meals to visiting family members. Phyllis Stensgaard remembered service members from Air Force bases in the area delivering donations to the seventh floor suite at BAMC.

As people in the wider San Antonio community became aware of the Marines' circumstances, they reached out to help, as well. "One woman walked into the hospital with sandwiches, baked goods and a washer basket full of food," related Army Lieutenant Colonel Kenneth Nolan, chief of social work services at BAMC. "Another lady offered a spare room for the out-of-town relatives." Care packages addressed "To the Fuji Marines" began arriving at the Marine Corps recruiting headquarters in the city. The boxes were stuffed with everything from underwear, cookies, and sunglasses to T-shirts imprinted with messages of encouragement. When more visitors were allowed on the wards, Frank Huerta remembered, San Antonio residents "came up to cheer us on, motivate us."

An association of restaurant owners in the San Antonio area began, every day, delivering dozens of meals to BAMC's seventh-floor suite. Member restaurants took turns providing the food to nourish family members and—as their conditions began to permit—the Marines themselves.

As patients' health improved, nasogastric feeding tubes were removed. When clear liquids were prescribed, Auxiliary members provided hundreds of liters of soft drinks. As surgeries continued in earnest, patients were transitioned to a high protein, high carbohydrate diet. The restaurant catering helped. "Every day—two, three times a day," Glenn Roberts recalled, "they would come up with just bags and bags of burritos and tacos and milkshakes . . . They wanted us on like seven thousand to eight thousand calories a day to help rebuild all the skin."

"Oh, take another one," nurse Catherine Syby remembered Auxiliary members encouraging as they carried huge trays of food to patients outside the ICU.

Following their commandant's orders, a steady stream of Marine generals had been checking in at BAMC. Mark Bedwell's sister, Lori, remembered the visitors as "very kind, very attentive. I just thought, 'Wow, it *is* like a family.'"

As San Antonio was Brigadier General Joe McMonagle's hometown, his call on the wards came soon after he landed in town to visit his parents. The general who had arrived at Camp Fuji the morning after the fire looked about for a familiar face. He wanted to say hello to the Marine with whom he had bantered on the Yokota flight line. The young man, he was told, had not survived.

Like many others first observing burn injuries in the muggy ward setting, some of the generals were disconcerted. Beforehand Carolyn Nelson, often an escort for such visits, would diplomatically try to prepare dignitaries for what they would see. "Sometimes I got the, you know, a hand wave-off," she remembered. "'I've been to Vietnam, I've seen everything that there is to see.'" When a visitor would begin to wobble, nurse Ron Hilliard recalled, "you just kind of discreetly take 'em out of the unit, get 'em by themselves." A bathroom just opposite the ICU afforded nearby respite. "They could get the general across the hall and into the toilet," ISR chief nurse Jean Truscott remembered, "and help them put themselves back together."

Fifteen-year-old Lori Bedwell had come to Brooke to support her brother. She would end up remaining at Fort Sam Houston for three months, forfeiting a good portion of her sophomore year at high school. Once her brother had been released from the ICU, she visited him daily.

When consuming calories became important to patients' healing, she helped feed him. Mark Bedwell's "mouth couldn't open very wide," she remembered. "It was like a little hole. I had to tear off the bites and poke it into the hole. And of course, he had a tracheotomy. Mark would be coughing and choking a lot from his burned lungs." When phlegm from the spasms pushed into the tracheotomy tube, the fifteen-year-old grabbed tissues or gauze patches to pull away any that blocked her brother's breathing.

Over time Lori Bedwell began visiting with other Marines on the wards, as well. Attractive, personable, and only three or four years younger than most of the injured young men, she updated each on how their friends were faring, and carried messages from one to another. "You know, 'So-and-so said hello to you,' and 'Keep up the good work.'"

"When you're eighteen years old," Mike Cummings said, "and you're in a hospital like that," the attention—"I do remember her being very good looking; she was blonde"—was encouraging. Decades later Lori Bedwell Corsaut remembered her goal at the time as "trying to be normal in an abnormal situation."

While the Marines and their clinical care teams focused on immediate concerns of life and health, they were doing so within a research institute. Much of the ISR's continuous experimentation involved comparing new care protocols against traditional practices. Nurse Clarence Wooten Jr. recalled having to be conscious of testing variables that might, for instance—with certain patients, but not others—require bandage wraps to be tied differently, or changed after differing numbers of days.

The Marines' en masse admission had put some such studies on hold. In at least four, though—mostly focused on endocrinological aspects of burn injury recovery—the Camp Fuji Marines made up the entirety of the group from which findings were drawn. Corpsman Robert Marchi recalled feeling particular sympathy when drawing blood samples or undertaking other procedures that bothered patients without providing immediate individual benefit. Parroting a phrase he had first heard Sergeant Major Leland Crawford use during his October 26 visit, he began jokingly telling patients that the annoyance was "for the good of the Corps."

Jon Jurgen recalled one day being unexpectedly reminded of the institute's research mission. His curiosity was piqued by a door he had not previously noticed. "I remember walking into a little closet storage room, looking up at shelves and seeing jars with names on 'em," he said. "I walked out of that room real quick."

In early November San Antonio's Catholic Archbishop Patrick Flores visited Marines on the burn wards. "I admire them for the courage and bravery they show constantly in their tremendous suffering," he said. The archbishop took photos with George Spotts, Patrick Schaefer and others. He invited "all my brothers and sisters in San Antonio to pray for [the injured Marines] . . . to support them in any way we can."

Late on the evening of Friday, November 9, in the crowded fourth-floor cube, Rodger Larson and Mike Cummings both found themselves sedated but unable to sleep. Their ICU beds next to one another, the two talked into the early hours. "I don't remember what the conversation was," Cummings conceded, but they kept each other company into the next day—the U.S. Marine Corps' 204th birthday. "When I woke up the next morning," he recalled, "him and the bed were both gone." During the three days beforehand, Larson had been battling burn wound sepsis. His body 80 percent burned, the twenty-year-old from Eau Claire, Wisconsin, had been particularly susceptible to invasive germs. At 4:32 a.m. the infection had prevailed. Larson had served in uniform for just eight months. The loss engulfed his parents, Ralph and Janice Madden, his three sisters, and three brothers—and classmates with whom he had studied at North High School.

Thirty-two Marines remained in the ISR wards—fourteen in critical condition, seven serious and eleven satisfactory. Seven of those in satisfactory condition were away on convalescent leave. At least one Marine evacuated from Camp Fuji—"he wasn't burnt very bad," Doreen Hunter recalled, "his hands was a little burnt"—was able to escort his mother to the San Antonio-area Marine Corps birthday ball. Freida Neal had been invited to the gala, but declined. With her son Steve undergoing painful treatment, she said, "I didn't feel like having that much fun."

The Marine Corps birthday occasioned a second letter from Bud Turner to General Robert Barrow. In it Turner expressed gratitude for the many who had come to his family's aid in San Antonio, "especially the Women's Auxiliary of the Marine Corp League." Praising a Marine he described as "the most professional gentleman I have ever met," Turner asked the commandant for a favor: "Please call Lt. Col. Reczek in San Antonio and personally thank him and his wonderful wife Lisa for the outstanding job they are doing."

Later in the day, those who were on hand in the burn ward—and able—took part in a Marine Corps birthday celebration. It was custom at such commemorations, wherever Marines were stationed around the world, to share a message from the Corps' commandant. For decades the missives had been sent by mail or teletype, then read aloud. More recently, commandants had begun making audio recordings to be played at the celebrations. While a generic message had been distributed to most of the Corps' commands, the words heard when the cassette player was clicked on in the ISR spaces were bespoke:

> This is the Commandant of the Marine Corps speaking to my fellow Marines at the Brooke Army Medical Center in San Antonio, Texas, on the occasion of our 204th Birthday. Today we celebrate our 204th year of dedicated service to the Nation. I realize that it is difficult under the circumstances for you to feel much enthusiasm for this occasion. But on this particular anniversary, I believe the day holds more meaning for you than for anyone else. Since our Corps' founding in 1775, Marines have been in the forefront of our Nation's defense during periods of peace and war. That great and honorable responsibility stems from the trust and confidence the public has that their Marines, when called upon, have the ability to always get the job done, quickly and efficiently. That ability is nurtured and sharpened at a variety of locations throughout the world. The efforts of Marines, like yourself, who keep their skills sharp in little known training areas, like Mount Fuji, are well recognized by myself, your fellow Marines, and a grateful American public. It is because of your training, and that of our Fleet Marine Forces the world over, that we can report to our Nation today, the Marines are ready. Your injuries, my dear Marines, are a matter of deep concern to me personally and, indeed, to all your fellow Marines. But while we are saddened by the tragedy you have endured, we have also been greatly inspired by the strength and courage each of you has displayed. On this 204th Birthday of our Corps I want you to know that Marines everywhere join me in wishing you a speedy recovery. We look forward to the day when you can return to full and productive lives. And so my fellow Marines, I leave you with this: keep up your courage, our prayers are with you, and God bless each of you.

Days beforehand San Antonio mayor Lila Cockrell had formally declared November 5–10, 1979, "Marine Corps Week" in the city. The proclamation she issued further specified that the Corps' Saturday birthday would be recognized in the city as "'Marine Day,' in commemoration of the 2nd Battalion, Fourth Marines, which were victims of a tragedy that occurred in Camp Fuji, Japan on October 19, 1979." Ornate parchment copies of the proclamation were distributed to the Marines.

A traditional cake-cutting ceremony followed, at which the first piece was presented to the youngest Marine present, the second to the oldest. "I was the youngest," Frank Huerta recalled. His eighteenth birthday was still two months in the offing. It is likely that the second piece of cake was presented to Colonel Russell McChesney Harwood, seven days away from his forty-ninth.

Russ Harwood had left his home in Brownsville, Texas, for San Antonio soon after the Marines had arrived there. During the 1960s and 1970s, he had thrived in the cotton business, growing and processing the fiber in Central America, Mexico, and south Texas. After a boll weevil infestation devastated cotton crops across the hemisphere, he had been able to transform his business. Refurbishing some two million square feet of warehouse space in Mexico, he had leased the structures to a variety of U.S. firms just then establishing manufacturing and warehousing facilities south of the border. In Texas he had transformed his warehouses into an industrial park between two international bridges in Brownsville. With trusted business managers in place, Harwood had embarked on a long part-time career in the Marine Corps Reserve. Assignments had taken him around the world. In Texas he had commanded the Fourth Reconnaissance Battalion.

Harwood's assignment to the burn ward was a volunteer mission. He had not been ordered there, nor was he being paid. "When it happened," his son Chris remembered, "it was very much a 'We need to pack our stuff and go.'" Harwood and his wife took the then-ten-year-old out of school to join them. Their presence would be helpful, the colonel told his son, because many of the Marines would not yet have the support of family members.

Carolyn Nelson was in the hospital when Harwood arrived. "He started introducing himself as 'Russ Harwood.' He's in civvies." Perhaps, she thought, he was related to one of the patients. There was something about him, though. "He's kind of got a little high and tight [haircut] going on. So, I said, 'I'm sorry, are you a Marine?' And he said, 'Oh, yeah. I'm Colonel Harwood.'"

"I'm here to help *them*," Nelson recalled him telling her. The colonel asked the lieutenant if she would help him carry something up from his car. She walked with him to a brown Cadillac Sedan de Ville parked just outside the hospital. "He opened up the trunk," she recalled, "and I'm looking in at a couple of brown grocery sacks filled with money. I just kind of looked at him. 'Yes, sir. What's this? Are we taking this with us?' He said, 'No. We're going to leave this here. But I wanted to let you know that it's here. It's for anybody that needs money. If somebody needs a ride, somebody needs food, somebody needs anything—the families, they need clothes. Whatever, this is here. This is for you to use for them; this is for me to use for them.'"

For at least five weeks—seven days a week, twelve to eighteen hours per day—Harwood served, records would later indicate, as "a special Marine Corps representative, ombudsman, expediter, and counselor of Marine victims, their families and their relatives." He telephoned the employers of many visiting family members, emphasizing the importance of the loved ones remaining by their Marine's bedside. His presence, Lieutenant Colonel Reczek maintained, "added reassurance."

"He interacted with the Marines," Carolyn Nelson remembered. "He interacted with the families a lot, up on the seventh floor. He would chat with Mrs. Reczek, and if there was anything she needed him to do, he would just volunteer to do." Nelson recalled a family needing to have something mailed from a post office. "He's a full-bird colonel and he's running to go do that." When Mark Bedwell was finally released from the cube, he learned that "you could have all you wanted to drink. Finally! And I wanted some orange juice." Harwood brought a bag of oranges into the burn ward and prepared the Marine a fresh glassful. "With his bare hands," Bedwell's father Mack remarked in wonder, "he squeezed it out for my boy, who is a lance corporal."

Harwood's signature contribution during the five weeks he would spend with the Marines, however, was as a mentor. "They were going to graft my ears," Glenn Roberts recalled, "and then the doctor goes, 'Well, we can't do it now, the infection hasn't really abated enough.' And I really had my heart set on getting home by Christmas." He could leave, nurses told him, if he signed a waiver acknowledging potentially attendant health risks. "And the old colonel came in," Roberts remembered. "He goes, 'You know, Marine, you don't want to do something for the sake of three days that you're going to regret for thirty years.' 'Ah, yes, sir—you're probably right.' So I stayed the extra time, waited for the infection to go. They did a nice ear graft and all was well. It was nice to have an older, calming influence."

As their burns and grafts healed, the Marines' skin grew together and tightened. It could continue to do so, they were told, for up to eighteen months. For long periods the Marines had remained in positions affording them least pain from burns and surgical procedures. As they did so, their bodies clenched. "You have to move your hands and stretch your skin to keep it from freezing in position," Bradley Cope explained. ISR physical therapists pushed, pulled and kneaded grafted arms, legs and hands. They applied splints to stretch out rigid joints. Their goal: to prevent skin covering hands, elbows and shoulders from over-tightening. That could inhibit movement and dexterity—or cause contractures: grafted skin shrinking and pulling apart at the edges. Craft activities were encouraged in hope of making the skin-stretching therapy interesting. Russ Harwood bought and distributed model car and airplane kits. His wife contributed pastel pencils and paper for those artistically inclined. The exercises, though, could be frustratingly repetitive; sometimes they seemed torturous. Carrie Beth Hogan remembered skin on Mark Bedwell's hands ripping as he tried to open small packages. "His hands would be bloodied. Oh, he'd get mad." Sometimes it would be necessary to cut a portion of the contracture and add more grafted skin.

The Marines had earned hard entry into a military service that prided itself on fit, strong bodies. With that came both confidence in what they could accomplish and a certain vanity in physical appearance. If both diminished, what then? "Disfigurement was a concern," Dr. Roger Yurt recalled, "particularly if it related to how they might function as far as returning to their duties."

Mike Cummings's badly scorched feet prevented him from walking; his burned face, hands and back caused him to wonder why he should *want* to get around. "I was in a clamshell at the time," he remembered decades later. "I didn't want to talk to anybody. I didn't want to do anything."

A burst of motivation would arrive from an unexpected source. As he sulked in a wheelchair one day, an odd noise caught Cummings's attention. "One of those plastic piss cups that they have in a hospital—I hear somebody kicking that damned thing, going down the hall. And you'd hear it hitting the walls." Glancing into a hallway, Cummings caught sight of seven-year-old Steven Tolbert. Second- and third-degree burns covered more than 30 percent of the boy's body—his face, arms, chest and part of one leg. Most of the thermal injuries were deep—"full thickness," as surgeons described them. The child had been burned September 28 near Lucedale, Mississippi—when an attempt to prime the carburetor of a truck that would not start went horribly awry.

By the time the Camp Fuji Marines arrived at BAMC, Steven had been moved to the third-floor "step down" ward and undergone at least eight skin graft operations. Everett Tolbert, though, worried that his young son seemed listless and depressed.

"Stevie was down in the dumps," he said—until, suddenly, Marines filled the burn wards. "Within two days of them arriving," the retired Air Force master sergeant observed, "the kid was on top of the world." Marines, the boy imagined, could overcome any obstacle. And they were all—he, they—dealing with the same hardship.

Marines who had progressed to Ward 13B came to know Stevie first. Soon, even those still on Wards 14A and 14B grew intrigued. "We used to go down to the next floor and visit him," Glenn Roberts recalled. "I remember his right hand—the fingers were burned down to the knuckle. He had like these titanium implants, they were going to try to rebuild him new ones."

"He never cried," observed twenty-one-year-old Lance Corporal Billie Stover of Leighton, Alabama. Shelby Waford watched Tolbert "walk into his physical therapy like a man." The lance corporal from Lawrence, Kentucky, thought the boy "the bravest guy in the ward."

Having himself been burn-injured as a child, Dr. William McManus had closely followed Tolbert's treatment. He saw that, rising to the role of surrogate older brothers, Marines who had themselves grown discouraged speeded their own healing. "When they saw him doing his exercises without a whimper," the surgeon said, "they started to do them, too, despite the pain."

Before Tolbert returned home December 18, the Marines presented him a certificate affirming their admiration of his "courage and fighting spirit." Using a longstanding nickname for Marines, it declared Steven Tolbert, "an honorary Leatherneck."

"When I wanted to die," Mike Cummings attested, "I watched Stevie. He never resisted painful therapy. If he can do it, I thought, so can I."

As a significant number of the Camp Fuji Marines moved into a routinized regimen of grafting and physical therapy, another adversary—boredom—encroached on their recovery.

A small group of fellow Marines on special duty in Los Angeles thought they might be able to diminish that dilemma. The Corps had posted four Marines in the U.S. Federal Building at 11000 Wilshire Boulevard. Their day-to-day job was to increase positive portrayals of Marines in movies and on television. In the course of their work, Major Patrick C. G. Coulter and newly minted Captain Michele Reese were in daily contact with studio executives, producers, and directors. In 1979 it was not uncommon for a significant number of those individuals to be military veterans.

The "Hollywood Marines" checked with senior officers in Washington, then began reaching out to motion picture firms. Would they consider loaning VHS copies of feature films to entertain the injured Marines? Michele Reese believed the first call she made was to the Walt Disney Company's executive vice president for film marketing. "After that," she remembered, "I called Jet Fore at 20th Century Fox, Herb Steinberg at Universal Studios, and many others." Fore, a senior publicity executive, had served as a Marine during World War II and been wounded in the battle for Tarawa. His boss, 20th Century Fox studio head Dennis Stanfill, had served in uniform for ten years after graduating from the U.S. Naval Academy. Universal's Steinberg had been an Army captain by the end of his World War II service. "The answers," Reese recalled, "were resoundingly positive." Every studio contacted agreed to loan tapes. Some promised, as well, to donate mint-condition movie posters.

They delivered quickly, Reese recalled. The first VHS cassettes arrived at the Los Angeles federal building in just days. As part of the deal, the Marines promised to protect the studios' intellectual property. To ensure that the tapes remained in Marine Corps control, were not copied, and were returned after their use—they were boxed up by Gunnery Sergeant Jim Bell and another Marine at the Wilshire Boulevard office. Boxes were then mailed to Captain Tom Sweatt, executive officer of the Corps' San Antonio recruiting station. "Often, we would get more than thirty in a single week," he recalled.

Sweatt would carry boxes of VHS cassettes into the ISR burn wards, pull video players up to some Marines' bedsides, and, in larger spaces, set up group screenings. Additional showtimes, for families, were arranged at the guest house. When screenings were completed, cassettes remained under guard at the recruiting station until being packed for return to Los Angeles.

Studios shared films they thought young military men might enjoy. Sweatt recalled the 1976 John Wayne western *The Shootist* being included in the fare. Many of the movies were chosen because Marine Corps characters figured in their plots. Most often these proved popular. One prompted winces.

In the 1953 science fiction thriller *The War of the Worlds*, spacecraft from Mars land outside Los Angeles. A radio reporter in the film notes that, in response, "the area is under control of Marines from El Toro base"—at the time, a post in California's Orange County. "You know, they're going to fight 'em," recalled Mark Bedwell, who watched the film with a roomful of fellow Fuji Fire survivors. "And there's the Marines shooting tanks and mortars and artillery at the Martians. 'Ooh-rah, Ooh-RAH. Yeah! Kill the Martians!'" On screen the extraterrestrial spacecraft responded with blazing ray guns. At thirty-eight minutes into the film—for thirteen seconds—three Marines are set afire, and run through their camp screaming in pain. "And we're all in there, going, 'Booooo!,'" Bedwell remembered. "Here's thirty patients, burned up. We're all booing *War of the Worlds*, because the Marines are being burned up by the Martians."

When eventually tallied the films—those few seconds excepted—had offered the Marines hundreds of hours of positive distraction. Their commandant expressed his appreciation. "Your generosity brought many hours of entertainment to the hospitalized Marines," Robert Barrow wrote to Dennis Stanfill at 20th Century Fox—and to Paramount Pictures Corporation President Michael Eisner—"helping them to pass the tedious, often painful, bedridden hours and easing their recovery."

By Monday, November 19, nearly nine full days had passed without the death of a Marine on the burn wards. Hopes that the fatalities had subsided were dashed at 3:50 p.m., when Roger Yurt formally declared the passing of Willie Davis Jr.

As a child in Detroit, Davis had enjoyed playing with GI Joes, then walkie-talkies. His sister remembered their taking turns washing dishes at home, and the wad of cash "Junior"—as he was known in the family—earned on his paper route. "I thought he was rich!" Doreen Hunter laughed decades later. In school he had been intrigued by architectural design; he worked at a drafting table in his bedroom. Corrine Davis remembered, when her son was a high school junior, planning a large Thanksgiving get-together. Discussing plans in a phone call, she said, "I told my mother that I was going to have [the many guests] bring their own plates, because I didn't have enough." Junior overheard. He surprised his mother with a set of dishes purchased with paper route proceeds. After his 1976 graduation from Northwestern High School, he spent time with relatives in Texas, looking for work. One had served as a Marine. At his suggestion Davis headed to the Parris Island recruit depot. His letters from boot camp had included no complaints, his mother remembered. When he returned home a Marine, she fussed over the South Carolina sand flea bites that mapped his body. Her son, she said, "acted like it was nothin', nothin' to worry about." His initial goal, Corrine Davis said, had been simply "to travel and to get an education." In his last letter home, though, he had told his mother that he was thinking about reenlisting. After three years' service, Corrine Davis said, her son was convinced that "the Marines were the best." In their time together in San Antonio, Junior and his mother had not been able to continue a verbal conversation. "He didn't say a word all the while he was there," she recalled. Davis's reputation among fellow mortarmen was one of positivity. "He never stopped smiling," Louis Sanford remembered. "He always had a smile on his face. He was happy as all get-out, all the time." Sanford swore that had been the case even when, on long hikes, Davis had had to heft a mortar baseplate or three nine-pound mortar rounds encased in a wooden crate. Part of what made Davis likable, his sister maintained soon after her brother's passing, was that he was the sort of person who "was proud of other people when they achieved."

With burns covering 55 percent of his body, seven days of septic shock complicated by pneumonia had done in the young man from Detroit. In the wake of her son's death, Corrine Davis planned to immediately depart for home. A Marine officer, though, convinced her that she should not travel alone. Volunteers enlisted the help of a cousin who frequently visited Mrs. Davis from Houston. "They told her to go back to Detroit with me, and they would make sure her car got back to Houston. So they got a plane ticket so she could come back with me." The Auxiliary paid for both tickets. Marines drove the cousin's car to her home in Houston.

A month or so after the flames had done their damage at Camp Fuji, a group of Army and Air Force medical and aviation teams convened in San Antonio. They had been gathered to discuss lessons learned from the Camp Fuji evacuation process. What had worked well? What could be improved in a future, similar scenario? Ninth AES flight nurse Dolly Velasquez had flown in from the Philippines. She and others visited patients in the ISR wards. One, still lying mostly uncovered, body-wide burns visible, made a lasting impression.

"They told him who we were," Velasquez remembered. "'These are the people that brought you home.'" The Marine struggled to sit up. "It was like he wanted to shake our hands. 'No, no, no, no, just stay down,'" she cautioned. "All he could say was 'Thank you. Thank you for saving my friends.' Even to this day, anytime I think of that, it tears me up. He was in such horrible shape. And he was so concerned in thanking us. 'Thank you for saving my friends. Thank you for saving my life.'"

By Thanksgiving Day 1979, some of the thirty-seven who had been admitted to the ISR October 21 had left the hospital for good. Steve Neal was discharged on the holiday itself. Others had been allowed convalescent leave at home, but would have to return for further treatment. Some had formally completed their military service; a handful had moved on to a next duty station.

Catholic bishop John J. O'Connor, a former chief of all U.S. Navy chaplains, visited the Marines and many family members around this time. In a letter to the Marine Corps commandant, Terence Cardinal Cooke, then the church's military vicar, praised the "dedicated support of patients and families alike" at BAMC. O'Connor, wrote Cooke, "tells me that during his own recently terminated twenty-seven years as a military chaplain, he has never observed greater professionalism or commitment."

A significant number of those celebrating survival on November 22 did so at the home of an Army pilot who knew well what the Marines were enduring. David Jayne had undergone three and a half years of treatment at the ISR after suffering burns in a 1959 helicopter fire. Despite a variety of lasting impairments—including amputation of the tips of all his fingers and thumbs—he had been able to remain on active duty and continue to fly. Generously, Jayne and his wife opened their home to the remaining Marines and their family members.

Frank Huerta was hosted at the family home of Corporal Diane Guzman. The corporal was one of many reserve center Marines who had been providing administrative support to hospitalized Marines.

By early December a significant number of the surviving Marines had shown signs of improvement. Fifteen were away from the hospital on convalescent leave. A number had been placed on the Marine Corps' Temporary Disability Retired List. In that status they would receive retirement and disability pay for a period until their condition could be reevaluated. At that point it would be determined if they could be returned to active duty, permanently retired with a pension, or discharged with or without ongoing disability payments. Some had moved out of hospital beds and into nearby barracks.

In order to minimize scarring, a number of the Marines were wearing pressure garments known as "jobsts." Custom-made of elastic, they fit tightly over areas where skin had been grafted, keeping healing wounds out of the sun and holding grafts in the intended healing shape. Those crafted to cover facial burns were hood-like, with small openings for a wearer's eyes, nostrils and mouth. A story circulated that the face covering of one of the Marines had startled a store clerk who believed the young man to be a masked robber.

Surgeries continued. Glenn Roberts and Lance Corporal Shelby Waford were among many of the remaining Marines continuing to trek to the ISR operating room. Jon Jurgen had developed an ear infection. Doctors "may cut and remove cartilage," Carolyn Nelson wrote in her notebook. From her conversations with her son's surgeons, Joanne Jurgen was confident that Jon would live. "It's a question of time now," she believed. "It isn't a question of danger." Such assurance was not universally shared. While the twenty-two-year-old's condition had been downgraded from very serious to serious, a December 6 report at Marine Corps headquarters continued to list Jurgen's fate as "questionable." He was one of ten so described. Filling out the list were Mark Bedwell, Steve Dye, Michael Freeman, Ernest Gutierrez, Frank Huerta, Craig Jackson, Gust Miller, Robert Turner, and Issac Williams.

Former Weapons Company Marine Lee Embrey visited the ISR around this time. Having stopped in San Antonio after transferring stateside, the lance corporal reported back to members of his former platoon that "I saw some of the people at the Hospital." All had been fine, he told them in a letter dated December 11, except for Mark Bedwell, Issac Williams, Robert Turner, and Ernest Gutierrez. He had been able to talk with the first three—assessing that "they were coming along very well"—though "the latter" of the four, he wrote, "I couldn't even see."

There was good, sad cause for that. Since mid-November, Ernest Eugene Gutierrez had been battling burn wound sepsis. Infecting germs had entered through the 56 percent of his body surface covered with burns. Respiratory issues had further complicated his precarious hold. On December 3 Gutierrez's kidneys had stopped filtering impurities from his blood. At 3:30 a.m. on Wednesday, December 12, the twenty-two-year-old from Moorpark, California, became the thirteenth and last Marine to die from immediate effects of the October 19 fire. "I heard a lot of screaming" on the ward, Frank Huerta recalled. The echoing sound of Gutierrez's family made the news clear. His friend was gone—the guitar-playing Marine that others sought out at the enlisted club, shouting that he should climb on stage. "Everywhere he went," Huerta remembered, "he sang," belting out 1950s and 1960s-era oldies. Huerta recalled that Gutierrez's singing had drawn Marines together across color lines—striking given that differing musical tastes on occasion sparked racial schism. Sometimes Gutierrez strummed his accompaniment; frequently he crooned a cappella. On Okinawa Lance Corporal Rob Krumwiede had bunked with Gutierrez while the two stood a weeks-long guard duty assignment. He recalled that "all the energy he had," had earned Gutierrez the nickname "Loco." "Only time will lessen the terrible hurt," Robert Barrow wrote to the Marine's parents, Manuel and Della Gutierrez, "but please know your many friends in the Marine Corps stand ready to help you in any possible way."

As more of the Marines were able to leave the burn wards, activities there receded from surge mode. Staffers once again resumed eight-hour shifts, five days a week. While escaping the hospital—for good, or for just awhile—was encouraging to those departing, it left Marines still hospitalized feeling oddly isolated. Fewer around them had shared the common experience that had brought them there. Those departing were again helped by the Auxiliary. "These guys were just fantastic," Glenn Roberts enthused. "If you were going home," he remembered, Auxiliary members would provide cash "to make sure you got new clothes, a coat, anything from the PX."

Donations to the Auxiliary-managed support fund continued to arrive from around the world. A December 3 Far East Network fundraising radiothon at Iwakuni, Japan yielded $9,000. Carole Darlington, the Auxiliary treasurer, received a $5 check mailed in by an individual lance corporal. A sergeant forwarded a check bundling contributions from his squad. At Camp Fuji, on December 7, Marines and Sailors of BLT 2/4 collected and forwarded $3,142.78. Five days later—as the Auxiliary tallied that it had so far directed more than $23,000 to the Marines' family members—a significant sum remained in the group's bank account. As 1980 dawned the group announced that no further donations were needed. Still they continued to arrive.

In Darien, Illinois, twenty-year-old Gust Miller was resting at home. That was an improvement after two months of hospitalization. He was far, though, from well. It would take a year, he had been told, for the burns over his entire back, most of his legs and chest, and part of his face to heal. A scar at the top of his right armpit was keeping him from being able to lift that heavily-grafted limb. "I'm trying to forget about it," he said. "I just don't want to think about it anymore."

By January 3, 1980, Mark Bedwell had finally regained health sufficient to return home. While he had been hospitalized, his paternal grandfather had died. The two had been close. Family members were convinced that the older man's heart attack had been prompted by the shock of his grandson's injury. Concerned that the news might impede the Marine's recovery, the Bedwell family had not let him know. At home he was finally informed. "After Paw-Paw died," Carrie Beth Hogan attested, "we had a lot of problems with Mark."

After having been allowed leave for the holidays, Jon Jurgen returned to San Antonio for outpatient treatment. "I kept to myself a lot," he said, though he recalled being approached by Auxiliary members who asked, "if I needed like, some money—or if I needed a car to go someplace," He took up the offer of a rental car and drove to Burkburnett, Texas where he visited Mark Bedwell. Later he heard a friend, "Corporal [Daryl K.] Perry asking [for a car rental] and they said, 'No.' And he said, 'Well, Corporal Jurgen gets it.'" It made Jurgen wonder if the largesse shown him had been targeted. While at home he had been interviewed for a profile in the *Hartford Courant* newspaper. The resulting Christmas Eve story—which appeared under the headline "Canton Marine Who Survived Fire Feels Lucky, but Also Bitter"—included Jurgen's observation that "a lot of us feel that the government was negligent, that they put that fuel dump on the top of the hill without any adequate safeguards around it." He felt bad that he had been afforded a perk disallowed his fellow NCO. "I think the Marine Corps did it to shut me up," he surmised.

By mid-January 1980 only Steve Dye and Issac Williams remained hospitalized. Both were still in "very serious" condition; questions persisted as to whether they would survive.

A newspaper reporter visiting Dye observed "ugly burn scars on his frail body. His left arm is bandaged," he wrote. "Yet, there is no bitterness in his voice." Rather, the twenty-year-old from Columbus, Ohio, reveled in his resilience. "I was burned over 82 percent of my body," Dye declared. "They tell me I had the second-highest burns of anyone who survived."

For more than four months, Dye and Williams had battled simply to continue to exist. They had been accompanied in that struggle by Steve's parents, James Dye and Irene Dye, and Issac's mother, Joan Williams. During the first week of March, the condition of the two Marines stabilized. "We were able," Dr. Basil Pruitt announced, "to begin skin grafts on them this week." Even after a significant number of grafting procedures, surgical nurse David Berry remembered, "both of them were so scarred up. Issac was really spotted. Everything visible was just spotted with scar tissue."

Physical therapists had done the best they could to help each injured Marine reacquire the dexterity needed in daily life. Social workers had accompanied their patients into the community, acclimating them to stares and other reactions their appearance would elicit once outside a medical center. Still, ISR team members worried.

"The last time we worked on Issac in the OR," Berry recalled, "Bill Goldfarb came over to me and said, 'Dave, I don't know if we've done this kid any favors.' And, of course, I've had the same worries myself. And I told him the truth, as we knew it and had to be reminded: it wasn't our call. Issac seemed happy to be alive."

At 11 a.m. on Tuesday, April 1, 1980—166 days after the fire at Camp Fuji, and 164 days after being admitted for burn treatment at Brooke Army Medical Center—Steve Dye walked out of Fort Sam Houston's Building 1000. Before returning to Ohio, the Marine and his parents stopped by the home of Hani Mansour. "Claudette [Mansour, the surgeon's wife] cooked a meal for them," the doctor remembered.

Two hours later Issac Williams was discharged from BAMC. He had regained 75 percent of his eyesight. Even after twenty-seven surgical procedures at the ISR, many months of additional skin grafting and physical therapy lay ahead. But he had survived. "He was determined," Bill Goldfarb affirmed. "He was determined he was going to live." Others inspecting his injuries, Williams knew, could "look at me and think there was no hope. But I never thought that way."

Observing that, at the time, only 50 percent of patients who experienced severe burn trauma lived long after injury, Basil Pruitt judged the Camp Fuji Marines' survival rate—nearing 80 percent—remarkable. While acknowledging that the Marines' youth and otherwise good health had contributed to their better than average survival rate, Jon Jurgen credited the ISR. "We had good doctors and nurses," he maintained. "The staff there was really good. And they cared, they really did."

So had scores of volunteers and thousands of donors across the globe. In the end financial contributions exceeding $115,000 had been provided for family members' financial assistance, lodging, food, and transportation. Factoring for inflation, in 2025 the collected funds would have been valued at more than $500,000. Money that remained in the Auxiliary's Camp

Fuji relief fund was put toward the purchase of burn center equipment and supplies.

"I'm really glad we were there for 'em," Phyllis Stensgaard concluded decades later, remembering the Camp Fuji Marines. "They were really hurtin'."

FIG. 1. (top) Training camp Quonset huts at the base of Mount Fuji. Courtesy David Luttenberger.
FIG. 2. (bottom) Marines of Echo Company, BLT 2/4 in their training camp Quonset hut. Courtesy Steven Holmes.

FIG. 3. Military satellite photograph of Typhoon Tip at its peak. Courtesy George Dunnavan.

FIG. 4. (top) Marines battered by Typhoon Tip make their way to the shelter of Quonset huts. Courtesy Alan Crook.

FIG. 5. (bottom) Accumulated rainwater disintegrated 15 to 20 feet of a 440-yard berm uphill of the Camp Fuji training camp. Fuel pumps atop the berm tumbled into the breach. A fuel bladder floated downhill into the opening. The sharp edge of a pump frame sliced the bladder, releasing 5,500 gallons of gasoline. Courtesy South Kanto Defense Bureau.

FIG. 6. (top) A Marine in rubberized rain gear and gas mask wields a portable fire extinguisher as a training camp Quonset hut burns. Courtesy TogetherWeServed.com, from a profile created in memory of Gregory L. Hassel.
FIG. 7. (bottom) Hut D-220 after the fire. The awning of the first side window is missing, likely ripped away as Marines pulled themselves through to escape. Courtesy South Kanto Defense Bureau.

FIG. 8. (top) Two Marines sift through ashen detritus inside a burned Quonset hut. Courtesy Keith Norred.

FIG. 9. (bottom) During the first hours of October 20, 1979, Navy Hospitalman Apprentice Dennis Zickefoose (center, wearing glasses) and others at the training camp transfer burn-injured Marines from Air Force ambulance buses to a Navy CH-46 helicopter for medical evacuation to a U.S. military hospital at Yokota. Ron Hatcher | © 1979, 2023 Stars and Stripes, all rights reserved.

FIG. 10. Stacked into litter-bearing frames and surrounded by medical life support equipment, Marines burned at Camp Fuji are transported from Yokota Air Base, Japan to Kelly Air Force Base, San Antonio. Curt Eddings | U.S. Air Force. Courtesy Mike Monahan.

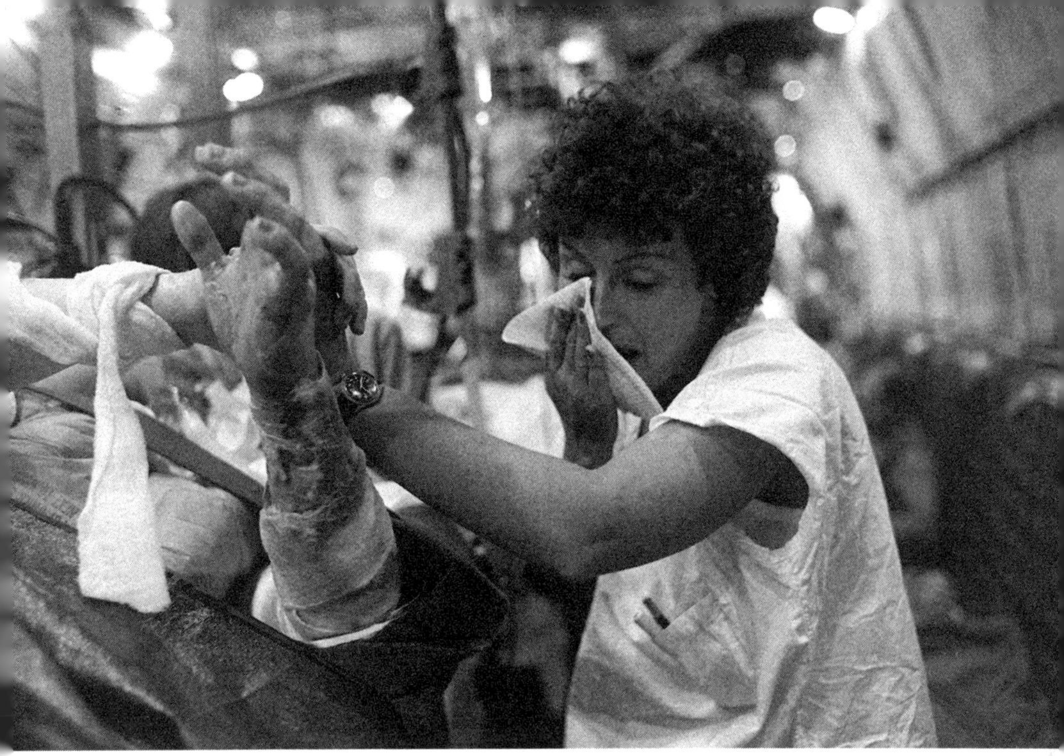

FIG. 11. (top) Captain Deanna Cox, an Air Force nurse, tends to Lance Corporal Tom Breunig aboard a MEDEVAC aircraft enroute from Japan to Texas. Curt Eddings | U.S. Air Force.

FIG. 12. (bottom) The Brooke General Hospital building, as seen while approaching by helicopter. Courtesy Hani Mansour.

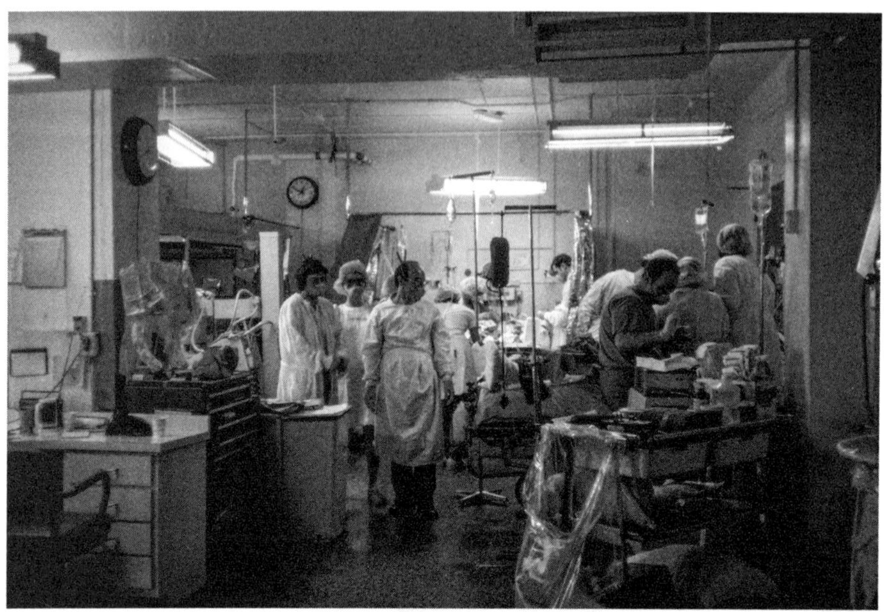

FIG. 13. (top) Army surgeon Hector Benitez (center, wearing glasses) and others care for burn patients in the intensive care "cube" on Ward 14A of Brooke General Hospital. Courtesy Hani Mansour.

FIG. 14. (bottom) The training camp soon after the fire, as seen from the direction of Mount Fuji. The left-most bladder pad remains in place; the gasoline bladder itself is trapped in the visible berm breach. Just uphill of the bladder positions are two trenches dug after the disaster to better direct rainwater around Quonset huts and other structures. Paul Long | © 1979, 2023 Stars and Stripes, all rights reserved.

FIG. 15. (above) A tank retriever pulls a Marine Corps M60 tank from an anti-erosion trench hastily constructed after the storm and fire at Camp Fuji. The tank fell into the deep trough on November 16, 1979. One Marine died in the incident. Courtesy John Paparone.
FIG. 16. (left) The Fuji Fire memorial stone on Camp Fuji in 2023. A model Quonset hut, in far better condition than those occupied in 1979, is situated as a memento in the background. Author photo.

FIG. 17. Colonel Allan W. Lamb, commanding officer of Range Company, Camp Fuji from July 18, 1979, to June 30, 1980. Kathy Ausra | U.S. Marine Corps.

FIG. 18. Lieutenant Colonel John H. Redgate, commanding officer of Second Battalion, Fourth Marines from June 21, 1979, to March 22, 1980, at Camp Fuji. Courtesy Michael Burbo.

FIG. 19. Sergeant Major Robert Hendrix, sergeant major of Second Battalion, Fourth Marines from March 6, 1979, to February 22, 1980, at Camp Fuji. Courtesy Michael Burbo.

FIG. 20. General Robert H. Barrow, commandant of the U.S. Marine Corps from July 1, 1979, to June 30, 1983. D. E. Williams | U.S. Marine Corps.

13

BACK AT THE CAMP

It was just like getting up from a rocket or mortar attack and taking off and kicking ass.

—Sergeant Major Robert Hendrix, U.S. Marine Corps

THROUGH ALARM AND angst, the disaster at Camp Fuji had impacted even those who had not suffered physical injury. Especially jolted were the nearly three hundred survivors who returned to uninhabitable incinerated huts. "Burnouts," as fellow Marines were calling them, had been left destitute.

"You don't have clothes," Fred Winters recounted, "you don't have money, you don't have a drivers license. I don't have an ID card, I don't have my own uniform." They wore a hodgepodge of sweatshirts, trousers, and shoes—some from the piles donated by families at Yokota, other pieces shared by Marines whose seabags had not been burned.

On Monday, October 22, two Marine Corps C-130 cargo aircraft delivered replacement uniforms. Accounting for size-matching and such, though, Mike Burbo remembered, "there were certain clothing articles that just plain nobody had." One Marine whose possessions were burned wore size 14 boots. With no replacements easily available, friends fashioned two shoeboxes to serve as his footwear.

To prevent theft and loss, service members overseas were encouraged to quickly convert payday cash into travelers checks. If the individual's cash was lost or stolen, it was gone. If the same happened to a travelers check, the buyer could provide the issuing company the stub of each misplaced check and be reimbursed. On October 19, the checks had been sold on Camp Fuji by a Japanese woman visiting from the American Express Bank at Atsugi. After the blaze destroyed checks *and* stubs locked inside Marines' footlockers, American Express for some time balked at offering refunds.

Don't dwell on the disaster, Tim Howell recalled being told. "'Hey, we're Marines, and we have to be ready to move on any given minute or day . . .' I don't remember counseling. It just seemed like they just pushed us through that."

"Every once in a while," though, Joe Macdonald remembered, "there would be word that another guy had died. And it was really horrible, because you didn't know when that number was going to end."

"It was hard," Thomas Moquino affirmed, "but, luckily, I was with some good guys."

Some BLT 2/4 Marines—faulting LSU 3/9 for the gasoline spill that fueled the fire—begin taking their anger out on Marines from that unit. "Weapons Company was not real happy with me," Rickey Lamon recalled. "A lot of them blamed me for it." As a lance corporal, the bulk fuel Marine had not selected the fuel farm site, nor been principal overseer of its construction. Yet, he mulled, decades later, "I can't blame 'em." By October 22 Lieutenant Colonel Redgate was warning his Marines to curb what apparently for a short time become a means of harassing the support unit. In a battalion staff meeting, Captain Leon Craig jotted Redgate's admonition: "Don't attempt to throw LSU out of chow line." Lamon—in the wake of the incident, "devastated, pretty much"—noted that the recrimination let up.

Even as cleanup efforts continued, small units had resumed training. Echo Company platoon commanders David Corderman and Jim Stallings took their Marines out to ranges to practice firing machine guns and mortars. Fox Company Marines were in the field doing machine gun drills and rehearsing squad tactics.

Worries persisted that gasoline and other impurities had leached into the Camp Fuji aquifer. During the battalion staff meeting Monday, October 22, Leon Craig recorded that officers were informed: "H2O is potable now." Two days later the Echo Company commander's meeting notes indicated alarm: "All H2O is contaminated—!!!"

By Friday, October 26, all fire-demolished Quonset huts had been cleared away from their concrete platforms. Around and above the slabs, combat engineers had shaped frames of wooden two-by-fours. General purpose tents were set atop the "hard-backs." Inside, displaced Marines and Sailors set up cots.

Fortunately, paper pay records in the training camp had remained intact. Captain Sam Sanders and his LSU disbursing team worked to put some money in the Marines' and Sailors' pockets. On Friday, October 26, they provided each individual eleven days' worth of their salary. In addition, claim forms were distributed. Though it would take time to process them, BLT and LSU members would be reimbursed for personal possessions lost in the fire.

While the unit's pace of training ramped up, it would be punctuated with opportunities to relax. Arrangements were made for helicopters on coming weekends to ferry Marines and Sailors to Yokota, Yokosuka, and Atsugi. Sam Sanders remembered helping to organize "a little basketball league and things like that to keep 'em focused."

On Sunday, October 28, Navy Lieutenant Commander Julian Sabbatini and Master Chief Constructionman B. Kilby of Naval Mobile Construction Battalion 4 arrived at the camp. Over the next four days, the Guam-based SeaBees surveyed fire and flood damage and begin planning a reconstruction effort. Walking the training camp with Colonel Lamb, Sabbatini recalled the Range Company commander as "receptive and anxious, I would say. They wanted to get any remembrance that the disaster occurred out of there. From the CO's perspective, he wanted it cleaned up." Remaining evidence of the fire damage, Sabbatini came to understand, "was a very bad hit on morale."

Monday, November 5, brought the assistant commandant of the Marine Corps to the camp. General Kenneth McLennan would spend three days there, assessing the state of the facility, and how Marines there were faring. He presented awards to a number of individuals recognized for heroism amid the fire; one, James Barnett, he promoted on the spot from private to private first class. McLennan—joined by Major General Kenneth Robinson, commanding general of the 3rd Marine Division, and 3rd Marine Aircraft Wing commander Major General William Maloney—also joined in the Camp Fuji Marines' early celebration of their Corps' November 10th 204th birthday.

The anniversary festivities continued into the evening. Inside one of the club huts, a four-member Japanese rock band entertained, playing pop hits.

They were fronted on stage by five American women dancers. Each member of the BLT and LSU had been allotted three beers for the party. On its face it was an opportunity for pleasant diversion. As the evening wore on, though, suppressed tensions emerged. At some point the women moved from dancing on stage to dancing with party attendees. With more than a thousand men on hand at the training camp, not everyone had an opportunity to dance with one of the few American women ever to appear at the site. "We had fights," Fred Winters recalled, "because one wanted to dance with her, the other guy wanted to dance with her. . . . The fights were not just in the e-club—the officers club was a brawl." Golf Company Marines quietly ushered their corpsman, Dennis Zickefoose, from the club after hearing other Marines—jealous that the women had danced with corpsmen as the band played the Village People favorite "In the Navy"—grouse that they would trounce the Sailors.

"Everybody was just getting their head together after the fire," Winters said, "and trying to get ready for a [combat readiness test]. Fight's on." It would not be the last such disturbance in coming months.

On November 6 and 7—in its final large-scale combat drill before the CRE—BLT 2/4 undertook a live-fire exercise in the East Fuji Maneuver Area. Having returned from visiting fire-injured Marines in San Antonio, Lieutenant Colonel Redgate, Chaplain Ferguson, and Sergeant Major Hendrix were able to observe the second day of the training.

Friday, November 16, found the entire BLT queued up for the most significant portion of CRE 3–79, a three-day mock battle. Interest in how it would all play out had been confirmed two days before with the arrival of the regiment's commanding officer, Colonel Charles Knowles, and its senior enlisted Marine, Sergeant Major Valdemar Vasquez.

The exercises began early. Randy Busk, then a sergeant with the BLT's tank platoon, recalled having to wake at around 3:30 a.m. By 4 his platoon had positioned its five M60-A1s at the lead of a column of men and machines stretching across the top of the training camp and down onto dirt roads beside unit huts.

"No moon," Busk recalled. "It was pitch black."

Because the BLT would be demonstrating covert movement, vehicles in the far-reaching file had switched headlights and taillights to blackout mode. That left visible only a thin horizontal line of illumination on each bulb. The "cat eyes" allowed a subdued point of reference. "You could see that little teeny illumination," Busk explained, "and that's how we followed the other tank."

At 5:30, when the BLT was ordered to move out, its five tanks led the procession of more than a thousand Marines and Sailors.

One by one the fifty-three-ton armored vehicles began churning their tracks across the volcanic soil—each following in trace of the one before. The movement was not high velocity. Sergeant Anthony Senatore, in an amphibious tractor just behind the tanks, likened it to "an elephant walk. You're just following the vehicle in front of you at a very slow pace."

Commanding the last of the five tanks was twenty-six-year-old Corporal Willie J. Hamilton Jr.—"Ham" to those on his crew. Hamilton sat high, the upper half of his body emerging from the tank's cupola. Grabbing a quick snack, he opened a box of C-rations.

Willie Hamilton was no stranger to early rising—or hard work. Growing up in Marion, South Carolina, he had in the winter gotten up early to hunt. In the summer farm work had begun during a day's first hours. There were "hogs to feed," his older brother Milton recalled, "the mule to take to work," cultivating crops of cotton, tobacco, and corn, "and the cows to put in the pasture." While he was in high school, football practice and a job at Dairy Queen had filled out long days. Graduating in the early 1970s, Hamilton had enlisted in the Marine Corps, served in Vietnam, then returned home. After a time life in Marion had seemed different. Maybe too much the same. He reenlisted. Back on active duty, Hamilton's professionalism had impressed his commanding officer at 29 Palms, California. "He was quiet, kind of unassuming, but always reliable," remembered then-Captain John Paparone. "His tank was always squared away, his crew was well trained." When Hamilton had been ordered "unaccompanied" to Okinawa, his wife Karen, daughter Natasha, and son Tarrell had remained in South Carolina.

In the dark the armored vehicles edged alongside the precipice of a drainage ditch fifteen feet deep. It was one of the trenches Colonel Lamb had ordered LSU 3/9 to dig, with safety in mind, soon after the October 19 typhoon and fire. In the event of another heavy storm, Lamb had reasoned, the deep furrow would divert rainwater away from the camp's center, toward its outer edges.

As each successive tank passed near the trench's upper lip, volcanic soil began to dislodge. Small bits crumbled into the pit. Amid the noise of vehicles moving out, and absent illuminated visibility, the crumbling developed into a cascade. The tracks of Willie Hamilton's M60-A1 chewed away the last portion of compacted edge.

In the troop commander's seat of the amtrac immediately behind Hamilton's tank, Anthony Senatore blinked. "We're going along," he recalled, "and all of a sudden the cat eye in front of us disappears."

From just ahead of the fifth tank, Randy Busk looked around in time to see cat eyes "flipped up." Willie Hamilton's heavy metal fighting machine had tipped into the abyss.

Senatore dismounted his amphibious tractor to see what had happened. As soon as his boots hit the ground, he tumbled into the ditch. "That's how close our amtrac was to it," he recalled. "I couldn't climb out. That's how far down it was."

Randy Busk tried three times to radio the tankers' platoon commander. Getting no response he left his team's gunner to continue trying. He and the rest of his crew jumped down from their tank and scrambled into the trench. By then screams were emanating from the fifth tank, which lay on its side, its top pressed hard against one of the furrow's walls. Inside the vehicle's driver, Private First Class Patrick Flanagan, lay bruised and bloodied, his pelvis fractured. Worse still, the nineteen-year-old from Mattydale, New York, could see what had happened to his tank commander.

Navy corpsman David Knapp, who had been riding in Anthony Senatore's amtrac, grabbed his Unit One bag, dropped into the ditch, and clambered into the escape hatch built into the tank's normally ground-facing bottom. He was able to do so safe from accumulating fumes because Flanagan, even in his distress, had had the presence of mind to shut off the tank's engines.

Randy Busk recalled Knapp eventually reemerging, shaken, but remarking, "Willie didn't feel a thing."

Hamilton's position when the tank overturned—in what tankers, because of its exposure, call the "suicide seat"—had left him vulnerable. When the tank fell against the trench wall, he was, as the BLT medical officer would report, "instantly killed, being decapitated, totally eviscerated, and nearly severed in two at the waist."

"I was a police officer for thirty years," Anthony Senatore would later observe. "I've seen a lot of stuff." Little of it, he said, remained as etched in his consciousness as the remains of Willie Hamilton. "I remember him holding a can of C-rations, the crackers."

The incident brought to a quick halt what had been the elongated column's first fits and starts of forward movement. "All of a sudden on the radios you could hear, 'Stop! Stop! Stop!'" Rob Ahrens recalled. "We've got a real-world fatality."

"Here we go again," thought Echo Company's Thomas Moquino, as the tragic news spread quickly throughout the column.

"At that point, you know," Fox Company commander Jeffrey Bearor recalled decades later, "I was thinking it. I'm sure other people were thinking it: 'Man, we are snake-bit.'"

Lieutenants Mac McDonald and Mel Ferguson were in jeeps far back in the convoy when a hollered directive—repeated down the line—finally reached them: "Battalion surgeon to the front! Chaplain to the front!"

The two raced to the head of the column, where an aurora of the day's first light was beginning to more clearly reveal what had happened—and where the tankers' platoon sergeant was upbraiding a couple Marines who had pointed cameras down into the trench.

An M88 tank retriever was called up from the base camp. The vehicle was owned by a team kept there to maintain armored vehicles. As Corporal Joe Grove maneuvered the heavy equipment uphill, the unit's commander hopped into a jeep and drove to the tip-over site. John Paparone's stomach sank when he heard mention of Hamilton, whose work he had valued while wargaming in the Southern California desert. He was shaken by the depth of the crevice that had swallowed the crew's vehicle: "That tank was sideways in the trench and you could have walked across the side of the tank to the other side." The captain watched as Corporal Grove's retriever vehicle did its heavy lifting. "He had to attach the retriever to both ends," Paparone recalled. "and move and maneuver the tank so you could get room to safely get somebody in there, the corpsman or whoever, to recover his body." Dawn was fully broken by the time Hamilton's remains could be extricated.

"I think somebody gave me a sleeping bag that I put the head in," Chaplain Ferguson recalled. "Doc McDonald had the rest of the body."

Three living Marines remained inside the leaning behemoth. "I remember two other tankers getting out," Anthony Senatore recalled—tankers recalled them as a Lance Corporal Serbin, the gunner, and PFC Carroll, the ammunition loader. Extricating the tank's injured driver, Patrick Flanagan, proved more complex. When he was eventually pulled out through the escape hatch, plans were made for his evacuation to the Yokosuka Naval Hospital.

For several hours the column of more than one thousand remained stationary in the frigid morning cold. Sergeants and corporals in Headquarters & Service Company began having Marines unload cases of C-rations from a truck packed full of the field chow. Once the vehicle bed was empty, the labor began in reverse. Its sole purpose: to keep the Marines warm.

Meantime, McDonald and Ferguson carried Hamilton's remains to the Battalion Aid Station. There, Ferguson remembered, "we basically put the body back together. [Dr. McDonald] had to take photographs, I recall that. And then I remember, both of us went out the back door of that Quonset hut, and we both vomited. And we just held one another. We got that out of our way. And we went back to do what we had to do."

"That is something that never should have happened," reflected former LSU commanding officer John Brosnan decades later, suggesting that the operational flaw was that "there was not a road guard walking with that tank. That was terrible."

Tank officer John Paparone held that he would not have expected to see Marines on foot guiding the tanks as they moved out. Such "ground guides," he contended, were rarely employed in the field. What Paparone wondered was "why the people who laid out the route from the assembly area to the line of departure had not reconnoitered that route far enough in advance to keep vehicles away from that ditch. You can mark the doggone ditch, you can put flags up, you can put ropes up, you can put flashlights on poles with red lights. You can do a lot of things to identify the location of that ditch and I saw no evidence that any of that had been done."

November 16 had become BLT 2/4's second fatal Friday at Camp Fuji. As Marine Corps leaders would later describe it, another "freak accident" had befallen the battalion.

After a time, the BLT column again began moving. "We had to walk past that tank as we went out," Leon Craig remembered.

During what Bill Meyers recalled as "cold, miserable, rainy, sloppy days," the BLT was put through its paces. Evaluators judged the unit's response to scenarios placing it on attack and in defense. Companies and platoons maneuvered. Weapons were fired for effect. An *Okinawa Marine* newspaper article described the Marines as having kept an aggressor force's "hands full defending against squad tactics, tank assaults, night attacks and reconnaissance missions" which eventually "destroyed" the exercise's opposition force.

On the last evening of the evaluation, Bill Meyers's Fox Company platoon had decamped to an area full of old-growth pine trees. "We're in these muddy holes in the ground," he recalled, "and water's seeping in." At some point he was told one of his Marines was shivering uncontrollably and only marginally coherent. At the Echo Company field position, the body temperature of one of Leon Craig's Marines had dropped dangerously low. The company corpsman's prescription, Craig remembered, until they could evacuate the Marine: "Get the person into a sleeping bag, then get somebody else in the sleeping bag with 'em." Quite a number, they eventually learned, were experiencing hypothermia.

At the end of the three-day mock battle, evaluators judged BLT 2/4 combat-ready. "That's not to say we were perfect," remembered then–executive officer Lance Woodburn, "but we passed the exam without any real difficulties." The battalion's logistics officer, Captain Roger Mauer, lauded what the Marines had achieved, "despite the fact that an integral part of the team, Weapons Company, was decimated by the fire. That's spirit."

"We really *were* tested," Leon Craig reflected. The fire and tank mishap had been "factors that we would have preferred not to have been tested against." As Chaplain Ferguson observed morale impacts of the tank tragedy—"the chaos, and the remorse"—an inquiry was underway to understand the disaster that had preceded it.

14

AN INFORMAL INVESTIGATION

> No person or persons is responsible for the fire that occurred at Camp Fuji on 19 October 1979; it was an act of God.
>
> —*Marine Corps investigators, November 9, 1979*

> There were too many manmade factors involved. It wasn't just the typhoon.
>
> —*General Robert H. Barrow, 27th commandant, U.S. Marine Corps, November 17, 1991*

WITHIN DAYS OF the fire at Camp Fuji, the Corps' commandant was referring to the incident as "the most serious peacetime disaster we've had in the Marine Corps in my time." He had served since 1942. He and other leaders promised a thorough inquiry into what had happened, and its impacts.

Marines at the camp had declined an inspection by the Japanese firefighters who had quelled the flames. "Because the fire occurred on Camp Fuji—legally U.S. property," firefighter Haruhiko Katsumata reminded, "as soon as the fire was out, we had to leave the base."

If the incident had taken place on a U.S. Navy installation, service regulations would have required a safety investigation. The Marine Corps would not adopt a similar rule until the 1990s.

The most detailed examination of what had happened at the camp would be guided by the Navy Department's *Judge Advocate General Manual.* An updated version of the legal guide had been issued in July 1978. In military jargon the inquiry would be a "JAGMAN investigation."

Four days after the fire—Major General Calhoun J. Killeen, commanding general of Marine Corps Base, Camp Smedley D. Butler, appointed two officers to look into what had happened at his command's remote training site below Mount Fuji. The subject line of Killeen's correspondence to Colonel James A. Poland and Captain Paul R. Smith summed up their task. They were to conduct an "investigation to inquire into all aspects and circumstances connected with the rupture of a rubber fuel bladder which occurred at Camp Fuji, Japan, on 19 October 1979, resulting in a fire which caused injuries to U.S. Armed Forces personnel and Japanese nationals and the destruction of U.S. property."

As was common practice, even in instances involving loss of life, the letter directed the two to conduct an "informal investigation." This differentiated their mission from a "formal investigation," which would have involved convening a board of investigating officers to conduct hearings in which witnesses would testify under oath and possibly be represented by counsel. Poland and Smith would instead gather evidence and statements, then report their findings, opinions, and recommendations to the commanding general. Based on that information, Killeen would take whatever action he felt necessary.

Colonel Poland was General Killeen's assistant chief of staff for logistics at Camp Butler. As such his day-to-day responsibilities involved him in issues related to Camp Fuji's upkeep and supply. Indeed, on Monday, August 27—fifty-four days before the fire, and forty-seven days after the fuel farm had been placed directly above the training camp—Poland had visited the camp to conduct a maintenance inspection. His familiarity with the installation likely influenced his selection to lead the inquiry. Having earlier seemed to confirm the camp's safety, however, could he probe objectively? The JAG Manual was silent on such considerations. The term "conflict of interest" did not appear in its index. Commanders were allowed great latitude in selecting investigators. They could be "commissioned or warrant officers, senior enlisted persons, or mature civilian employees of the Department of the Navy." The only other criterion, and it was not binding, was that those conducting an informal investigation "should not be junior [in rank] to any person whose conduct or performance of duty will be subject to inquiry." Assisting Colonel Poland, Captain Smith—a Marine Corps attorney—came to the task from Camp Butler's Office of the Staff Judge Advocate.

Members of multiple military organizations had been involved in and impacted by the events of October 19. The Range Company Marines who oversaw camp operations fell under Marine Corps Base, Camp Butler—Major General Killeen's command. BLT 2/4 was an operational unit of the 3rd Marine Division, led by another Okinawa-based major general. Logistics Support Unit 3/9, while temporarily "attached" to the BLT, was on loan from the 3rd Force Service Support Group—also Okinawa-based, and led by a brigadier general. While Poland and Smith were directed to comprehensively explore the causes of the fire, other portions of their investigation would be limited to issues related to people and equipment assigned to units under Killeen's purview. Determinations as to whether "members of units other than Marine Corps Base, Camp S. D. Butler," had been hurt or killed in the line of duty or their injuries had resulted from misconduct, for instance, Killeen instructed, would "be handled by their respective commands." Finally, anticipating that Japanese civilians hurt in the incident might make claims against the U.S. government, the two were directed to include in their report information related to those individuals' injuries.

Flying up from Okinawa, the two arrived at Camp Fuji on Tuesday, October 23—the day their appointment letter was signed. The training camp they observed looked considerably different than it had in the immediate aftermath of the blaze.

"The destroyed buildings had been torn down and tents with strongbacks [wooden frames] erected in their places," they wrote. "The soil that had washed down into the training camp had been removed from around the buildings and from the culverts and drainage ditches. The breach in the berm had been filled and the fuel farm removed."

Three dozen or so photographs would serve as their visual point of reference. A Marine Corps photographer attached to BLT 2/4, Sergeant Richard P. Hill, provided prints of thirty-three images he had captured soon after the fire. Lance Corporal James N. West of the LSU offered up four prefire snapshots depicting the fuel farm area in which he worked.

Prior to their arrival, the Range Company executive officer—second in command of the training site—had begun an advance inquiry of sorts. Major Richard M. Reilly had been assigned to the camp since July 19, one week after the fuel farm had been put in place. Immediately after the fire, he ordered a handful of Marines from Weapons Company and LSU 3/9 to handwrite statements. On October 22 he collected Lieutenant Colonel John Fitzgerald's confusing statement about when Fitzgerald had conducted a safety inspection at the camp and what he had found. Given Reilly's post with Range Company, which bore responsibility for operating the camp, he was not a disinterested party. He reported directly to Colonel Lamb, who described his laissez-faire approach to activities allowed at the camp as a "policy not to interfere with the training of the BLT." Reilly's "pre-investigative interviews," Poland and Smith wrote, "enabled us to proceed in an orderly and time-saving manner in the conduct of the investigation."

During some five days situated in an office at the base camp, the two investigators would gather the recollections of eleven individuals. While 2nd Battalion, Fourth Marines—particularly the unit's Weapons Company—had borne the terrible brunt of the Fuji Fire, they would take no statements from any member of the battalion.

Poland and Smith began conducting formal interviews on Thursday, October 25—speaking that day with seven Marines assigned to LSU 3/9. At a quarter after eight that morning, they took the statement of First Lieutenant Jacob Evans. The combat engineer officer commanded the LSU's landing support platoon. Its engineers and bulk fuel specialists had set up and operated the fuel farm.

"It was hard for [the investigating officers] to grasp what really took place in such a short period of time," Evans would later recall—"within four to five hours, this much destruction."

He found it difficult to grasp a rumor Colonel Poland told him he had heard: that a fuel farm Marine had intentionally knifed open the bladder. "And the investigator asked me [if that was true] and I said, 'No.' And I took him up and showed him exactly what happened." The false allegation bothered Evans. "Who said it?" he recalled. "I don't know. They didn't reveal that to me."

Forty-five minutes after sitting down with Evans, Poland and Smith spoke with Staff Sergeant Henry Simmons, platoon sergeant of the landing support platoon. At 9:20 a.m. the LSU's Andrew Stowell made a formal statement. He had been corporal of the guard on October 19. As such he had posted, then, when ordered to do so, pulled PFC Ki Lewis Smith back from the fuel farm sentry post. The investigators spoke with Smith himself at 9:45.

By 10 a.m. the LSU commanding officer was sitting before Colonel Poland, who asked why he had sited the bladders above the camp. "And I explained to him why," John Brosnan would later recall: "based on my previous experience at the camp."

Lance Corporal Rickey Lamon was the next summoned by Colonel Poland. Even many years later, he remembered the experience as nerve-wracking. "I went down there and talked to him," Lamon related. "And he said this was a preinvestigation to see if there was a court-martial warranted. Well, that didn't make me feel too happy, too comfortable." Poland queried the fuel farm's recently appointed NCOIC on operating procedures, Lamon recalled—and the events of October 19. "I give him the truthful answers. And he gets through, and he tells me, 'Lance Corporal Lamon'—he didn't think there was grounds for a court martial."

After lunch Poland and Smith took the statement of Sergeant Anton Koncaba of the LSU's maintenance platoon. He offered a reminiscence of seeing what he believed to have been the first MOGAS ignition.

On Friday, October 26, one week after the fire, Colonel Poland met at 8 a.m. with the Range Company commanding officer. Allan Lamb detailed Typhoon Tip's severity and noted that at 11:30 a.m. on October 19, after "setting up a disaster control team," he had ordered everyone in the base camp to safe quarters, leaving only one Marine in the headquarters on telephone watch. Japanese civilian employees under his command were among those he ordered to safety; those working in various stores on the camp had not been evacuated. "[The Navy Exchange at] Yokosuka," he stated, was "responsible for securing the PX employees." Lamb noted having received a telephone call at 12:45 from Major Lance Woodburn, reporting that, in advance of the bad weather, BLT Marines had organized a disaster control team and had been cleaning up loose objects in the training camp area. Lamb said his first knowledge of an unfolding disaster on October 19 was a 1:45 p.m. telephone call from the LSU commanding officer. Major Brosnan, Lamb recounted, "called and said that there was a stove fire in one of the huts. The operator [Range Company's assigned 'phone watch'] broke in [on the telephone line] and I was informed that there were multiple fires and that the local fire department had been called." The Range Company commander described moving up toward the training camp to get a sense of what was happening. He said he "saw that the Marines were heading for the helicopter pad. I directed that they be put up in the hangar." As he watched many barely clad Marines running back into the training camp to help others, Lamb observed BLT 2/4 Sergeant Major Robert Hendrix and Navy dentist Miles Wilhelm "trying to sort out the most seriously injured casualties and getting them on trucks." Lamb recounted how he dispatched Japanese–English translators to clinics where Marines had been sent for treatment.

At one o'clock on the afternoon of October 26, the investigators' attention turned to Japanese citizens at the camp. First, they spoke with Masao Satoh. The Range Company fuel supply specialist explained how, weeks before the fire, he had raised concerns about the LSU's storage site selection.

After taking Satoh's statement, Poland and Smith turned to issues related to Yasuko Nakayama. The woman remained hospitalized. Four days beforehand, Japanese military authorities had provided Nakayama a 20,000 yen (~$85) emergency relief payment. Similar 5,000 yen (~$20) stipends had been presented to Sumiko Yuasa and Kimio Hata. The Marine investigators' task: to determine if the U.S. government might be required to pay for Nakayama's treatment. At the time doctors at Gotemba Hospital were estimating that she would require at least a month of hospitalization, then follow-on reconstructive surgeries. C. J. Wagner, manager of NEX activities at the camp, advised the investigators that Nakayama did not per se work for the exchange. Rather, she was a staff member of "Charlie Hama, who had the contract for laundry services at Camp Fuji. Under the terms of our contact with Mr. Hama, he is required to carry insurance for his employees."

Finally that day the investigators took a statement from Major Reilly. It provided information they had—the day before—asked him to collect on their behalf. Reilly provided an inventory of buildings destroyed during the storm and fire and an accounting of "burn victims and where they were injured."

He also offered greater detail on the two instances in which padlocks had apparently been used to secure hut doors. "One lock," he wrote, "was located on the ground adjacent to the east exit of quonset hut #220. This 'lock' consisted only of a 'U' bolt; the remainder of the lock could not be found. The other lock was found on the ground next to the west exit of quonset hut #316. Both were still connected to the door hasps and the nails that connected the hasps to the door frames were still attached. It appears that both doors these locks came from had to be forced open by the occupants while the buildings were burning." Concluding his testimony the Range Company executive officer validated that the photographs he had given the investigators were taken before initiation of the postfire cleanup effort.

By Wednesday, October 31, Poland and Smith were back on Okinawa. At 10:30 that morning, they took a statement from Corporal David Marlow. Ten days before the fire, the former fuel farm noncommissioned officer in charge had returned to Okinawa. A school-trained bulk fuel specialist since May 1977, Marlow noted that the LSU executive officer, "Captain [Joseph] Bryant told us where to put the fuel farm. He picked that location because there was already a large berm in place, it was near a road, and it was accessible to both wheeled and tracked vehicles. . . . I have checked TM-3835–15/1 and I feel that the fuel farm we built at Camp Fuji met the requirements established there."

With these statements in hand—and feeling confident, as they would write, that "all persons interviewed were cooperative and forthright in their views"—James Poland and Paul Smith began drafting their report.

They started by noting key observations. First, they wrote, the fuel farm site "was at least 100 yards from the nearest building and 250 yards from the nearest Quonset hut used as a barracks." That seemingly placed it in compliance with the Marine Corps training manual's requirement that it be "isolated from living quarters and at least 250 feet away from buildings or structures." The north end of the long berm, they noted,

> appeared to be newly constructed. It curved slightly to the northwest and was connected to a small knoll next to Gotemba Trail, a highway that runs along the northern edge of the camp. That end of the berm showed little signs of wash-out or deterioration. The south end of the berm was intact, but the area to the south and west showed evidence of considerable water run-off. The berm was overgrown with vegetation except at its northern end and in the area where the fuel farm had been.

A plans officer with the 3rd Force Service Support Group told Poland and Smith that it would have been imprudent for LSU 3/9 to not carry an Amphibious Assault Fuel System to Camp Fuji, given a requirement that the unit be prepared to support BLT 2/4 if it was called away to conduct an expeditionary operation.

As information arrived from Camp Fuji, the investigators were able to tally the financial loss of the storm and fire. Property damage alone totaled $569,000. Beyond that there had been loss of what the military termed "garrison property"—small items, including blankets and sheets. "Some of the linen," Range Company supply officer Kathryn A. Papenhausen informed them, "was lost as a result of [medical teams] using it in the first aid of burn victims." The second lieutenant tallied a loss of $72,514.35 in such small and reusable items. Finally, the investigators estimated that $11,024.27 in personal combat gear issued to Marines in the BLT and LSU had been destroyed during the disaster.

In the end Poland and Smith compiled eighty-two findings of fact in their report. The investigators tallied fifty-one injured, noted which huts they had been in at the time of the fire, and where they were eventually transported for treatment. They acknowledged that Yasuko Nakayama's face had been burned, but did not mention thermal injuries Japanese investigators noted on the woman's chest and back. Apparently misconstruing Lieutenant Colonel Fitzgerald's disordered statement, the pair's findings stated as fact that Navy Lieutenant Commander John Rever had—along with Fitzgerald—in September 1979 certified the structural stability of fuel farm berms. Finally, the findings acknowledged the many training camp safety deficiencies fire inspectors had found on October 3; none, though, they asserted, had related to the fuel farm.

The findings were followed by opinions the two investigators drew from them. They had come to believe, they wrote, that the probable cause of the berm breach was a combination of "abnormally excessive rainfall"; Typhoon Tip; characteristics of the camp's volcanic soil; excessive drainage runoff; and pressures placed on the long berm—by heavy pumps atop the structure and the hard press of floodwaters against its side. In turn, the fire's probable cause, they inferred, resulted from the MOGAS bladder rupture, runoff of the spilled fuel into the training camp, and "the ignition of the MOGAS in the vicinity of Buildings D-215 and D-216 from an undetermined source." The fire, they reported, was probable cause of all the October 19 injuries—and property damage resulted from "the combination of fire in the training camp area and the heavy run-off of water and soil as a result of Typhoon Tip."

The fifth of the pair's ten opinions absolved any human blame. "No person or persons," they concluded, "is responsible for the fire that occurred at Camp Fuji on 19 October 1979; it was an act of God." Following that line of reasoning, they added, in Opinion 9, that "no Japanese national employee has a claim against the United States as a result of injuries incurred in the fire as there was no negligence on the part of the United States Government." Poland and Smith also opined that the extension of the north end of the long berm "did not materially contribute to the circumstances which caused the main berm to be breached."

Six recommendations followed, key among them that "no administrative or disciplinary action should be taken against any member of the United States Marine Corps as a result of this investigation," and that "no further inquiry into Mrs. Nakayama's injuries should be made until such time as a claim [against the U.S. government] is submitted by her or on her behalf."

Among family members of those who had been hurt at Camp Fuji, interest in the investigation had been growing. On November 8—twelve days after her nephew Robbie Smith had died at Yokota—Ann Page mailed a letter to the Navy Judge Advocate General asking for a copy of the investigators' findings. The following day, Poland and Smith sent their report to Major General Killeen.

Killeen reviewed the work of his appointed investigators. On Saturday, November 24, as he forwarded a copy of the investigation to his next higher headquarters, Killeen "suspended indefinitely" the use of Amphibious Assault Fuel Systems at Camp Fuji. His concern: similar "potential act-of-God dangers."

In Hawai'i Lieutenant General Andrew W. O'Donnell—the general officer overseeing all Marine Corps Bases in the Pacific—felt Poland and Smith's report begged questions. On Sunday, January 3, 1980, O'Donnell messaged the Marines on Okinawa, asking for greater detail. Specifically, he wanted to know more about the handling of Masao Satoh's objections to the fuel farm placement. He also sought deeper understanding of safety issues fire inspectors had raised before the incident; fire prevention measures in place at the camp; how the fire had moved through the camp; and who battled the blaze. Additional questions sought information about the extent to which blocking and locking of doors and windows—and the fifteen-to-twenty-hour delay in getting the injured to Yokota—had impacted health outcomes of the injured. Final queries on the list included: Had it really been impossible for anyone to observe the breach as it occurred? To what extent had the placement of the fuel farm played a key role in incident? And should fuel bladder use doctrine be changed as a result of what happened?

The Camp Butler leadership began gathering information useful to answering O'Donnell's questions. The task would fall to Camp Fuji's executive officer. In a letter dated January 7, Allan Lamb formally appointed Richard Reilly to conduct a supplementary informal investigation. At 7:30 that morning, he began by conducting a more detailed interview with Masao Satoh.

Satoh offered additional background on anxieties he had expressed to his supervisor, First Lieutenant Steven C. Miller, when LSU 3/9 shifted the fuel farm site. His warning that rainfall drainage could negatively impact the bladder and pump system, he told Reilly, had not prompted any near-term reaction. Satoh added, though, that

> sometime in August an earth moving project was carried out above the fuel farm to change the contour of the ground and thereby divert water run-off away from the fuel farm. When this project was completed I thought the drainage problem was solved for this rainy season. But I was still concerned about future years. I told Mr. Takasugi, a representative from the Japanese Defense Facilities Administration Office, about my concerns when he visited me in August and asked if his office could build a drainage control ditch in the area above Camp Fuji. Mr. Takasugi told me that such a project was planned, but not until 1980. With this information I felt that the points I objected to regarding the location of the fuel farm were taken care of.

In his October 26 interview with Colonel Poland and Captain Smith, Satoh had not mentioned that his apprehensions had been alleviated prior to the fire. It cannot be known whether his January 1980 declaration was influenced by clarity of memory or the fact that the fuel supply specialist was being interviewed by Reilly, an officer in his chain of command—indeed, his boss's boss. Range company leaders would not have appeared in a good light if they had done little to address Satoh's safety concerns.

At 9 o'clock that same day, Reilly took a follow-on statement from John Brosnan. The LSU commander noted that removing Ki Lewis Smith from dangerous storm exposure at the fuel farm sentry post had conformed with "the SOP for Tropical Storm Condition One Emergency." Brosnan reasserted that no drainage dilemmas had been encountered during the passage of Typhoon Owen, or other heavy rainstorms since early July. "Had drainage problems been suspected," Brosnan held, "provisions for some type of watch in the area of the main berm could have been made." As regarded Masao Satoh's apprehensions, Brosnan maintained, "at no time was Mr. Satoh's objection made known to the LSU." Finally, he weighed in against the idea of curbing employment of Amphibious Assault Fuel Systems. "These tanks ideally fit the purpose for which they were designed," he declared.

Later that Monday the Camp Fuji executive officer collected a statement prepared by the BLT 2/4 medical officer. In Colonel Lamb's initial remarks to investigators, he had described difficulties encountered in obtaining medical care for the burn-injured Marines. The statement had not referenced immediate assistance administered by Dr. McDonald, Dr. Wilhelm, and the BLT's 30-some corpsmen. "The initial treatment of burns," Mac McDonald explained, "consists of primarily supportive care of the patient." That *had* been provided, he affirmed. The fifteen to twenty hours it had taken to eventually transport the Marines to Yokota, he maintained, had not "significantly impaired the morbidity or mortality of the patients."

The following day Reilly prepared a statement of his own addressing certain of the questions put to the command by O'Donnell and the headquarters staff in Hawai'i. Most of the concerns expressed, and recommendations made, by fire inspectors who had visited the camp, he maintained, addressed issues that "did not relate" to the October 19 incident. He noted that 225 fire extinguishers the Range Company supply section had ordered arrived at the camp in late October, after the fire. Crowded conditions in training camp Quonset huts, he noted, continued to preclude the ease of passage sought by visiting fire inspectors. He provided a timeline claiming that the very minute the fire erupted—when even most people in the training camp were unaware of what was happening—the "telephone watch" at base camp headquarters, far downhill, began summoning Japanese first responders.

Even as Reilly drafted those answers, and prepared to forward them with the other statements to General Killeen and his staff on Okinawa, a Marine public affairs officer on the southern Japanese island was about to publicly announce the outcome of the investigation.

Prematurely gray and fancying himself a dashing character, Major John Woggon was known for an *Okinawa Marine* newspaper column he wrote under the pen name "The Silver Fox." That Tuesday, January 8, acting as the Marine Corps' spokesman on Okinawa, Woggon echoed the investigators' "act of God" determination, reiterating that Poland and Smith had found "no culpable negligence" in the placement of a fuel storage area above the training camp, or in any other respect. "This wasn't a matter of not being conscious of safety," he was quoted as saying, "but a matter of an overwhelming effect of the typhoon."

A *Pacific Stars and Stripes* article published two days later included inaccurate claims that may have resulted from Woggon's explanations or misunderstanding on the part of the article's author. The report indicated that the public affairs officer "said safety inspectors had inspected the site routinely since the bladders were placed there in 1973 and had never recommended that they be moved." While the long berm above the training camp had been in place since 1973, investigators had acknowledged that "construction on the fuel farm began on about 3 July 1979, and was completed by about 12 July 1979." The article also mistakenly reported that the ripped bladder had been the "middle" of the three; as one looked uphill, the MOGAS bladder had actually been farthest to the right.

On reading the article-topping headline—"Probe: Fuji Fire Act of God, Not Negligence"—Major John Brosnan breathed a sigh of relief. The LSU 3/9 commanding officer had "sweated bullets waiting to see the results of the investigation," he would recall decades later. Because the investigation had been forwarded up the chain of command, neither Brosnan, nor most others who had lived through the fire, were shown copies of the official report. "I never read it," he said, "and I was never asked if I wanted to see it."

The same day the *Pacific Stars and Stripes* article detailed the investigation's conclusions, Major Reilly took a statement from First Lieutenant Duane Schattle. His would be the first statement by a Marine assigned to

2nd Battalion, Fourth Marines to be included in the command-directed investigation. The twenty-five-year-old had been at Camp Fuji on October 19, awaiting formal appointment as Weapons Company commanding officer. That had come four days after the fire. At 9 a.m. on Thursday, January 10, Schattle noted that he had just that day been made aware that "a statement made by the Executive Officer of Range Company, Camp Fuji which is part of the Investigating Officer's Investigation of 9 November 1979, made reference to conditions existing in some of the buildings which caught fire." That statement, Schattle wrote, "requires elaboration." As best the young officer could—eighty-two days after the fact—he documented the October 19 memories of the handful of fire survivors who remained at the camp.

The same day Reilly collected Schattle's statement, he presented Colonel Lamb the supplementary investigation containing his findings and opinions. The report confirmed the pre-July 1979 fuel storage locations. It summarized Masao Satoh's new statement and noted that the supply officer to whom Satoh had raised safety concerns was no longer stationed at the camp. Steven Miller had in September 1979 been transferred to California State University, Bakersfield; the Marine Corps was affording him time there to earn a graduate degree. Reilly did not indicate whether he had queried Miller about the officer's actions in response to Satoh's concerns. He did, though, include the supply officer's mailing address, "should there be any need for higher headquarters to contact [the since-promoted] Captain Miller."

Reilly reported that BLT 2/4 had "standard fire prevention and fire fighting procedures" in place prior to the incident. He validated Duane Schattle's summary of Weapons Company's experience of the disaster and affirmed that Marines' escape from Buildings D-214 and D-215 had not been impeded by blocked doors or windows. Whether that had been the case in Building D-220, Reilly wrote, could not be determined by anyone remaining in the camp. Echoing Dr. McDonald's statement, he contended that evacuation delays and initial limited care capacity "did not significantly contribute to the morbidity or mortality rate of the burn victims." While conceding that earlier warning of the fuel spill might have been available had a sentry been kept at the fuel farm, Reilly supported the view that hazardous weather conditions had merited removing the sentry from his post. Finally, the Range Company executive officer reported that, given the number of buildings crowded into the training camp's comparatively small tract of land, "any available space for the installation of the fuel farm would place it uphill from troops billets or workshops, or uphill from civilian installations." Still, he stated in his findings, no changes should be made in how fuel bladders of the sort involved in the fire were used in training. The fire, Reilly opined, had been "beyond the ability of Marines at Camp Fuji to contain or put out due to its fuel-fed nature and its intensity." Because of the camp's terrain and crowded conditions, he admitted, "above-ground fuel storage facilities may continue to pose threats to safety in the future." Allan Lamb forwarded Reilly's report to the base commander on Okinawa.

In coming days the findings of Marine Corps investigators generated a good deal of conversation among American service members posted in Asia. From one Marine—a young man named Barry S. Evans—it also prompted a letter to the *Pacific Stars and Stripes*. The newspaper published it on January 22 in its "Readers' Forum" section. In military jargon, Evans was "short"—that is, he would soon complete his enlistment. The circumstance had ingrained in him a certain liberty to speak his mind. He did so, regarding what he believed were unsafe living conditions at Camp Fuji. While Evans's present posting was listed as "Yokohama, Japan," he referenced having trained at the camp not long before BLT 2/4's arrival.

"My words may sound strong from here on out," Evans wrote, "but I feel you should have a story about that camp."

> I lived at Fuji for three months last year. In the three years in the Marine Corps (I get out in April) I have never lived in such difficult if not dangerous conditions. . . . I lived through one typhoon and a part of another, and it was downright scary. I can't argue about the bladder inspection (the cause of the fire) but I can about the inspection in general. Any inspector labeled that camp as safe was a fool. I will argue to his face if you want! I remember telling 3 to 4 Marines one night at the club that something would happen that will prove to be disastrous. I haven't much to complain about the bad food and the totally bad living conditions. I never expected much of living conditions with the government anyway. The only complaint I have is: If it was so safe, why did I sleep over a gas leak for over two months? I feel sorry for the innocent person who had to inform parents of such a false investigation.

On Monday, February 11, Major General Killeen replied to the questions Lieutenant General O'Donnell had raised about Colonel Poland and Captain Smith's investigation. In large measure his message repeated the findings of Major Reilly's supplemental inquiry.

Killeen reiterated his intent to bar future use of expeditionary fuel bladders in Camp Fuji's training camp. Such a change would only slightly impair the logistical training, Killeen contended: "The safety consideration is paramount."

On March 21 Andrew O'Donnell affirmed most of the submitted investigation report, but rejected Killeen's call to curb Amphibious Assault Fuel System use at the camp. Removing that opportunity, he assessed, would be "neither necessary nor wise." Instead, he suggested refining the Corps' fuel handling regulations.

15

AFTERMATH

> Once the storm is over, you won't remember how you made it through, how you managed to survive. You won't even be sure, in fact, whether the storm is really over. But one thing is certain. When you come out of the storm you won't be the same person who walked in.
>
> —*Haruki Murakami, Kafka on the Shore*

JUST AFTER THANKSGIVING 1979, the USO helicoptered a group of recent Miss America pageant contestants into Camp Fuji. Inside one of the Quonset huts used as a club, pageant winners from six states sang pop hits and danced to Broadway tunes. It is not clear that any in the troupe had been made aware of what those at the camp had recently endured. "I don't believe we were told the extent of the damage and injuries and deaths," recalled then–Miss Ohio Sher Patrick, who performed a belly-dance routine. "That would have broken my heart at the time, and I would surely remember."

Soon thereafter a twenty-member SeaBee detachment arrived from Guam to begin assembling improved 20-feet-by-48-feet structures—Butler Buildings—on concrete pads now cleared of burned Quonset huts. The team from Naval Mobile Construction Battalion-4 was joined by twenty-five Japan-based Marine Corps combat engineers. "Immediate steps were taken," twenty-four-year-old Lieutenant (junior grade) Richard Hunter wrote at the time, "to initiate the formation of a single Fuji Detail." The officer in charge of the SeaBee detachment and twenty-six-year-old Marine

First Lieutenant Walter Whitfield merged their respective teams into work crews mingling the Sailors and Marines. They were given ninety days to install the replacement structures. “I remember telling Rich Hunter to do it faster,” then-NMCB-4 operations officer Julian Sabbatini reflected.

The teams strengthened each new hut to withstand winds greater than 125 miles per hour. The work entailed draping steel tie-down cables over the front and back ends of each structure as it took shape, then anchoring the lines into its concrete slab foundation. In addition, they inserted a fortifying layer of wood inside each building’s sheet metal exterior.

The Japanese winter made the work challenging. The group found itself in frequent need of new drill bits under 1/4 inch in diameter. They were constantly shearing—likely from the internal stress of rapidly heating while they were being used, then, as quickly, cooling to outdoor temperatures ranging between 27 to 37 degrees Fahrenheit. “We had the same issues,” former SeaBee Guy Tincher recalled, “with the hut guns we used to secure the metal siding and roofing to the frames.” The crews would use the power tools until they would no longer drive pins, then switch them out for others being warmed in front of a space heater.

Extreme cold and winter humidity also impacted the humans wielding the tools. “It was a damp coldness,” Walter Whitfield remembered. “You never got dry.” He recalled SeaBees and Marines having to keep metal sufficiently warm—and construction team members amply clothed and gloved—so that metal pieces would bend as needed and not dangerously adhere to workers’ skin.

Even in the frigid environment, work teams “pushed each other,” the Marine officer recalled. “When we did knock off, guys would still be out there working, just to beat the timeline and outdo each other.”

On Okinawa public affairs teams brainstormed ways to boost the morale of those who had borne tragedy at Camp Fuji. They decided to publish a number of articles in the *Okinawa Marine* newspaper about units there successfully continuing to train. A staff sergeant who wrote under the byline “J. Vina” was dispatched to the camp.

When Judy Vina completed recruit training in 1968, she became one of 2,700-some women on active duty in the Marine Corps. In 1979 it was still unusual for most male Marines to encounter a woman in Marine uniform—or to assume that a woman could write knowledgeably about Marine Corps operations. Hence her ambiguous writing credit.

Vina was ordered to report to Range Company. "They told me," she recalled, "'You're to go there, and you're *not* to be an investigative reporter. You're just to go there and do normal stories. They're trying to move forward. . . . Stay positive.'"

Her reception at the base camp was dismissive. "I don't think they wanted me there," she remembered decades later. "They may have had their fill of everything that had gone on. The investigators had been there." So had an array of general officers. "And here *I* was."

Shortly after her arrival, the staff sergeant was ushered into the Quonset hut office of a senior Range Company staff NCO. She heard others, laughing, lock the room from outside. The walls of the space were covered with sexual imagery involving humans and animals. "He had a nasty mouth and his hooch [the office hut] was pretty sickening," Vina recalled. While shaken, she remained confident. "Never let anybody disrespect you," she remembered leaders on Okinawa reinforcing. "You're a Marine and you don't let that happen." Before the other staff NCO could move toward her, she pounded on the office door, ordering junior Marines outside to unlock it immediately. They did.

Vina grabbed her seabag and marched uphill. From a telephone in the training camp office of Sergeant Major Hendrix, she reported the base camp incident to her supervisors on Okinawa. "Don't you dare pull me out of here," she said. "I told my leaders, '[The abusive staff NCO] is your problem, he's not mine. You take care of him.'" She was anxious to begin working. As the only woman in the training camp, she was moved alone into a decrepit Quonset hut. SeaBees quickly refurbished the structure to at least nominal comfort and safety.

The military journalist wrote about BLT 2/4's undertaking of the combat readiness evaluation. With the exception of not being allowed to walk the ground where the fuel spill had occurred, she had free run of the area. "They were just very cooperative," she said, "and very positive about having me there." She attributed a good deal of the assistance to Hendrix, "the epitome, to me, of what a sergeant major should be, or an enlisted leader: compassionate but firm, knowledgeable. . . . There was just a difference in the atmosphere between the base [camp] and 2/4. I think about it sometimes and I ask myself, 'Why?'"

Beyond Vina's uplifting stories in the *Okinawa Marine*, she took on a role in the training camp as a therapeutic listener. At Hendrix's prompting she would sit at a table in the enlisted club, attentive to stories shared by young Marines who would come talk with her. It would be cathartic, the sergeant major told Vina, for the young men to unburden anxiety in conversation with a woman. Some shared daunting recollections of the disaster. Setting her recorder and notebook aside, Vina tried to steer conversations toward their hopes for the future.

At 8:45 a. m., on Friday, December 14, hundreds of BLT 2/4 Marines formed up in front of Building T-115, the training camp mess hall. Just outside the building that fixty-six days earlier had served as a disaster triage site, a white sheet covered a large block of gray stone. The polished slab sat in a garden of gravel on the flattened top of a three-foot-tall white concrete pyramid. In front of the formation, also facing the soon-to-be-revealed monument, stood fourteen middle-aged and older Japanese men in dark business suits. The solemn group was joined by a kimono-clad Japanese girl seven or eight years of age. As the brief ceremony progressed, the girl, aided by one of the older Japanese men, pulled the sheet away, revealing the block, and its engraved sentiment:

IN MEMORY OF
THE
MARINES AND SAILORS
OF
BLT 2/4
WHO DIED OR WERE INJURED
DURING THE TYPHOON AND FIRE
19 OCTOBER 1979

Etched on the reverse side was the name of the group of Japanese community leaders that had commissioned and paid for the memorial: the Camp Fuji Cooperative Association.

Two days later a Weapons Company fire survivor who had taken part in memorializing platoon mates killed or injured, found himself compelled to rush into another set of uncontrolled flames. As his Saturday night liberty in Gotemba eased into the first hours of Sunday, December 16, twenty-one-year-old Lance Corporal Robert L. King became aware of nearby noise and mayhem. He and other Americans—Lance Corporal Andy Bonwit and BLT 2/4 Chaplain Mel Ferguson among them— began sprinting toward the sound. In a small commercial district, Bonwit recalled, they ran up to a street-level fish shop. A residence above the store "was going up like a match." On a small balcony eight or nine feet above the street, smoke poured through an open sliding glass window. "[Lance Corporal King says], 'Well, we gotta get these people out of there,'" Bonwit remembered. "I say, 'Yeah.' So he jumps up, and he grabs the railing and he pulls himself up. I tried to do the same thing, and to tell you the truth, my courage was not as strong as his. I'm trying to pull up, but I feel like I can't, and there's too much smoke." King vaulted over the railing onto the balcony, then rushed inside the house. There he found sixty-four-year-old grandfather and fish seller Shigeo Sato. Overcome by smoke and confused, Sato at first refused to leave his upstairs apartment. King had to forcefully pull him out onto the balcony. After rushing back inside, slapping at futons to ensure no one remained, the Marine withdrew and lowered Sato down to Ferguson and Bonwit. "I still remember [King] sitting there, afterwards," Bonwit recalled, "the firefighters or somebody giving him some water, and he's coughing, and he says, 'Does anybody have a cigarette?'"

As SeaBees and Marine engineers moved toward completing their barracks replacement project at the camp, Colonel Lamb approached them about undertaking additional renovations. "You could be inside [some uphill huts] and look at the ground," Walter Whitfield recalled. "There was no flooring." That contrasted with the better-maintained base camp. Whitfield inferred that Range Company commanders had focused repair efforts on the downhill site "because they lived there longer" than Marines rotating through for exercises. Where they could the construction teams improved facilities in the training camp.

On Monday, December 10, bearing a full combat load, the Marines and Sailors of BLT 2/4 stepped off on a particularly long unit hike. "Twenty-five miles in eight hours, or something like that," Leon Craig remembered. Given the BLT's twin traumas and passage of other tactical assessment tests, he said, "that was easy. Anybody can walk." When the last of the more than one thousand in column returned to the training camp, the unit had checked the final block of its combat readiness evaluation.

As the holiday season neared, some in the training camp formed a rag-tag choir, practicing singing Christmas carols in Japanese, then performing for children at the Yamanaka Seibi Home. Occasional spikes in bad behavior continued. Sometimes they occurred in the base enlisted club, when Marines who had joined the BLT after the fire grew tired of hearing raised-drink toasts "To Weapons Company!" Sharing no experience-informed empathy, one might retort, "Fuck Weapons Company!" October 19 veterans would feel the affront. Fights would ensue.

Beginning Sunday, January 13, and continuing through the following Tuesday, the Marines and Sailors first of LSU 3/9, then of BLT 2/4, departed Camp Fuji for Okinawa. Most were able to make their way onto ships and other means of transport for the journey. Along Imazawa Beach, though, inclement weather conditions and troubled sea states forced ships to leave harbor before everyone and everything could make it onboard. Some 35 percent of the units' cargo—and 15 percent of its Marines and Sailors—would be left stranded on Honshu for a period of days.

On February 2, 1980, the teams that had worked to reconstruct the training camp retreated to their respective bases. The SeaBee detachment returned to Guam and the Marine combat engineers to their posts elsewhere in Japan. Despite having faced adverse weather, and taking on extra "while you're here" work, the detail had completed its fifteen-structure replacement project in just two-thirds of the time allotted.

Two years after the fire, echoes of the disaster continued to provoke wariness in some deploying to Camp Fuji. A 1981 Marine Corps news release seemed intended to assuage such reticence. "Both the Base and Training Camp have undergone extensive fire safety changes," it claimed encouragingly. Among them were installation of "fire safety locks so people inside can get out even if the door is locked," and installation of circuit breakers. The camp motor transport chief, it reported—Gunnery Sergeant Donald Brunker, who from 1964 to 1966 had captained a fire department in Downey Ville, Colorado—was doubling as the camp's fire marshal. He had trained ten or so Marines to operate a pumper truck and one-thousand-gallon tanker truck that had been added to the Range Company motor pool.

The release touted placement of "fire extinguishers in every hooch," though a companion *Pacific Stars and Stripes* article—written by a Marine captain also touting fire safety improvements—claimed that "the pumper vehicle is extremely important because the training camp has no fire extinguishers." The camp's auxiliary fire brigade, which had access to heavy canvas-type firefighting jackets, trousers, and boots, conducted twice-monthly drills. "Our major need now," Gunnery Sergeant Brunker was quoted as saying, "is to get the men fire-fighter trained."

A permanent fire safety solution was brought to fruition in March 1983, with completion of a purpose-built, professionally staffed fire station. The following month, nearing the end of his tenure as Marine commandant, General Robert Barrow visited Camp Fuji as part of a preretirement tour of Marine Corps installations. Accompanied by outgoing Sergeant Major of the Marine Corps Leland Crawford, the general who had been so impacted by the October 1979 fire visited Building 95 and met with the Japanese firefighters who would, from that point on, wield capabilities better protecting Marines and Sailors at the camp.

Back in the United States, veterans of the events at Camp Fuji did their best to move on.

"When I came home from Texas," Issac Williams recalled, "it was like no one knew what had happened to us. It was strange."

Principally, that could be attributed to the nation's focus on the hostage situation in Iran. In addition, though, the Marine Corps seemed disinclined to encourage discussion of the October "freak fire" and November "freak accident."

Early responses by military leaders in Japan had reflected a certain defensiveness. U.S. forces at the time did not enjoy the same esteem they had in years preceding the war in Vietnam. Indeed, some World War II veterans at the time implied that those in uniform during the 1960s and 1970s were somehow of lesser caliber.

A comment by the Range Company commander seemed to at once validate and contradict that view. "The way men of BLT 2/4 handled themselves and the situation brings back memories of the pre-60s," Allan Lamb said, "when everyone worked for the good of others in a superbly professional manner." In the *Pacific Stars and Stripes*, Brigadier General Joe McMonagle was quoted as saying the Marines at Camp Fuji and their rescuers "are every bit the men we had in World War II or anytime since."

A handful of media outlets internal to the military printed articles about the events at Camp Fuji—the *Okinawa Marine* and the *Chevron* principal among them. Coverage in the latter, the newspaper of Marine Corps Recruit Depot, San Diego, likely resulted from its deputy commanding general's involvement in overseeing care of the Marines in San Antonio.

A number of base newspapers, on the other hand—Camp Pendleton, California's *The Scout*, for instance—printed no stories about the fire or those impacted. The Marine Corps Association's *Leatherneck* magazine, which since 1917 billed itself as "The Magazine of the Marines," never published an article about the Fuji Fire or its aftermath. A six-page 1989 profile of the camp in the magazine made no mention of the incident.

In March 1980 the *Marine Corps Gazette*—an MCA publication targeted toward officers—did include an essay in which John Redgate credited his Marines' quick response to outstanding preparation. In the piece "Our Training Pays Off," the lieutenant colonel did not address what had precipitated the fire, other than to write that "the intensity of Typhoon Tip on 19 October 1979 increased more rapidly than any storm anyone could remember," and that "the explosion and fire struck suddenly and without warning."

Writing, he said, in tribute to the Marines and Sailors of BLT 2/4, Redgate posited that the fact each "instinctively knew his responsibilities in the midst of a crisis" resulted from his battalion's emphasis beforehand on such skills as "physical training and military courtesy (the fundamentals) to embarkation planning, shipboard life and field tactics." It had created, he wrote, a state of alertness in which "every officer and enlisted man practiced the attitudes and state of mind incident to being and remaining 'up on the step,' combat ready."

The lieutenant colonel derided those who implied that such practices as "close order drill, unit formations, daily mustering, [and] the requirement for strict accountability of every man's whereabouts" might be anachronistic. "Many things military people traditionally have done are criticized by others (or, occasionally, by novices within our own ranks) as being meaningless 'Mickey Mouse' drills." Such training, the battalion commander concluded, had at Camp Fuji "saved many lives."

"All 1,300 men were evacuated from danger in less than 30 minutes," Redgate claimed in the article, "and all were accounted for an hour and a half later."

"This is one of the things that we kind of snickered about," Michael Weltsch remembered decades later. "That was not true. We knew some of the missing, we didn't know 'em all." Weltsch remembered finally getting a handle on casualty figures after four or five hours of driving to various hospitals, then, during the post midnight hours of October 20, smoothing the list. In the interim period, he remembered, "we were, I won't say clueless, but there was a lot of confusion."

Institutional defensiveness was evident even in late 1982, as significant structural improvements were being made at Camp Fuji. "There were a lot of discrepancies brought out because of the fire," a civilian engineer told the *Pacific Stars and Stripes*. "It focused the attention of a lot of high-ranking dignitaries on the camp." Indeed, though he did not weigh in publicly in 1979, General Robert Barrow noted in a candid 1991 oral history interview that the disaster, "among other things, moved me to make it look like a place where people should be secure and reasonably comfortable." In 1982, however, the Marine Corps seemed keen to remove the incident from cause-effect equations. "The rebuilding was going to take place anyway," said the Marines' senior spokesman on Okinawa.

Though the fuel spill and fire had been contained within the confines of Camp Fuji, it disquieted Japanese leaders. A considerable number of towns and villages closely abutted the dozen or more U.S. military facilities in the country. "Numerous questions were posed by the Defense Facilities Administration Agency concerning the status of petroleum, oil, and lubricants storage at Camp Fuji and other locations in Japan," noted officials at the U.S. Pacific Command.

On November 6, 1979, during a special session of Japan's national legislature, Shin'ei Kyan, an at-large representative from Okinawa, put forward questions about the Camp Fuji incident. The fire had not occurred on Okinawa, but Kyan represented a prefecture with a large U.S. military presence. Some on the island were applying political pressure to remove or downsize American bases there. Kyan suggested to prime minister Masayoshi Ohira that Japanese residents near fuel storage sites at other U.S. bases might be at risk. He asked the prime minister to "consider applying domestic laws such as the Fire Safety Act to U.S. military bases."

Ohira responded that "Japan's laws and regulations do not apply to the maintenance and management of facilities and oil storage facilities in the area conducted by the United States Armed Forces." He affirmed a belief, though, that "the Armed Forces respect Japanese laws and regulations and pay due consideration to public safety." His government, he said, was requesting greater U.S. attention to such matters.

Soon after, similar issues were being raised by lawmakers in the prefecture where the fire occurred. "Nearby residents had long been nervous about the facility," noted one speaker in a November 1979 meeting of the Shizuoka Prefectural Assembly, "and this accident has deeply affected them."

"Regretfully," contended another, the incident pointed up "glaring issues with how the fuel was stored and managed." Facilities on the camp needed to be strengthened, he argued. "Although this cannot be accomplished through Japanese law due to extraterritoriality, and there are difficult problems between Japan and the U.S., I believe that we must work with the government to create storage facilities and safety facilities for fuel, ammunition, et cetera, to ensure that this never happens again." It was noted that Colonel Lamb had "recently visited the prefectural office to apologize and express gratitude for local cooperation."

In response to their queries, American military leaders provided the Japanese government "locations and general information concerning collapsible storage tanks, with emphasis on their inherent durability and safety," U.S. Pacific Command officials indicated. "Specifics on capacities and safety procedures at each location were not provided, however. By year's end," they wrote, "the matter appeared to have quietly closed."

The recovery journey of injured laundry employee Yasuko Nakayama would be similarly muted. Though a draft U.S. Naval Forces Japan news release in November 1979 declared Nakayama "well on the way to recovery," she would require what friend and former neighbor Taeko Matsuzaki described as scores of reconstructive surgeries. "She basically lost her nose and had severe burns around her mouth," Matsuzaki recalled. "But the surgery wasn't quite successful because of her age." Nakayama lived for thirty-some years after the fire, her friend said. "She mentioned to me that she would wait until it was dark at night to take out the trash, so that no one would see her."

Patients discharged from hospitals after surviving serious burns are not as far down the road of recovery as those released after other sorts of treatment. "You're still hurting and limited," Mark Bedwell remembered. "You've still got another two or three years to go of just getting well."

After Issac Williams returned home to Louisiana, he sought help from a Veterans Administration hospital near his home. It did not offer specialized burn care. The VA made plans to send him to Washington DC. Further reconstructive surgery, they told him, could be done at Walter Reed Army Medical Center. The medically retired Marine, though, was wary of strangers. He wanted to continue treatment with Dr. Goldfarb. "He understood what was going on with my body," Williams explained. "He understood what was going on with my life."

Bill Goldfarb had by this time completed military service and returned home to Pittsburgh. There, he had accepted a post as associate director of the burn center at Western Pennsylvania Hospital.

"I asked him," Issac Williams remembered, "'Could I come up there?'"

Goldfarb agreed to see if that could be arranged. While he and the burn center's director, plastic surgeon John Gaisford, were willing to donate their services, they could not waive costs of a hospital stay. Goldfarb sought the help of John Heinz, one of Pennsylvania's U.S. senators. At Heinz's insistent urging, the VA agreed to reimburse the medical center charges.

On October 5, 1980, 187 days after he had been discharged from BAMC, Issac Williams moved into Room 312A at "West Penn." Another round of surgeries began.

"He had developed contractures," Dr. Goldfarb recalled. They were limiting movement of Williams's shoulders and elbows. In West Penn operating rooms, those problems would be addressed while plastic surgery procedures better reconstructed the Marine's face, ears, nose, neck, and hands.

Millie Brenlove, a legislative assistant to Senator Heinz would look in on Issac once or twice each week. His injuries "didn't seem to bother him," she remembered, but she could see continuing impacts to "his eyes and face, you know, how sometimes the skin gets pulled in a very taut way." On her visits Brenlove would drop off magazines and other things she thought the young man might find interesting. She "was one of my main connections," Williams recalled. "She took care of me real good."

So did the city of Pittsburgh, when word got out about Issac's stay. Hundreds of encouragement cards arrived, many from local schoolchildren. Someone sent him a radio. A local men's hairstyling firm provided the Marine prosthetic hair, eyebrows, and a mustache. They also identified and donated a cosmetic that could safely smooth asymmetries in his still-sensitive skin. Pittsburgh Steelers wide receiver Lynn Swann visited. "We talked about football," Swann recalled, observing that Williams was in the midst of "a battle tougher than any football game."

Thursday, December 11—sixty-eight days after he had arrived in Pittsburgh—Issac Williams checked out of West Penn. The surgeries had made a positive medical and aesthetic difference. After a celebratory dinner at the Goldfarb family home, he returned to Louisiana. The *Pittsburgh Press* published Williams's thank-you note to the city. Senator Heinz credited the Veterans Administration for having allowed the unusual treatment arrangement. The VA "had a heart," he said, "and came through for a courageous Marine."

Grief permeated the homes of families whose loved ones had been lost or maimed at Camp Fuji. Nine months after the fire, the mother of a Marine who had survived, badly burned, replied to a letter from the father of a Marine whose son had died of fire-related injuries. "This may sound cold and heartless," she wrote, "but death is a final thing; [my son] and many others will bear these scars for the rest of their lives." When Robert Brees's father, Bill, returned home to South Dakota, Lori Beesley remembered, he "went into a shell." Over the years Bill Brees's anxiety would create for his son an unsettled rest. In early November 1979, the Marine was buried in South Dakota. Later, when Bill's work as a construction contractor led him to relocate to Washington state, he had Rob's remains disinterred and reburied there. The process was repeated in reverse years later, when Bill again took up residence in South Dakota.

For some, like Robert Breunig, accountability remained front of mind. In St. Paul, Minnesota, he, his wife, and three remaining children ached at

Tom Breunig's passing. By the summer of 1980, he believed the U.S. government should pay for what had happened. As a Minnesota district court judge, Breunig knew something of trials seeking damages. He also knew lawyers who had built successful practices pursuing such claims.

In July 1980 letters to other parents of Marines killed or injured at Camp Fuji, Judge Breunig noted a plan to take legal action. "I have retained the law firm of Cochrane and Bresnahan in St. Paul, Minnesota," he wrote, "to represent Mrs. [Jean] Breunig and myself in an action for damages due to the accident resulting in the death of our son.

"Mr. Cochrane," the judge continued, "advises us that we may be entitled to make a claim under the Military Claims Act and in addition, he is investigating the possibility of an action against certain manufacturers, fabricators, suppliers and contractors associated with the design and layout of the billeting area as well as the fuel storage facility in Japan." In the event others chose to join in a lawsuit, Breunig shared the law firm's address and telephone number.

Reactions to the offer varied. Corrine Davis and Freida Neal deferred. So did Joan du Pont: "I guess it just really pissed me off," she remembered. "It wasn't about to bring Philip back."

Four months after receiving Breunig's letter, Joanne Jurgen, mother of Jon Jurgen, wrote back that "Mr. Jurgen and I and our attorney all feel that any action is futile. The U.S. government is faultless and will wiggle out of all blame."

John Cochrane felt otherwise. The merchant seaman-turned-personal injury lawyer had developed a reputation for prevailing in class actions against large corporations. Over a period of years, he assembled a group of twenty-two plaintiffs. On April 6, 1983, in U.S. District Court for the District of Minnesota, Cochrane filed a lawsuit on behalf of fifteen injured Marines and seven parents of Marines who had died. The action sought damages for personal injuries and wrongful death under the Federal Tort Claims Act. Dating to 1946, the law allowed private individuals to seek damages if they could prove harm or loss because of a non-criminal act by individuals acting on behalf of the federal government.

Underpinning the suit were claims that military leaders had been negligent in designing, locating and maintaining fuel bladders; that they should have known better than to place fuel uphill of living quarters; that barracks doors and windows should not have been nailed or locked shut; that the camp should have had in place sufficient firefighting plans and equipment; and that the camp's use of kerosene heating systems had created inappropriate danger.

Claims requested for the five worst-burned Marines ranged from $501,000 to $1.5 million. Others' injuries were noted as meriting amounts between $100,000 and $250,000. For each set of parents who had lost a son, the action sought $526,000.

On September 6, 1983, the U.S. Attorney's Office advised that it would ask the court to dismiss the lawsuit. The law, assistant U.S. attorney Robert Small argued, did not allow civil court damage claims in the cases of men and women killed or injured while serving in the military.

Just before 10 a.m., on October 5, 1983—as lawyers gathered in Courtroom 4 of the federal courthouse in Minneapolis, Patrick W. Parmater stepped up to argue on the Marines' behalf. Parmater was a veteran—though not necessarily of the courtroom. Serving in the Army from 1969 to 1971, the enlisted-Soldier-turned-chief warrant officer had fought in Vietnam, earning a Bronze Star Medal for valor and an Air Medal. The junior associate with Cochrane and Bresnahan had earned his law degree and bar membership the year the fire occurred. Parmater would face the task of convincing Judge Diana E. Murphy that the Marines' and families' case should be heard.

Arguing for dismissal, Robert Small noted that because the incident occurred in Japan, the claim was not eligible for consideration under the Federal Tort Claims Act, which focused on remedying mishaps that had occurred in the United States. He then invoked a legal precedent created in 1950: the "Feres doctrine."

In late 1947 Army First Lieutenant Rudolph J. Feres had deployed from his 82nd Airborne Division post in North Carolina for cold weather training at Pine Camp (now Fort Drum), New York. Thirty-one years old at the time, the paratrooper had 304 jumps under his belt—including an airborne descent into France during the Normandy invasion. He had fought in Belgium during the Battle of the Bulge. His bravery in combat had earned him three Bronze Stars and a commission into the officer ranks.

At Pine Camp Feres and other officers were billeted in rickety two-story wooden barracks. At around 2:30 a.m. on December 10, 1947, fire and smoke spread through the building. The blaze killed Feres and four others.

In 1948 the Soldier's widow, Bernice Feres, went to court seeking damages. A U.S. district court judge in northern New York ruled that, under the Federal Tort Claims Act, the government was not liable for injuries military members sustained while on active duty. The act had been previously understood to preclude claims for injuries and death sustained during combat operations. Scholars had disagreed, though, as to whether it protected the government in instances where harm occurred *off* the battlefield. When an appellate court confirmed that it did, Bernice Feres and the others asked the U.S. Supreme Court to consider the matter. In 1950 the high court concluded that, even when involving aspects of negligence, "the Government is not liable under the Federal Tort Claims Act for injuries to servicemen where the injuries arise out of or are in the course of activity incident to service."

Judge Murphy, during the hearing, described the *Feres* decision as "good doctrine, too, I think it is fair to say." Parmater ventured that the precedent was "not that popular with anybody except the United States government." He argued that Typhoon Tip had not harmed his clients. Rather, "it was the negligent activity which occurred that resulted in that injury."

Two days after the hearing—on October 7, 1983—Judge Murphy granted the government's request to dismiss the case for lack of jurisdiction. The Cochrane and Bresnahan firm appealed, but on May 29, 1984, a panel of the U.S. Court of Appeals for the Eighth Circuit affirmed the decision against the Marines and surviving family members.

A second legal controversy would soon embroil Tom Breunig's family. In March 1980 the late Marine's former girlfriend Tammy Richard, not yet seventeen, gave birth to a boy she named Jesse. When the child was four years old or so, the mother went to court. Claiming that Tom Breunig was the child's father, she asked a judge to order that the Marine's body be exhumed from its grave—an action necessary, prior to easy availability of DNA testing, to establish paternity. Breunig's parents did not believe Richard's claim. "It really seemed like this was a chance to take advantage of the situation," Tom's sister Patty Thornton said. The judge hearing the case ruled against Richard's request. The young mother made other attempts to reconnect with the Breunig family, but eventually moved on.

Jesse Richard grew up with a photo of Tom Breunig in his bedroom. Not having had a father during his early years had been difficult. As he entered his mid-thirties, he found himself drawn to know more. In the winter of 2016, he left a voicemail message for Tom's sister Carol. The family did not immediately respond, though Carol saved the recording. Jesse followed up with a request to connect with her via Facebook. When the two did, Carol and her sister Patty browsed through photos posted on Richard's page. "That looks so much like Tom," Patty Thornton remembered saying. "Wow. He had a son."

By the time Tom Breunig's siblings met Jesse Richard face to face, Robert and Jean Breunig had both passed away. Jesse's mannerisms and speech struck the Breunigs as eerily similar. Patty proposed a means of better connecting the son and the father.

On August 3, 2017, a memorial service was held at the Jordan, Minnesota cemetery where Tom Breunig had been laid to rest. It mirrored the 1979 ceremony, except this time thirty-seven-year-old Jesse Richard was presented the folded American flag originally handed to Tom's parents. The crowd assembled on the windy, drizzly day intermingled members of both of Jesse's families. Many in attendance had been at Tom's funeral. Patty Thornton's daughter, thinking other Marines who had been impacted by the Fuji Fire might want to be part, had encouraged her mother to publicize the ceremony. That's how Jerry Holt ended up being on hand.

In late 1979 the medically retired Weapons Company Marine told a reporter in his hometown of Boyle, Mississippi, that he had enrolled in college with a specific goal in mind: "I want to go into photography." He had done so, eventually joining the photojournalism staff of the *Minneapolis Star-Tribune*.

Some years later, a newspaper assignment in San Antonio surfaced memories of the fire, and the painful, healing months he and fellow Marines had spent there. Few had remained in touch with each other. His interest rekindled, Holt pored over old newspapers. They offered lists of the names and hometowns of those who had been injured at Camp Fuji. Holt had not been aware of his fellow Marine's south St. Paul roots; he tried unsuccessfully to locate Breunig's grave. A 2017 Facebook message from a fellow veteran alerted Holt to the planned second memorial. At the ceremony, he sat with Jesse Richard, then lingered over Breunig's grave. "I found it an extreme necessity to be part of this," Holt told a colleague. "I guess the word is closure, probably. . . . The only thing I have is that."

The many who had converged amid the Fuji Fire crisis had very quickly spun away in disparate directions. The injured had departed by MEDEVAC. Those who had responded from outside the camp quickly returned to routine duties. Every day, it seemed, overseas rotation dates pulled veterans of the incident back to the United States. Some went home; others continued service at other military installations. Many people they encountered had heard little or nothing of the fire. It left individuals feeling disconnected.

"There was never one event where we all got to say goodbye to each other," Jerry Holt observed. "Back in Mississippi it took me a year, a year and a half, to heal my body. During that time there was no connection to those Marines that were involved."

Chaplain Mel Ferguson had remained with BLT 2/4 until early 1980. The evening after he returned home to Arlington, Virginia, he and his wife set out for a celebratory dinner. At some point into the meal at a crowded neighborhood steakhouse, Ferguson recalled, the feeling arose "that I'm now safe. And a relief came over me, and I started to cry. Then Linda started to weep. We're making the guests at the other tables very nervous." Unable to finish their meals, they paid and left. "I never did that in that time with 2/4. You know, 'Be strong, because they're suffering more than you.'" It struck him that he had "allowed myself no personal reflection."

When Mike Cummings departed the ISR burn ward, he was allowed thirty days of convalescent leave, then reported to Parris Island, South Carolina. Shortly after arriving he was sent to the Washington DC area for two months of follow-up burn treatment. Tightening skin around his eyes was becoming a problem. Surgeons at the Bethesda Naval Hospital took healthy skin from over his right ribs. One graft they placed on his nose, another under his left eye. Cummings's assignment at Parris Island was "light duty." He finished out the two remaining years of his enlistment working as a driver—one day on, two days off. Similar assignments awaited some others who returned to units after significant time at BAMC. At Camp Lejeune, North Carolina,

Corporal Patrick Schaefer was assigned to manage a fitness center. Leaders at Marine Corps Base Quantico put Jesse Lugo to work at the base bowling alley.

Some of those not physically injured, but jarred by narrow escapes, found themselves well received at units where leaders knew what they had been through. Fredric Britton Jr. remembered arriving with four other former 2/4 Marines at Camp Pendleton, California. Their belongings having all burned in the fire, they wore ragtag civilian clothes as they checked into Lima Company, 3rd Battalion, Seventh Marines. They were met by a first lieutenant surnamed Luster. "Hey, you guys just relax," Britton remembered him saying. "Take the pack off your back for a while until we get you squared away and into some military clothing.'" At Camp Lejeune, North Carolina, Captain Bud Meador, commanding India Company, 3rd Battalion, Second Marines, paged through the service record of a disaster survivor who had transferred into his unit. "Several pages inside had been fire damaged," he recalled decades later. The entire folder "smelled of smoke."

Other Camp Fuji veterans joined units less familiar with the Fuji Fire. At Camp Pendleton Anthony Senatore found that "nobody talked about it. Not the COs, not the XO, not the company gunny. Nobody asked, 'Hey, what happened over there?' It was just never discussed." After joining the Camp Lejeune–based 2nd Battalion, Second Marines, Terrance Stokes remembered, "people was trying to tell me, 'You wasn't at Fuji, because you didn't get burned.'"

For the injured who hung up their uniforms soon after experiencing the fire or being discharged from the burn center, the separation was quick, complete, and, in many cases, difficult. Several suffered through what they termed a "bad decade." For others difficulties diminished but remained.

Mark Bedwell, his sister Carrie Beth Hogan remembered, "was very angry at a lot of things." There were times, she recalled in years thereafter, when "it was hard to know how to love him." Through a tenuous grapevine, rumors spread. Terrance Stokes and others remembered hearing that Bedwell had taken his own life. He had not, though life had been difficult.

Jon Jurgen faced similar challenges. "Took a long time for me to straighten myself out," he related. Over the years Jurgen spent time in college, but stopped just short of graduating. He studied the crafting of precious metals and stones, then for years ran his own jewelry business. "I'm good at what I do," he said, but lingering effects of the fire seemed to rob him of drive. "It's only been recently," he said in 2021, "that I've really started to get my head together."

Glenn Roberts attained significant personal and professional success after recovering from burns over nearly half his body. The achievement remained weighed down, though, by lingering trauma. "I've got four kids, three stepkids, two dogs, fourteen chickens, three goats. I'm on my fourth career," he tallied. "The two degrees—I cannot say enough good about the VA, I'm their biggest advocate." He had survived cancer and pursued scuba diving. His work afforded him global travel. "On the downside," he shared, "I still sleep with a window cracked open. I have to have one arm out of the sheets all the time. This has been like this for forty years. You never know when you're going to have to jump out. I don't wear a seatbelt. I would rather be flung out of a car and have my neck broken than be trapped in something burning."

Many who survived the 1979 events—those who were injured and those who dodged danger, alike—described troubled dreams in the aftermath. About a year after the fire, Charlie Dickerson dozed off on a couch at his father's home. Before he could wake from a moment-by-moment flashback of events inside Hut D-214, he had punched his fist through a window in the house. Tim Terrell embarked on a post-Navy career as a radiology technician. Hospital colleagues, knowing of his service as a corpsman, frequently called on him to help with patients in distress. The work offered no shortage of tragic moments. None, though, seemed to return unbidden. It was a Camp Fuji phantasm that disquieted Terrell's sleep: "Seeing this subject I got out of the storm to treat: boom, the burn victim."

Post-traumatic stress manifested itself differently for Steven Haishuk. Though grieving at the funerals of his father, then his mother, he shed no tears. "But I watch a video of a service guy coming home and greeting his dog," he said, "I cry. . . . Forty-some-odd years since this happened. And it's still with me."

Initially, Murray Simpkins noted, "I couldn't be close to an open-flame gas stove, a charcoal grill, a candle." For many years the retired corpsman found himself quickly nauseated by the odor of gasoline, or being lost in a surrounding fog. "If I talk about it, my voice still shakes," Bill Dyer said; his hands, as well. Steve Holmes choked up, after having for decades suppressed the memory of fire leaping up Sumiko Yuasa. "I can picture her right now," he said. "I did probably what most people do in traumatic situations like that. I just buried it."

For many fire date anniversaries have sparked memories. "There has not been an October 19th that I have not reflected back on that day in 1979," Dennis Zickefoose professed. The Fuji Fire so influenced Zickefoose that, after being commissioned into the Navy Medical Service Corps, he fought to serve his final tour of active duty as officer in charge of the medical clinic at Camp Schwab. Some arrivals of the anniversary have prompted retired Sergeant Major Mike Tuttle to reach out to friends with whom he served in 2/4. On other occasions he has found himself gone quiet, reflecting. For Steve Neal each Memorial Day brings to mind Stephan Turner. The two had discussed dreams of aviation. Neal went on to a career piloting jetliners for TWA and American Airlines; Turner's death precluded similar possibility.

Over time many impacted by the Fuji Fire received laudable assistance from the Veterans Administration. Early on it was primarily medical care for those who had suffered physical injury. Educational subsidies helped a significant number earn college and graduate degrees. VA housing loans provided them a path to homeownership. As years went by, however, some with less visible injuries encountered challenges eliciting help for post-traumatic stress. Few providers had heard of the 1979 tragedies; if an individual had not been seriously injured, it was unlikely their service records referenced the incident. In some measure that changed over time, but still a burden fell on veterans to provide newspaper articles or other proof of what had occurred.

After Rickey Lamon's twenty-year marriage fell apart, and he was arrested for driving while impaired, he was ordered into counseling. His case was assigned to a therapist specializing in work with veterans. "She had me give her my life story," Lamon recalled. It included memories of the fire. "Other than my brother and my ex-wife, she was probably the first person I'd ever talked to about it. I sat there and cried like a baby the whole time I talked to her about it. And she says, 'Huh. That's part of why you drink like you was drinking. You've got PTSD.'" Lamon did not think so. "I said, 'No, that's for people who was in war situations. I was never in a war situation.'"

John Redgate would eventually be promoted to colonel. Friends say the senior officer carried the weight of what his battalion had suffered. "He was distraught about this whole situation," recalled Colonel Warren Weidhahn, a friend and senior officer. "Anytime I ever met or talked to Johnny socially, invariably the fire would come up somehow in conversation."

"You knew it affected him," Jeffrey Bearor remembered, though in subsequent years, "he never treated anybody any differently. He was always a hundred percent upfront. He was a very gregarious and outgoing guy. . . . Although I'm sure he had bad days, you never knew it."

Having faced the tragedy together bonded Redgate and officers with whom he served in 2/4. Over the years he would keep in touch with a number of them. "I would hear from him out of the blue," Mac McDonald recalled, even after the physician had left the Navy to pursue a civilian career in emergency medicine. "He would check on me, how I was doing," and share news about others who had served in the battalion.

On July 10, 1980, the Marine Corps issued an order directing a "pen change" revision to the service's fuel handling manual. Every unit holding a copy of TM-3835–15/1 was directed to handwrite and "add [a] warning page as follows: '*Avoid sites on slopes and in vicinity of drainage structures. These sites pose a strong risk hazard which could cause a waterborne fire hazard to personnel and equipment from a catastrophic failure of fuel storage facilities.*'"

After the 1984 creation of an on-site fire department at Camp Fuji, Marine Corps leaders there formalized an "agreement for mutual fire and emergency service assistance" with the Gotemba-Oyama Fire Department. The decade also found the U.S. military reducing its inventory of equipment fueled by MOGAS.

In August 2009 medically retired Lance Corporal Steve Dye passed away after a short illness. He had lived to be forty-nine. Dye spent the best of those years with his son Hunter, who followed his father's footsteps into military service. Returning to his hometown, Issac Williams went on to marry. "I've got four children," he marveled, "I have about twenty grandchildren. And I've got some great-grandchildren." As of 2021 he served as a church deacon and choir president, and commanded Veterans of Foreign Wars Post 8852. Mark Bedwell's postfire life was rocky at times, but rewarding nonetheless. He completed college, then worked for years in Texas and Oklahoma oil fields. Later he earned a master's degree and was inducted into the National Political Science Honor Society. In a Texas community not far from his birthplace, Bedwell and his wife went on to serve as directors of a three-thousand-member nonprofit providing conservation and outdoor opportunities for young people. In 2021 Jerry Holt shared in the *Minneapolis Star-Tribune*'s Pulitzer Prize for breaking news reporting. Three years after first hanging up his Marine Corps uniform, Mike Cummings reenlisted for another seven years, serving in California and Louisiana. For years former Lance Corporal Donald Fox maintained the online site Warriors Den, which reminded people of what had happened at Camp Fuji and offered a digital gathering space for those who had been there.

After a security career at the Sandia National Laboratory, Thomas Moquino served multiple terms as governor of Santo Domingo Pueblo in New Mexico. Watching Mac McDonald respond to the fire crisis had impressed infantry Lance Corporal Andy Bonwit; he went on to become a medical doctor. Louis Sanford completed his Marine Corps service not long after the fire; enlisting in the Air Force, he flew with crews that had evacuated Camp Fuji Marines from Japan.

John Brosnan returned to artillery assignments after his tour leading LSU 3/9. He retired from the Marine Corps as a colonel. John Redgate, after military retirement, taught writing and served as dean of students at his prep school alma mater. He died at age eighty-three in 2020. Colonel Allan Lamb died in Ogden, Utah, in 2021. He was ninety-one.

A significant number of the surgeons who treated Camp Fuji Marines in San Antonio continued in remarkable public service. On September 11, 2001, scores who suffered burns when terrorists attacked New York City's twin towers were taken to New York-Presbyterian hospital. Their care was overseen by burn center director Roger Yurt. The surgeon's experience responding to the Marines' mass casualty incident, he said, "enabled me to set up a unit and be prepared for a lot of burn patients all coming in in a very catastrophic situation." Hani Mansour went on to lead the burn center at New Jersey's St. Barnabas Medical Center. Not long after having organized Issac Williams's treatment at Western Pennsylvania Hospital, Bill Goldfarb was appointed director of that institution's burn center. Cleon

Goodwin would serve as president of the American Burn Association, then director of the Army's Institute of Surgical Research.

At some point after the 1979 incident, Marines and Sailors stationed at Camp Fuji adopted a custom of annually memorializing those who died or were injured in the fire. Over the years at least three fire survivors would return to Camp Fuji to take part in the poignant ceremonies. In 2012, Jesse Lugo spoke briefly to those assembled. At the 2017 observance, Joseph Macdonald attended with his namesake son. The following year former Lance Corporal Donald Fox described for those in attendance his experience in the "fire and darkness." In 2020 First Lieutenant D. J. Glover was among those continuing to organize commemorations at the camp. "It was a truly painful time that both Marines and our Japanese partners overcame," he explained—difficult circumstances not to be forgotten. "We will continue to remember those that sacrificed in that fire," he promised. "We'll continue to honor them."

After the tragedy many survivors questioned the decision to place the fuel farm directly above the camp. "I thought that was something that was swept under the rug," Joe Macdonald contended. "Why *there*?" Mel Ferguson had asked, among other questions: "I have a Quonset hut that was up on blocks. Why weren't they all that way? Because it's not the first rainstorm that's ever hit Camp Fuji."

Few, though, expressed bitter resentment. "I was in the wrong place at the wrong time," Mike Tuttle reasoned, though the events, he said, led him to appreciate the Marine Corps' later requirement to apply risk management criteria in training plans.

"I do not hold the Marine Corps responsible for this," Glenn Roberts affirmed, "You'll never, ever get me to believe that the American military, let alone the Marine Corps, would put their people in harm's way deliberately." Frank Huerta chalked the disaster to "some crazy weather"—his greatest regret being the trauma it pressed upon his mother.

More haunting have been questions of "What if?" Glenn Roberts mulled what might have been if, after dashing in from the storm, he had not immediately stripped off his water-soaked uniform. Thirty seconds later it could have protected his body from burning. Mike Tuttle wondered how his fate might have been different if, on moving into Hut D-214, he had chosen a different rack. "Some made it out alive, and some didn't," he mused, "and the difference was, 'Where was your bunk?'" Former Navy corpsman Dennis Zickefoose asked himself, "What if I had studied harder in Corps School? What if I had responded quicker?"

Among those unhurt, or suffering only minor injury during the 1979 events, life perspectives shifted. "What problem was going to be big after that?" Richard DesLauriers ruminated. Jim Stallings agreed: "I haven't had a bad day since October 19, 1979."

In others survivor guilt arose. "I was twenty feet away, maybe," Tim Howell remembered. "And I was saved from that. Why?" "Knowing all those guys got hurt," Paul Verdier admitted, "you wonder, 'What could I have done different? Could I have helped somebody else?' You feel like shit." Despite having been a lance corporal at the time, trained on-the-job in bulk fuel handling, Rickey Lamon felt that he should have better understood the porous aspect of lava soil.

"You know, you always look back," former LSU commander John Brosnan reflected decades later. "Woulda, coulda, shoulda." Retired combat engineer Jacob Evans surmised that "regardless of where we put those bladders, that storm would have come in, we would have still had the same problem. I believe that today. Maybe not the gas in the camp, but somewhere." "If we hadn't had a typhoon," Brosnan contended, "everything would have been fine."

There is little doubt that Typhoon Tip precipitated the tragedy that unfolded at Camp Fuji on October 19, 1979. As of February 2025, it remained the most intense tropical cyclone ever recorded. Had the massive storm not deluged the camp with rain, the Marines and Sailors of BLT 2/4 would almost certainly have been spared.

While the record-setting cyclone was a *necessary* cause of the Fuji Fire, however, it seems in retrospect not entirely *sufficient* to have provoked the resulting pain and destruction. Additional contributing factors were required. They came in the form of constant organizational and personnel flux, a poorly maintained training facility, deprioritizing safety, and simple bad luck.

Staffing shortages in 1979 left some positions in Marine Corps units unfilled, and others occupied by people with less-than-optimal experience. Of necessity, some individuals—officers and enlisted Marines—were placed in positions for which they had not been formally trained.

The constant shifting of individuals serving staggered twelve-month overseas tours mitigated against Marines in a unit getting to know and trust one another. It also reduced a sense of individual or shared accountability. Additionally, because senior commanders wanted to provide promising young officers an opportunity to command—the experience increased their likelihood of promotion—a company of Marines might find itself led by a new commanding officer every three months or so.

For those assigned to installation staffs abroad, every assignment began with limited understanding of the areas in which they would serve. If transfer dates had not been aligned to allow direct handover of authority from one individual to another, as often happened, individuals reporting into a new post would arrive with no counterpart briefing on significant events encountered the previous year. LSU 3/9's moving of the fuel storage point occurred after one Range Company commanding officer had departed and before his replacement arrived. Once in an assignment, individuals would experience each annual season just once. They would gain only limited understanding of recurring patterns—regarding weather and erosion, for instance. The short tours did not encourage vested interest in long-term improvement of facilities or operations.

In addition, amid Corps-wide shape-shifting, relationships among component organizations were not always clear. As an example, when Logistics Support Unit 3/9 was dispatched to Camp Fuji to support BLT 3/9, the BLT did not include the logistics unit on its rolls. When BLT 2/4 arrived at the camp, it counted LSU 3/9 among its "attached units." Other attached units included an artillery battery and platoons of tank and amphibious tractor crews, combat engineers, and reconnaissance specialists over which the BLT commander exercised direct control. Decades later, though, former BLT 2/4 executive officer Lance Woodburn would aver, "I don't remember any real interrelationship with the LSU as a distinct unit. With logistics people, yes—but not with the LSU as a distinct unit."

Further complicating command relationships at Camp Fuji was the Range Company commander's tasking of LSU 3/9 to undertake physical improvement projects on the camp. Allan Lamb was not part of either BLT 2/4's or LSU 3/9's chain of command. As a colonel, however, he was the senior-ranking officer at the camp. While he claimed a "policy not to interfere with the training of the BLTs," it was not uncommon for him to directly approach the LSU commander, a major, and encourage his provision of engineering assistance. Indeed, former LSU 3/9 commanding officer John Brosnan conjectured that the Lamb-directed project "extending the north end of the berm" as a means of covering a trash pit may have caused water to "run along behind the berm"—accumulating uphill of the man-made ridge, rather than, to the extent it had beforehand, flowing around the north end of the berm and away from Quonset huts.

Moreover, to the minds of some in the camp during October 1979, it was not clear who controlled fuel operations. "My understanding—apparently a fallacious one," retired Colonel Woodburn offered decades later, "was that the base camp was responsible for the fuel farm."

Numerous issues factored into Camp Fuji's dilapidated condition in 1979. Not insignificant among them, though, was successive Range Company commanders favoring improvement of facilities at the base camp over those in the training camp. The disproportionate placement of available fire extinguishers is just one example.

A general sense that because warfare is customarily dangerous, training for it is as well, seems also to have led the Marine Corps of the time to deprioritize safety in noncombat settings. The slim fuel-handling manual in use during 1979 focused on employment of fuel bladders on risk-inherent battlefields; less emphasis was placed on the sort of safety measures evident at the time in guidance issued by other U.S. military services.

Finally, a key element of misfortune was that the October 1979 spill involved the bladder containing MOGAS rather than those filled with Diesel or JP-5. All three of the uphill-stored fuels, if spilled, would have streamed over the surface of flowing rainwater. On reaching the huts, however, the other two—with lower vapor density and higher flashpoints—would have been less likely to quickly ignite. At the very least, they might have allowed Marines and Sailors greater escape time.

On detailed reflection it seems overly simplistic to—as Marine Corps investigators did—ascribe the Fuji Fire entirely to the doings of a deity. Similarly inadequate, though, would be to too-narrowly lay specific individual blame. The combined circumstances that led to the events of October 19, 1979, more precisely constitute what organizational theorist Charles Perrow has termed a "system accident."

Studying "the role of organizations and management in preventing failures—or causing them," Perrow claims that human foible is unavoidable. Ignored warnings, unnecessary risks, sloppy work, he writes, are "part of the human condition." When incorporated into systems, however, "operating in an unforgiving, hostile environment," the social scientist suggests, "these routine sins of organizations have very non-routine consequences."

"System accidents," Perrow posits, "as with all accidents, start with a component failure, most commonly the failure of a part, say a valve or an operator error." What distinguishes a system accident is the "presence or not of multiple failures that interact in unanticipated ways." Applying Perrow's reasoning, the Fuji Fire illustrates how it is "the *interaction* of the multiple failures that explains the accident."

Approaching five decades distance from the 1979 tragedies at Camp Fuji—whatever one's analysis of this particular set of interacting failures—there seems little value in imagining counterfactual outcomes. "You can't look back on it and say what might have been," survivor Mike Cummings said he had concluded. "You've just got to deal with what happened."

ADDENDUM 1

THOSE WHO DIED

THIRTEEN U.S. MARINES died as a direct result of injuries sustained during the October 19, 1979, fire at Camp Fuji. They ranged in age from 17 to 22. Seven were white, four Black, two of Hispanic heritage. Twelve were born in the United States; one was born in South America.

October 19	LCpl **L. C. Malveaux**, 21, of Beaumont, Texas
October 21	PFC **Tyrone Chris Elem**, 19, of Alexandria, Virginia
October 21	LCpl **Thomas Joseph Breunig**, 19, of St. Paul, Minnesota
October 24	Cpl **Colin Miller**, 21, of Brooklyn, New York (b. Georgetown, Guyana)
October 25	LCpl **Philip Everett du Pont**, 21, of Bluemont, Virginia
October 27	LCpl **Robert Vinson Smith, Jr.**, 19, of Spartanburg, South Carolina
October 31	PFC **Robert Lee Brees**, 17, of Dell Rapids, South Dakota
November 2	LCpl **Stephan Ray Turner**, 22, of Tipp City, Ohio
November 4	LCpl **Orlando Eloy Sandoval**, 20, of Pueblo, Colorado
November 6	PFC **Gregory Lawrence Hassel**, 20, of Chicago, Illinois
November 10	PFC **Rodger Allen Larson**, 20, of Eau Claire, Wisconsin

November 19	LCpl **Willie Davis, Jr.**, 22, of Detroit, Michigan
December 12	LCpl **Ernest Eugene Gutierrez**, 22, of Moorpark, California

+ Additionally related: the November 16, 1979 death of Cpl **Willie J. Hamilton**, 26, of Marion, South Carolina. The tank Cpl Hamilton commanded during an exercise at Camp Fuji tipped into a deep flood diversion trench excavated after the fire.

ADDENDUM 2

THOSE WHO WERE INJURED

AT LEAST SEVENTY-THREE people—seventy-one men and two women—were physically hurt at Camp Fuji on October 19, 1979. Sixty-nine were U.S. Marines, three were Japanese civilians, and one was a U.S. Navy Sailor. At least fifty-four of them suffered thermal injury.

The list below is drawn from rosters created at the BLT 2/4 battalion aid station, a 3rd Marine Division command history, military teletype messages of the time, a Japanese military investigation, and contemporaneous news reports. It includes thirteen individuals whose injuries led to their death—on October 19 or during fifty-four days thereafter.

After immediate treatment on Camp Fuji, then at nearby Japanese medical facilities and the U.S. Air Force Hospital at Yokota Air Base, forty-seven of those listed below were evacuated elsewhere. Of those, thirty-eight were flown from Japan to San Antonio, Texas for treatment by U.S. Army Institute of Surgical Research teams at Brooke Army Medical Center. Six others were transported for care to Naval Hospital, Yokosuka, Japan. An additional three were flown to Okinawa for treatment at Naval Regional Medical Center, Kuwae. Two of the injured were in such critical condition that doctors determined they would not survive aerial evacuation; the two were kept at the Yokota hospital, where they died. The remaining injured Marines were treated at the BLT 2/4 battalion aid station, then rejoined their units on the camp. The worst injured of the three Japanese workers on Camp Fuji was hospitalized for a month at Gotemba Hospital before undergoing multiple reconstructive operations by Japanese military surgeons. The two other Japanese NEX employees' minor injuries were treated on an outpatient basis.

Because some of the documents informing this list were created amid the chaos of the incident, they include misspellings, mistaken ranks, and imprecise or incomplete initial diagnoses. In several cases—but likely not all—data from other sources allowed correction of those errors. The compilation below is almost certainly incomplete. It is probable, for instance, that some who experienced physical trauma at the camp that day—observing others whose suffering was far greater—did not seek treatment in ways that would have been immediately recorded. Finally and importantly, casualty figures collected at the time did not include instances of immediate, much less subsequent, post-traumatic stress.

Among those injured were:

Lance Corporal **Douglas B. Adams** (Lacerated Feet) † † †
Private First Class **Nicholas C. Albert** (Burned Ear, Twisted Ankle) † †
Private First Class **L. D. Alcorn** (Laceration) ※
Private First Class **J. M. Barr** (Lacerated Foot) ※
Lance Corporal **Mark C. Bedwell** (2nd and 3rd Degree Burns: Face, Arms and Back) †
Private **Robert L. Brees** (2nd and 3rd Degree Burns: 95% of Body) †, ‡
Lance Corporal **Thomas J. Breunig** (2nd and 3rd Degree Burns: 85% of Body) †, ‡
Private First Class **W. E. Bufford** (Back Sprain) ※
Private First Class **Keith J. Burleigh** (2nd and 3rd Degree Burns: 9% of Body) †
Lance Corporal **Bradley E. Cope** (2nd Degree Burns: Face and Hands) †
Lance Corporal **Mike Cummings** (2nd and 3rd Degree Burns: 75% of Body) †
Lance Corporal **Willie Davis Jr.** (2nd and 3rd Degree Burns: 70% of Body) †, ‡
Lance Corporal **Charles W. Degnim** (Burned Ear and Lip) † †
Corporal **Fernando L. DeJesus** (Foreign Object in Eye) † † †
Lance Corporal **K. L. Delaney** (Lacerated Foot) ※
Captain **Richard E. DesLauriers** (Knee Sprain) ※
Private First Class **Charles A. Dickerson** (Burned Ear and Hand) † †

Lance Corporal **Philip E. du Pont** (2nd and 3rd Degree Burns: 80% of Body) †, ‡

Private First Class **George S. "Steve" Dye** (2nd Degree Burns: 80% of Body) †

Private First Class **Tyrone C. Elem** (Multiple Severe Burns) ‡

Private First Class **L. T. Embrey** (Minor Burns) ※

Private First Class **J. R. Escalante** (Lacerated Foot) ※

Private First Class **Isagani F. Fajotina** (Minor Burns, Laceration) † †

Private First Class **Mark W. Ferrara** (1st and 2nd Degree Burns: 10% of Body) †

Private First Class **Donald J. Fox Jr.** (Burned Neck) † †

Lance Corporal **Michael A. Freeman** (2nd Degree Burns: 60% of Body) †

Lance Corporal **Donald L. Fullerton** (2nd Degree Burns: 50% of Body) †

Lance Corporal **C. D. Giles** (Lacerated Leg) ※

Lance Corporal **Thomas A. Glasper Jr.** (3rd Degree Burns: 60% of Body) †

Gunnery Sergeant **H. D. Gould** (Laceration) ※

Lance Corporal **Ernest E. Gutierrez** (2nd and 3rd Degree Burns: 70% of Body) †, ‡

Lance Corporal **Steven D. Haishuk** (2nd Degree Burns: 55% of Body) †

Mr. **Kimio Hata** (Minor Burns: Both Arms)

Private **Gregory L. Hassel** (2nd Degree Burns: 85% of Body) †, ‡

Lance Corporal **J. M. Hayes** (Lacerated Leg) ※

Lance Corporal **G. L. Hickins** (Minor Burns and Laceration) ※

Private First Class **Richard J. Hill** (Burned Face and Ankle) † †

Lance Corporal **Jerry G. Holt** (2nd and 3rd Degree Burns: 85% of Body) †

Private First Class **Francisco "Frank" P. Huerta** (2nd and 3rd Degree Burns: 90% of Body) †

Private First Class **Craig X. Jackson** (3rd Degree Burns: 40% of Body) †

Lance Corporal **B. G. Johnson** (Minor Laceration) ※

Corporal **Jon L. Jurgen** (2nd Degree Burns: 50% of Body) †

Lance Corporal **W. Kemp** (Foot Laceration) ※

Private First Class **R. Kriska** (Possible Broken Nose) ※

Private First Class **Rodger A. Larson** (2nd and 3rd Degree Burns: 80% of Body; Obstructed Airway) †, ‡

Private **Billy J. Lennon** (2nd and 3rd Degree Burns: Face, Hands and Neck) †

Lance Corporal **K. L. Lollie** (Lacerated Foot) ※

Lance Corporal **Jesus A. Lugo** (2nd Degree Burns: 30% of Body) †

Lance Corporal **L. C. Malveaux** (Multiple Severe Burns) ‡

Corporal **Colin Miller** (2nd and 3rd Degree Burns: 85% of Body) † † † †, ‡

Lance Corporal **Gust L. Miller** (2nd and 3rd Degree Burns: 85% of Body) †

Ms. **Yasuko Nakayama** (2nd Degree Burns: ~33% of Body; Face, Chest and Back)

Corporal **Steve L. Neal** (1st and 2nd Degree Burns: 50% of Body) †

Private First Class **Craig J. Patane** (1st and 2nd Degree Burns: 12% of Body) †

Corporal **Daryl K. Perry** (2nd Degree Burns: 50% of Body) †

Sergeant **J. L. Qualman** (Jammed Toe) ※

Corporal **Glenn L. Roberts** (2nd Degree Burns: 45% of Body) †

Private First Class **Roosevelt Ross** (2nd and 3rd Degree Burns: 25% of Body) †

Lance Corporal **Orlando E. Sandoval** (2nd and 3rd Degree Burns: 70% of Body) †, ‡

Corporal **Patrick T. Schaefer** (2nd and 3rd Degree Burns: 50% of Body) †

Lance Corporal **M. R. Scott** (Lacerated Foot) ※

Lance Corporal **Robert V. Smith Jr.** (2nd and 3rd Degree Burns: 90% of Body) † † † †, ‡

Private First Class **George S. Spotts** (2nd Degree Burns: 50% of Body) †

Lance Corporal **Billy R. Stover** (2nd Degree Burns: Hands, Legs, Face + Obstructed Airway) †

Corporal **T. J. Thornton** (Sprained Back) ※

Corporal **Mark A. Tipton** (Sprained Ankle) ※

Lance Corporal **Robert L. Turner** (2nd and 3rd Degree Burns: 45% of Body) †, ‡

Lance Corporal **Stephan R. Turner** (2nd and 3rd Degree Burns: 90% of Body) †, ‡

Ms. **Sumiko Yuasa** (Minor Burns: Back, Arm, Left Ear, Under Both Knees)

Lance Corporal **Shelby T. Waford** (2nd and 3rd Degree Burns: 75% of Body) †

Hospitalman Apprentice **Joseph G. Williams** (1st and 2nd Degree Burns: 5% of Body) † † †

Lance Corporal **Issac Williams** (2nd and 3rd Degree Burns: 95% of Body; Respiratory Failure) †

Private **Thomas L. Woolery** (1st and 2nd Degree Burns, 30% of Body) †

※ Treated at BLT 2/4 Battalion Aid Station, then released to unit

† Evacuated for treatment to U.S. Army Institute of Surgical Research, San Antonio, Texas

† † Evacuated for treatment to Naval Hospital, Yokosuka, Japan

† † † Evacuated for treatment to Naval Regional Medical Center, Kuwae, Okinawa

† † † † Remained at U.S. Air Force Hospital, Yokota, Japan

‡ Died of fire-related injuries

+ Additionally related: the November 16, 1979, injury of PFC Patrick Flanagan, 19, of Mattydale, New York. The tank PFC Flanagan drove during an exercise at Camp Fuji tipped into a deep flood diversion trench excavated after the fire.

ADDENDUM 3

THOSE WHO RECEIVED AWARDS

A NUMBER OF individuals and units were formally recognized for their extraordinary actions amid, and in the wake of, the Fuji Fire. Some were presented military decorations. The list below was compiled from military teletype messages, newspaper articles, and unit historical documents. It is almost certainly incomplete.

NAVY AND MARINE CORPS MEDAL, THE DEPARTMENT OF THE NAVY'S HIGHEST NONCOMBAT DECORATION FOR HEROISM

Private First Class **James D. Barnett**, USMC
Private First Class **Keith J. Burleigh**, USMC
Lance Corporal **Bradley E. Cope**, USMC
Private First Class **Charles A. Dickerson**, USMC
Lance Corporal **Steven D. Haishuk**, USMC
Lance Corporal **Roger V. Rearick**, USMC
Corporal **Patrick T. Schaefer**, USMC
Corporal **David W. Skaggs**, USMC
Corporal **Mark A. Tipton**, USMC
Second Lieutenant **Frederick Winters**, USMC

A Marine Corps news release issued in November 1979 noted that "though records are not maintained for such," this number of Navy and Marine Corps Medals might have been the largest "ever presented at one time for heroism occurring in the same incident."

Note: For his December 16, 1979 rescue of Shigeo Sato from a burning building in Gotemba, Japan, Lance Corporal Robert L. King was also nominated to receive the Navy and Marine Corps Medal.

LEGION OF MERIT

Colonel **Russell M. Harwood**, USMCR
Lieutenant Colonel **Gerald S. Reczek**, USMC

MERITORIOUS SERVICE MEDAL

Lieutenant Colonel (Dr.) **Philip M. Long**, USAF
Major (Dr.) **Cesar F. Sarmiento**, USAF
Captain (Dr.) **Salvatore J. De Vincenzo**, USAF
Colonel (Dr.) **Clarence K. Whiteside**, USAF

NAVY COMMENDATION MEDAL

Hospitalman Apprentice **Fred E. Odom**, USN
Hospitalman Apprentice **Timothy L. Terrell**, USN

NAVY ACHIEVEMENT MEDAL

Sergeant **Richard P. Hill**, USMC
Lieutenant (Dr.) **Wilbur E. McDonald Jr.**, USN
Lieutenant (Dr.) **Miles L. Wilhelm**, USN

HUMANITARIAN SERVICE MEDAL

All in the 375th Aeromedical Airlift Wing who took part in evacuating burn-injured Marines from Yokota, Japan to San Antonio, Texas

NAVY MERITORIOUS UNIT COMMENDATION

U.S. Air Force Hospital, Yokota, Japan
U.S. Army Institute of Surgical Research
U.S. Naval Regional Medical Center, Yokosuka, Japan

MARINE CORPS CERTIFICATE OF COMMENDATION

Alamo Detachment, Marine Corps League Auxiliary

ARMY CERTIFICATE OF ACHIEVEMENT

U.S. Army Aviation Detachment, Camp Zama, Japan
U.S. Army Health Clinic, Honshu

MERITORIOUS MAST

All BLT 2/4 Navy hospital corpsmen who cared for injured Marines on October 19, 1979

Lance Corporal **Saul Del Toro**, credited with creating the incident's first written casualty list

NAVY HELICOPTER ASSOCIATION SEARCH AND RESCUE CREW OF THE YEAR

Naval Helicopter Combat Support Squadron-3, Detachment 106 crew members who participated in the MEDEVAC of Marines from Camp Fuji to Yokota Air Base

ACKNOWLEDGMENTS

THIS BOOK GREW from the seeds of a social media post I made in August 2020. Under a photo of myself as a young corporal training at Camp Fuji in early 1978, I mentioned that it had been taken a year or so before the disastrous fire there. I was startled by the number of people who responded, "What fire?" The incident's strikingly high peacetime casualty count jolted Marines of the time. I had not been at the camp in October 1979 but was disheartened that few seemed aware of the tragedy fellow Marines experienced there.

Early supporters of this project were Gunnery Sergeant David Luttenberger, USMC (Ret.), a friend who in 1979 served with Weapons Company, BLT 2/4 and survived the Fuji Fire; Captain D. J. Glover, USMC, who in 2020 was posted at what is now Combined Arms Training Center, Camp Fuji; Colonel (Dr.) Lee Cancio, USA (Ret.), director of the U.S. Army Institute of Surgical Research burn center; and Chief Hospitalman Murray Simpkins, USN (Ret.).

Documents curated and shared by my friend Charles W. Henderson—the international best-selling author and retired Marine Corps chief warrant officer—provided a critical springboard as I began exploring these events.

One hundred and thirty individuals directly impacted by the Fuji Fire shared memories of the incident and its aftermath—despite the tears often generated as they did. You have met most in the preceding chapters. Their graciously offered recollections made this work possible.

Finding these men and women was a primary challenge. Genealogical researcher Mark Parson valuably assisted in this regard, as did Brian Foster and Kim Craft of TogetherWeServed.com; Colonel Kevin Lavin, USAF (Ret.) of the Air Weather Association; and the Reverend (Capt.) Lyman M. Smith, USN (Ret.) of the Military Chaplains Association. Similarly helpful were Dan Clare, Rob Lewis, and Matt Saintsing of the veterans service organization Disabled American Veterans; Ron Corey of American Legion Fyre-Vaughn Post 264 in Burkburnett, Texas; Niles Eggleston and Erin Lucero of the Virginia Commonwealth University Medical Center; Barbara Jaffe of Assemblies of God Chaplaincy Ministries; Jarrod Metzgar and Ron Nicholas of the Marble Falls, Texas, Chamber of Commerce; Colonel John Rader, USMC (Ret.) of the Marine Corps Aviation Association; and former Machinist's Mate Third Class Eliese Rumbolt-Adams, USN.

Scores of archivists, public affairs officers, librarians and others, compelled by the story of what happened at Camp Fuji, provided remarkable research assistance. Andrew Hayt, formerly of the U.S. Marine Corps History Division—now with the National Archives and Records Administration—stands out among this group, as do Deborah Rexon of the Marine Corps Research Library; Ayano Quentin and Song Jordan of CATC, Camp Fuji; and U.S. Air Force historians Captain Keith Loney, USAF (Ret.) and Lesleigh Jones. Lieutenant Commander George Dunnavan, USN (Ret.), principal author of the definitive 1979 scientific journal article about Typhoon Tip, expertly analyzed additional meteorological data; David Ray of the Defense Logistics Agency kindly explained the history of military fuel usage; Dennis Rubin, former chief of fire and emergency services in Washington DC thoughtfully shared fire science instruction; and Captain Janet Quinn, USN (Ret.) and Captain John Quinn, USN (Ret.) offered gracious counsel on military legal issues.

Colonel Neil J. Owens, USMC; Major Brad Hull, USMC; and Sergeant Major Restituto Paz, USMC, provided generous access to the enhanced-by-orders-of-magnitude modern Camp Fuji. Crucial help was also furnished by Major General Juan Ayala, USMC (Ret.), director of the City of San Antonio Office of Military and Veteran Affairs; Captain Dale Dye, USMC (Ret.); Colonel Walt Ford, USMC (Ret.); Lieutenant General Robert E. Milstead, USMC (Ret.); Master Gunnery Sergeant Emanuel Pacheco, USMC (Ret.); Lieutenant Colonel Ralph Peters, USA (Ret.); Commander Don Savage, USN (Ret.); Lieutenant Colonel Ammin Spencer, USMC (Ret.); Colonel Michael D. Visconage, USMC (Ret.), director of the U.S. Department of Veterans Affairs History Office; and Lieutenant Colonel Jud Whitlock, USMC (Ret.)

Additionally appreciated contributions were made by Carlos Alvarado of the U.S. Army Medical Department Center of History and Heritage; Amy W. Barrett of *Army Aviation Digest*; Sara Bock of *Leatherneck Magazine* and

Marine Corps Gazette; Christi Bayha of the Marine Corps Research Library; Joshua Botts of the office of the U.S. State Department Historian; Megan Lynn Casey of the Navy Department Library; Dominic Amaral, Stephen Coode, Dieter Stenger, and Nancy Whitfield of the U.S. Marine Corps History Division; Captain Anthony Cooper, USN (Ret.), of the Naval Facilities Engineering Systems Command; U.S. Army Aviation Branch historian Billy G. Croslow Jr.; former *Pacific Stars and Stripes* editor Robert Cullick; Yoshie Eddings, widow of the late, gifted photographer Master Sergeant Curt Eddings, USAF (Ret.); Lisa Ellis-Shooks of the Naval Safety Center; Jeremy Farmer of the National Archives and Records Administration, Chicago; Bryan Howard, PhD, director of the Fort Sam Houston Museum; Eiichi Ito of the Library of Congress; Jennifer Parsons Kangas and John Manning of the Air Force Reserve Command; Marine Heavy Helicopter Squadron-361 veteran Paul Kelley; U.S. Indo-Pacific Command historian Rana Lynn Kennedy; Holland Kessinger and Nancy Heath of the Marine Corps Recruit Depot, San Diego Library; Kevin Krejcarek of U.S. Army, Japan; Erin Lasley of the 62nd Airlift Wing; Jeffrey S. Michalke of Air Mobility Command; Gregory Mitchell of Naval Air Facility, Atsugi; Michael Rhodes of the Naval History and Heritage Command; Jessica Russo of the Marine Corps Base Camp Lejeune Library; Master Sergeant Roman Rusynko, USAF (Ret.); Veterans Benefits Administration historian Jeffrey Seiken, PhD; Navy Bureau of Medicine and Surgery historian André Sobocinski; Kelley Woolley and Mark Harrison of the Marine Corps Base Camp Pendleton Library; Mark Wilderman of the 375th Air Mobility Wing; George C. Wunderlich, director of the Fort Sam Houston Museum Activity; and Julie Zecher of the Naval War College Library.

Thanks are due, as well, to Kate Abel of the Austin, Texas Public Library; Ian Barker of the Tyrrell Historical Library in Beaumont, Texas; Tamara Blackwell of the Bolivar County Library System in Cleveland, Mississippi; Ian Bloomfield of the Elmont, New York Memorial Library; Colonel J. Clarke Bursley, USA (Ret.); Bentley Clark of the Roswell, New Mexico Public Library; Julia Corrin of the Carnegie Mellon University Archives; Rachel Costantino and Emily Morgan of the Leesburg, Florida, Public Library; Andrew Crews and Matt DeWaelsche of the San Antonio, Texas, Public Library; Torrey Crossman of the Fairfield, Vermont, Historical Society; Shane Curtin of the San José Public Library; Jacqueline B. Davis, docent at the Fort Sam Houston Museum; Suzanne Dungan of the Paris-Bourbon County Public Library, Kentucky; Valerie Ellis of the Mobile, Alabama, Public Library; Kate Feighery of the Archives of the Catholic Archdiocese of New York; Jill Fleck of the Milwaukee Public Library; S. Victor Fleischer, Archivist of the University of Akron; Rusty Gaspard of the Rapides Parish Library, Alexandria, Louisiana; Frank Harris of the Los Angeles County Library; Maureen Heher of the Hartford, Connecticut, Public Library; Jamie Helle of the Boyle County Public Library, Kentucky; Jordan Hunt of the Indianapolis Public Library; John Larson of the St. Paul Public Library; Morgan Lewis of the Chicago Public Library; Jenny Martin of the Chicago Heights Library; Ann Marie Megoulas of the Dauphine County, Pennsylvania, Library System; Nat Norton, City Archivist of San Antonio, Texas; Rebeccah Parks of the U.S. District Court, District of Minnesota; Ilona Perry of the Tacoma, Washington, Public Library; the L. E. Phillips Memorial Public Library in Eau Claire, Wisconsin; Joe Popowitch of the Darien, Illinois, Indian Prairie Library; Cade Rensmeyer, senior property manager of the Old BAMC complex on Fort Sam Houston; Martha Riley of the Bernard Becker Medical Library at the Washington University School of Medicine; Scott Rosario of the Greater San Antonio Chapter of the American Red Cross; Charlene Garcia Simms of the Pueblo, Colorado, Public Library; Crystal Smith and Liliya Gusakova of the NIH National Library of Medicine; Medical historian Dale Smith, PhD, of the Uniformed Services University of the Health Sciences; Brent Stauffer of the Archives of the Catholic Archdiocese of San Antonio, Texas; Nicole Sutton of the Columbus, Ohio, Metropolitan Library; Robert Tucker of the Wichita, Kansas, Public Library; Janet Wall of the National Oceanographic and Atmospheric Administration's National Climatic Data Center; Kelly Wallace of the Los Angeles Public Library; Jackie Walters of the American Red Cross; Jonathan Wuepper of the Cass County, Michigan, District Library; and Mark Zoeter of the Alexandria, Virginia, Public Library.

In Japan immeasurable aid was provided by former *Tokyo Shimbun* editorial writer Yoshikazu Imazato; Yousuke Itakura of *Chunichi Shimbun*; former Camp Fuji employee Hidetoshi Iwanaga; Jieitai Captain Masanobu Katsumata; Takafumi Katsumata, Toshimitsu Tsuchiya, and Masakado Tsuchiya of the Gotemba International Association; Mayuko Kasai and Kazuki Yasui of the Japan Meteorological Agency; Assistant Chief Sotaro

Magasaki and Battalion Chief Takanobu Tsuchiya of CATC Camp Fuji Fire Station 7; Jieitai Major Yosuke Moriya; Hideko Shirakawa, owner of the Pasadena Restaurant and Bar in Gotemba; Rie Suetomi, director general of the South Kanto Defense Bureau; Takashi Yamada of the Gotemba-Oyama Fire Department; Jieitai veteran Makato Yamamoto; Jieitai Command Sergeant Major Yoshihiko Yamamoto; Dr. Youichi Yanagawa of Shizuoka Hospital and Juntendo University; researchers at the National Archives of Japan and legislative materials analysts at the National Diet Library.

Yuki Henninger's superb translation skills were crucial to including Japanese perspectives in this recounting—as were Ayano Quentin's remarkable abilities as an interpreter. Lea Chang, Miki Ichimura Guido, Lyal Miller, Sae Robinson, and Chisato Takeya also helped me gain insights from myriad Japanese speakers and source materials.

In undertaking this work, I have been inspired and encouraged by the advice and friendship of eminent Asia scholar Kongdon Oh Hassig, PhD; respected military historian and fellow Marine Richard B. Meixsel, PhD; the brilliant Soldier-diplomat-gentleman Colonel Richard Downie, PhD, USA (Ret.); and my eighth grade English teacher, the author Sharon Giacomazzi.

The generous assistance of individuals listed above, and so many others, was invaluable to telling this story. Any errors in interpreting or presenting the documents, memories, and expert analyses they so kindly shared are entirely my own.

Finally and eternally, I am grateful to my wife, Rosemary. She endured with grace my four-year, single-focus devotion to this inquiry. As a Marine spouse, she understood.